CASE STUDIES IN
CULTURAL ANTHROPOLOGY

GENERAL EDITORS

George and Louise Spindler

STANFORD UNIVERSITY

A SINHALESE VILLAGE IN SRI LANKA
Coping with Uncertainty

Location of Sri Lanka in Asia

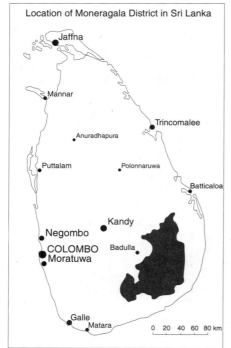

Location of Moneragala District in Sri Lanka

Location of Suduwatura Ara Village in Moneragala District

A SINHALESE VILLAGE IN SRI LANKA
Coping with Uncertainty

VICTORIA J. BAKER

Eckerd College

HARCOURT BRACE COLLEGE PUBLISHERS

Fort Worth   Philadelphia   San Diego   New York   Orlando   Austin   San Antonio
Toronto   Montreal   London   Sydney   Tokyo

Publisher	Christopher P. Klein
Product Manager	Julie McBurney
Project Editor	Tamara Neff Vardy
Senior Production Manager	Cynthia Young
Art Director	Carol Kincaid
Electronic Publishing Coordinator	Lisa Rawlinson

Address editorial correspondence to:
Harcourt Brace College Publishers
301 Commerce Street, Suite 3700
Fort Worth, TX 76102

Address orders to:
Harcourt Brace & Company
6277 Sea Harbor Drive
Orlando, FL 32887-6777
1-800-782-4479

Harcourt Brace may provide complimentary instructional aids and supplements or supplement packages to those adopters qualified under our adoption policy. Please contact your sales representative for more information. If as an adopter or potential user you receive supplements you do not need, please return them to your sales representative or send them to:

Attn: Returns Department
Troy Warehouse
465 South Lincoln Drive
Troy, MO 63379

Printed in the United States of America

ISBN: 0-15-505176-8

Library of Congress Catalog Card Number: 96-79968

7 8 9 0 1 2 3 4 5 6 039 9 8 7 6 5 4 3 2 1

Foreword

ABOUT THE SERIES

These case studies in cultural anthropology are designed for students in beginning and intermediate courses in the social sciences, to bring them insights into the richness and complexity of human life as it is lived in different ways, in different places. The authors are men and women who have lived in the societies they write about and who are professionally trained as observers and interpreters of human behavior. Also, the authors are teachers; in their writing, the needs of the student reader remain foremost. It is our belief that when an understanding of ways of life very different from one's own is gained, abstractions and generalizations about the human condition become meaningful.

The scope and character of the series has changed constantly since we published the first case studies in 1960, in keeping with our intention to represent anthropology as it is. We are concerned with the ways in which human groups and communities are coping with the massive changes wrought in their physical and sociopolitical environments in recent decades. We are also concerned with the ways in which established cultures have solved life's problems. And we want to include representation of the various modes of communication and emphasis that are being formed and reformed as anthropology itself changes.

We think of this series as an instructional series, intended for use in the classroom. We, the editors, have always used case studies in our teaching, whether for beginning students or advanced graduate students. We start with case studies, whether from our own series or from elsewhere, and weave our way into theory, and then turn again to cases. For us, they are the grounding of our discipline.

ABOUT THE AUTHOR

Victoria J. Baker was born in Austin, Texas, but she has spent more than half her life outside the United States. As a child of a military family stationed in Europe, she acquired a taste for comparing cultures even in primary school. She received her B.A. in French from Sweet Briar College and was a language teacher at the American International School of The Hague for ten years. She started studying anthropology at the University of Leiden (Netherlands) as a hobby and went on to get her M.A. (1982) and Ph.D. (1988) from there.

Her specialization is anthropology and education, and Baker has done comparative case studies of rural schools on all the inhabited continents, in more than twelve developing countries, from Senegal to Malawi, from Bangladesh to Vietnam. She has written numerous articles in that field in addition to her book *The Blackboard in the Jungle* (1988).

Baker has taught at the University of Colombo, the University of Leiden, Webster University (Leiden campus), and is presently in the Collegium of Comparative Cultures at Eckerd College. She spends about four months of every year traveling and gathering comparative anthropological material to use in her courses, advising students on their projects, and savoring the fascination of cultural diversity.

ABOUT THIS CASE STUDY

This case study is remarkable in three ways. It is a study of a village community established in the 1960s and 1970s in the jungles of Sri Lanka. It is a study of a village that is representative of thousands of other small communities in developing countries around the world. And it is a study that is both ethnographically solid and yet thoroughly reflexive. The reader comes to understand the place and people described in exacting detail and the ethnographer as well—as ethnographer—and her interaction with the people.

This case study can be assigned to students with the assurance that from it they will learn a lesson that is integral to the anthropological insight—that people are much the same everywhere and that in every place people are different. Perhaps this should be phrased as such: People are the same everywhere but their cultures are different. The ability to convince the reader of the truth of this axiom is both the strength of anthropological ethnography and the source of certain difficulties.

As the culture historian and literary critic James Clifton has pointed out, an ethnography is a construction, fabricated from the observed behavior of people in place and the interpretations placed upon that behavior by the ethnographer. The word *fiction* has been used as an appellation for this construction. While granting the validity of this term as a step toward understanding any ethnography, one must also understand that a good ethnography goes well beyond fiction in its usual novelistic sense. The reader is taken into the confidence of the author-ethnographer in the attempt to understand and portray behavior and motivations that are quite different than those of either the reader or the ethnographer. A good ethnography is a true story, where the characters and their characteristic behavior emerge early on and remain in character as the plot, the story line, unfolds; and where the author-ethnographer's character and perceptions also emerge early on and remain true to form as the story is told.

The "story" in this case study—the life and times of the residents of a small village in a developing country—is unusually complete. The history of the village, subsistence and living standards, beliefs in the supernatural and the rituals that put them into action, healing and health, kinship and family, childhood and socialization, formal education, the position of women, factionalism, and the village in relation to the nation are all displayed in living detail. The negative aspects of village life are not neglected, but on the whole the interpretation is positive and hopeful. Throughout the telling of the story of this village the author-ethnographer is a vital and enduring presence. She tells it like it is, and tells how it was for her.

As a representation of the strengths of an anthropological approach to understanding this complex, vexing, changing world we live in, this case study is unparalleled. An instructor can assign it to students knowing that what they will learn will contribute positively to the course being taught and that anthropology is well represented. No higher recommendation can be made for the use of any case study in the teaching and learning of anthropology.

George and Louise Spindler
Series Editors
Ethnographics
Box 38
Calistoga, CA 94515-0038

Preface

This book is a case study of a village in Sri Lanka, the teardrop-shaped island of more than 18 million people located off the southeastern tip of India. Sri Lanka is a nation of villages—some 30,000 of them in an area about the size of West Virginia. The village studied here is in numerous ways representative of hundreds of thousands of villages in the developing world, especially those in the populous subcontinent of South Asia.

The six countries of South Asia—Pakistan, Nepal, Bhutan, Bangladesh, India, and Sri Lanka—constitute a single region, divided by multitudinous ethnic groups, more than a hundred languages, differing political systems, and a great diversity of religious beliefs. These differences notwithstanding, there are many commonalities. Seventy-five percent of the people are farmers with small holdings who inhabit villages and earn their living with simple technology. Almost the whole region is located in the monsoon belt, and the erratic weather presents a problem for farmers living at subsistence level. The Indo-Gangetic Plain, stretching from the Punjab to Bangladesh, and reaching south along eastern India to Sri Lanka, is the world's largest rice-growing zone; and most South Asians eat rice as their staple food. The region's traditional agricultural and economic life is punctuated by the weekly market, which provides for a lively exchange of produce and services as well as an opportunity for communication.

With the exception of Nepal, the nations of South Asia share a British colonial past. Although every country achieved its independence, this did not bring economic liberation or in most cases political stability. South Asian nations are perpetually launching programs of rural development and industrial development, and they are perennially in need of foreign aid in loans and grants. The diversity of ethnic and religious groups has led to political unrest in most of these nations, or even to separatist wars. This was the case in Bangladesh, which separated from Pakistan in 1971; and it is now the situation ravaging Sri Lanka, as the Tamil minority fights for independence from the Sinhalese majority state.

The social systems of South Asia are largely hierarchical, with castes or caste-like groupings that play an important role in society. Even in the Muslim nations of Pakistan and Bangladesh there is a strong hierarchy in ranking from landholders down to peasants and manual laborers. The social sphere is family oriented, emphasizing respect for elders, cooperative and community values rather than priority of the individual, and extensive familial obligations.

Perhaps the most pervasive feature of all the South Asian nations is their religious orientation. The lives of the people are largely determined by beliefs and rituals that can be found in every sphere: economic, social, political, and aesthetic. These beliefs help provide a sense of security, especially for the poor who are engaged in an elemental struggle for survival, striving to improve their standard of living against countless odds.

The subject of this case study is Suduwatura Ara, a remote agricultural village in southeastern Sri Lanka, and a place that well exemplifies the ways in which supernatural beliefs permeate all human activities. It is a relatively new village of settlers who began arriving in the 1960s and 1970s, encroaching on plots of crown land they cleared in an area of scrub jungle. There I lived and worked for sixteen months in 1984–1985, returning in 1994–1995 to spend my sabbatical year of leave in the same little mud house the villagers had built for me a decade earlier. Just as Suduwatura Ara is representative of thousands of villages in South Asia and the developing world, so too are my experiences as a fieldworker in a remote agrarian setting in many ways similar to those of other anthropologists in the field. I have tried to share my personal reflections throughout this work.

In the first research period I focused on formal education in disadvantaged rural areas, visiting village schools in the largely undeveloped Moneragala District for a study that was to become my doctoral dissertation. Although I was looking mainly at education, I was continually intrigued by other phenomena unfolding around me in a subsistence village. In the second research period I was free to delve into all aspects of village life as well as note the developments that had taken place in the interim years.

Returning to Suduwatura Ara allowed me to document a village culture that must constantly cope with perils and uncertainties, and one that has taken this process of coping to great lengths. The villagers employ a complex variety of ritual practices and beliefs in supernatural forces that can be manipulated, appeased, or dispelled to reduce misfortune. Transecting every chapter of this book—which attempts to give a broad overview of village life—are examples of ways in which the people seek to minimize risks and dangers, many practices having evolved into institutionalized rituals.

The theme of coping with uncertainty lies at the very core of Sinhalese village life. It was this kind of fascinating anthropological phenomena that kept me going as I attempted to cope in my own way with many uncertainties, using my Western strategies and values. Sometimes I was tempted to back these up with an amulet or an offering to a local deity.

In their various ways the villagers kept me free from harm during my sojourn. Once again—as they had a decade ago—they gave generously, allowing my presence in their homes, their school, their fields, their meetings, their social events, and their ritual ceremonies, enduring and answering my endless questions. We have come to know each other with renewed and deeper insights. I hope this book does justice to them and to their culture.

Contents

1 / Fieldwork on the Sinhalese Frontier

With a new appreciation I thought of my own life, of my country and our civilization. I had learned here to appreciate the riches of comfort and learning. . . . Secure in our heritage we are often blind to it. Surrounded by so much, we are often too lazy to stretch out our hands for even the nearest. . . . I had come from one world to live in another. These two worlds judged by standards so greatly different that translation was often impossible.
—from Return to Laughter by Elenore Smith Bowen, 1954

In October 1983 I went to Sri Lanka to lecture at the University of Colombo as a team member of the Dutch Inter-University Cooperation Project for Training, Teaching and Research. My departure had been postponed for two months, and my plans had almost been canceled, for the past summer had witnessed the worst ethnic rioting and violence in the history of the nation. With some trepidation I got off the plane and set foot on what felt like a different planet in spite of all my preparations. After a brief introduction with the project manager, we set off for Colombo. The project car honked and careened its way over the crowded road from the airport, the driver—like those in the other cars—making more use of his horn than his brakes.

Notwithstanding my initial anxiety, I was soon enthralled by the exoticism of the local color that was unwinding like an ethnographic film on all sides: three-wheeler taxis with squawking horns darting among slow-moving ox carts and occasional luxury automobiles; barefooted laborers in hoisted sarongs unloading trucks and shuffling along with incredible loads on their backs; people washing at roadside pumps, pouring buckets of water over their heads and their soaked bathing cloths.

There were tiny, squalid-looking roadside stalls with orange-colored king coconuts and heaps of the discarded shells decaying in the sun. The smell of rancid rice and spices rose from small garbage dumps as crows picked through them and skirmished over bits of stale bread. Walls were covered with tattered political posters and gaudy hand-painted billboards that touted sentimental love scenes in the latest Indian films or martial arts from the Far East. Buses and smaller private vans, packed to beyond capacity, tilted and strained as more passengers jumped onto the steps, hanging outside, while the crier shouted the destination in tongue-twisting blurts. Amid the potholes and litter and stray dogs strode elegantly clad ladies in their saris with gold chains and yards of draped cloth that fell in flowing trains from their left shoulders. Buddha statues were seated in roadside shrines with wilted offering flowers on small altars before them, yellow paint peeling from their serene and unflinching faces as the noisy street scenes continued in urban rhythms.

My senses feasted on the unfolding scenarios with an enthusiastic and naive anthropological gluttony. Contrasting the exotica we also passed air-conditioned first-class hotels, private clubs in colonial mansions with immaculate lawns, and exquisite restaurants catering to the discriminating taste. The future looked promising and exciting. I stepped immediately into the infatuation stage of culture shock.

It did not take long for disillusion to set in when I began my job as guest lecturer at the University of Colombo. The draining heat, the transportation problems, the slow pace and lack of efficiency and punctuality, the communication handicaps—not only primary ones through the language and culture, but secondary ones due to the archaic technology: power outages, phones and typewriters and copying machines that didn't work—all added to my frustration. Preparing a lesson while my papers were flying around and flapping in the breeze of a ceiling fan is an art that I mastered. I never got used to the nonchalant way in which appointments were not kept, however; people always had some family funeral to attend.

On the other hand, many of the M.A. students I taught—the cream of the crop—were bright and stimulating. Some were even eager to do a field project in a remote district. By the end of the first term I was infinitely glad that my contract allowed me to do research in a village for my doctoral dissertation, serving as adviser to my students doing projects in other villages.

FIRST FIELDWORK, 1984–85

The remote Moneragala District in southeastern Sri Lanka had for several years been the target area of the Leiden–Colombo NUFFIC Project. In its broadest scope this project focused on "sociological aspects of rural and regional development," and formal education was an aspect yet to be covered. Informal visiting of the schools in the district began in December 1983 in order to make a specific choice of research location. During several trips to the district I casually observed some forty schools, often with the help of two excellent contact persons who were familiar with the district. One of these, a retired education officer for Moneragala, Mr. D. D. K. Senanayaka, was later to become my indispensable assistant for the research. The District Education Department was only of minor assistance in the search for a school—an understandable situation, for they preferred to show the "model" schools that were considered to be faring well.

A tip came from an Education Department jeep driver that there was a small school in a jungle area south of Moneragala town, over dirt roads, with only one teacher. Notwithstanding the eroded path with deep ridges, the rocks, gullies, gorges, streams, mud bogs, and jungle growth, the project car managed to forge its way out to the little hamlet of widely scattered homesteads. The school grounds were deserted upon arrival, but the weathered tables and chairs and the homemade blackboards on rickety easels verified the fact that the wattle-and-daub structure was indeed a school. Together with the others in our small party and a few village children, I climbed to the top of a colossal rock near the school, pausing with a sense of adventure as the children pointed out some fresh elephant dung on the rock. Taking in the bird's eye view of the surrounding area—with rugged boulders jutting haphazardly throughout the landscape of *illuk*-grass fields, nestled in a valley between two forested mountain ranges—I quickly assessed the advantages and disadvantages of such a location:

- There were only simple mud houses without any conveniences, thus probably no appropriate boarding place. Being a relatively new encroacher village, however, it was a type typical for the fast-growing Moneragala District and therefore quite interesting.
- It was not easily accessible, but within an hour's drive by motor vehicle to Moneragala town, where not only the District Education Department is located but also a more developed infrastructure.
- It obviously had a needy school, one where a contribution in the way of teaching English, which was in the curriculum but lacking due to teacher shortage, would likely be appreciated.

I must admit that the peaceful and scenic environment and the idyllic pond nearby with its trickling waterfall, luscious ferns, and vine-covered rocks, swayed my hopes that this would be my research location.

Chatting with the villagers who had gathered in the schoolhouse, curious at the arrival of any vehicles and especially one carrying a white woman, I found out that this was a new village, named Suduwatura Ara, with mainly migrants from the up-country in central Sri Lanka. They had built the school themselves and had run it on a volunteer basis for two years before it was taken over as a government school. Further conversations revealed that there was a 50-year-old woman principal/teacher who walked 6 km to school and frequently stayed in the somber, dusty room at the end of the open school hall. Things were taking shape and my hopes grew with each new bit of information.

Inquiries about possible accommodations with a family in Suduwatura Ara met with surprise and hospitable reactions, but also some skepticism as to whether there would be a suitable place. Quickly, however, a villager suggested that they build a small house on the school grounds, so I would have use of the school latrine—the only one in the village with a concrete slab—and the nearby pond; it would also give easy access to the focal point of my research on education. Others agreed with the idea, and there was discussion about possibly building the house in a *shramadana* (free community labor) effort.

The warmth of these Sinhalese villagers continued to radiate as I went to the pond to bathe, accompanied by a bevy of chattering girls and women. We all put on our bathing cloths, and they giggled as I clumsily struggled with mine. While some soaped my back, others scooped up water in buckets to pour over me in the traditional bathing fashion. Laughing together, I ventured my first basic Sinhala sentences, but more communication was carried on through gestures and smiles. I walked back to the school, still surrounded by girls holding on to my hand or arm and pulling the sandspurs from my skirt. The first mutual feelings of attachment were already made.

By now the teacher and the local carpenter had arrived. All were enthusiastic about the prospects of a guest coming to live in their village. Putting up a wattle-and-daub house in short order was apparently no problem, but they recommended a cement floor rather than one of cow dung as in all the other houses, and a corrugated iron roof rather than the customary grass thatch to reduce the danger of poisonous snakes. I gulped at these remarks but remained undaunted. I already felt a sense of affinity with these people who accepted a stranger in their midst without hesitation or suspicion. The choice of this village was made on the spot. With the aid of the teacher a date was set for a general village meeting in the school on the next full moon day *(poya),* February 16, 1984, when an official introduction would be made.

There was a large turnout at the schoolhouse on that day as the Education Department's jeep, filled to capacity with local dignitaries, chugged out to "my" village of Suduwatura Ara. The welcome was hospitable and the appropriate mood of importance and acceptability had been created by the time it was my turn to make a speech, telling of the purpose and goals of coming to live there. The people listened with necks craning to get a look at the white woman who so unexpectedly and unexplainably had chosen this place out of many possibilities. Mothers nursed their babies and people whispered comments to one another as the business moved to the subject of my house. It was designed and planned then and there, the local carpenter and mason giving advice.

The Assistant Government Agent (AGA) gave permission to fell the trees necessary for construction, and estimates were made for the costs of cement, corrugated iron sheets, and carpentry work. As is the case for all important endeavors in these surroundings of imminent evil forces and uncertainty about outcomes, plans were made for starting work on my house on the auspicious day and time *(neketa)* the astrologer would determine. This would help counteract any bad fortune that might be ahead during the house building and my subsequent living there.

Bouncing and jolting over the washed-out paths back to Moneragala town, it was clear I would have to invest in a jeep if I did not want to walk to and from the village. In Colombo, after many frustrating comparisons of broken-down vehicles, I settled on an old second-hand Mitsubishi. It would serve as village bus and ambulance in the months to follow, gradually becoming a pathetically ramshackle jalopy on the jungle roads and in the makeshift repair shops lacking spare parts.

I stayed in Suduwatura Ara for sixteen months, with intermittent short trips back to Colombo to touch base with the project. I came to know the people well, holding in-depth interviews in all forty-three households within the loosely defined boundaries of the village at that time. Teaching English in the school, I became personally acquainted with the children and the problems faced by teachers and learners in remote rural villages.

In October 1985 my house was officially turned over to the village as a "Learning and Development Centre," with a small lending library. The local Member of Parliament came for the opening ceremony and promised that the village would be given a permanent school building. At an elaborate and emotional farewell party shortly thereafter, I left part of me behind in Suduwatura Ara.

THE INTERIM

Back in the Netherlands in 1986 I received a letter from my assistant, Mr. Senanayaka, who wrote about another American anthropologist in Sri Lanka whom he had met. My assistant had told him about the village and the existence of my house as a possible home base for his research. Shortly thereafter I received a letter from Michael Woost of the University of Texas, asking if I would have any objections to his carrying out a study in Suduwatura Ara.

An irrational feeling of possessiveness swept over me, which I tried to fight with rational arguments. I also felt guilty as thoughts like "But what if he should come to totally different conclusions and discredit my research?" flooded my mind. At the same time I reasoned that it would be anthropologically interesting to have two lengthy, consecutive, but completely independent field researches in a single village. Besides, having another Westerner in Suduwatura Ara would mean that possible development attention would focus on the village and benefit the people. I wrote back that he was welcome to use the "Learning and Development Centre" as his abode, and I wished him the best of luck.

Like my research, his was written into a Ph.D. thesis (1990), although on an entirely different topic. Woost looked at the routines and rituals of development, the ideologies of national community, and the process of state formation. Like me, he is now a college anthropology professor (Hartwick College), and we occasionally enjoy exchanging tales and sharing news of events on the Suduwatura Ara scene: our old data-hunting grounds.

During the interim nine years I continued contact with the people of Suduwatura Ara through my assistant, Mr. D. D. K. Senanayaka, who made regular visits and reports, managing the small contributions sent for maintenance and expansion of the library. The villagers' letters were answered with a twinge of guilt: "I miss you all, and I will return, but I can't yet tell you when."

I was pleased when the Swedish International Development Authority (SIDA) selected the Suduwatura Ara school to participate in its program, which brought such advantages as the building of teachers' quarters and school cabinets and bookshelves. More significantly, it was a pleasure to hear that the village was selected to participate in the government's "Village Re-Awakening" campaign in 1991, through which Suduwatura Ara received a prescribed development package.

The number of homesteads had grown from 43 to 108, and a few outward development changes could be perceived, such as road culverts, a community hall, and six new wells. But for the most part, the slow-beating rhythm of agricultural life, and the struggle for a decent and hunger-free existence in the Dry Zone—filled with risks and uncertainties— were unchanged. The feel of the village, its pulse, its essence, were just the same as when I left there nine years before.

THE "HOMECOMING" IN 1994

Taking my sabbatical year of leave from Eckerd College in September 1994, I arrived in Colombo with only two suitcases of goods to see me through, but with a much larger baggage of experience and a modest knowledge of the language, which was slowly coming back. Four days in the sultry, noisy, boisterous capital city were enough to make preparations and purchase a list of needed items that completed my survival kit: kerosene lamps and a single-pit cooker, plastic buckets and water jugs, and chlorine to purify my water. The charm of the big city quickly evaporated under the intense, exhausting sun. I was eager to get back to familiar territory.

The villagers, knowing I was coming but not knowing when I would arrive in Suduwatura Ara, sent an emissary, an energetic and independent neighbor woman, on the twelve-hour trip by foot and bus. Leela arrived at 1:00 A.M. at my assistant's house and saw me for an emotional few minutes at breakfast. With a true sense of mission, she immediately got back on a bus for the long return trip, able to tell the villagers when to be ready with the welcoming reception.

This time I would not have a jeep, as I did not need to visit schools throughout the district as part of the research. Looking back in my old journals, which told the tale of many headaches the jeep had caused and the endless days it was in the shop waiting for unavailable parts to be made, I was relieved to be relegated to my own two feet for transportation—although I knew the people would be disappointed: Any four-wheeled vehicle lends status to a poor village like Suduwatura Ara.

As my assistant and I turned off the main road in an old rented car with driver for the last 8.5 km, all my senses were functioning with keenest acuity, hungrily assimilating the sights and sounds and smells that hurtled me back a decade in time. Nearing the school and central point among the widely scattered homesteads, I felt a rush of emotion, which kept me on a high through the long welcoming ceremony. I passed between two lines of smiling well-wishers offering sheaves of betel leaves and bouquets of plastic flowers. I embraced Sudu-Menike (pronounced Sudu-Mani-Kay), the woman who had been my dearest and most loyal friend, for a mutual tearful moment of reunion. The faces passed as in a dream, some well known but mellowed by age, children I had taught earlier still looking vaguely familiar, and a few carrying an infant of their own.

1.1 Villagers line up to greet the ethnographer when she returns to Suduwatura Ara after a decade. Village matriarch, Bandara Menike, is in the center.

The program reflected the respect and sentimentality of the villagers: blessings by the Buddhist monk, traditional songs by solo performers, dances by the children, humorous skits, and endless speeches. I was somewhat embarrassed to hear the repeated praises in which I was given credit for everything good that had ever happened to the village.

My house of the previous research period had recently been painted and given a new covering of grass thatch to insulate the corrugated iron roof from the blazing tropical sun. It was a joy to see that the mango, jackfruit, and lime trees I had planted were now quite large and bearing fruit. The flowering trees that graced the garden had grown from cuttings the schoolchildren had brought a decade earlier. On my first night back in this small house I called my "hut"—with the mild fumes of kerosene lamps, watching a gecko scamper along the top of the mud walls, listening to the night calls of the jungle, and gazing out at stars so clear and bright it was no longer a wonder that they played a large role in the people's beliefs—it felt like I'd never been away.

It was the second night that the villagers nearly did me in through their finest intentions. In my honor an all-night *pirith* chanting ceremony had been organized. This chanting, to invoke the blessings of "the triple gem" (the Buddha, his teachings, and the Buddhist monks) as well as the gods and deities in the area, would normally have been held just before the start of the main *(maha)* cultivation season; but when the villagers heard I was coming, they postponed it until my arrival.

The school hall was bustling on my second day there, with young men carefully constructing an elaborate enclosure *(mandape)* decorated with blue and white tissue paper. This was the place to sit for the eight village men who would do the chanting. Construction was done according to sacred prescriptions, with nine kinds of plants hanging from the *mandape*'s ceiling. This time (much to my secret dismay) the Women's Society had spent Rs. 500 (about $10.50—a huge sum in a poor subsistence village) to rent a battery-operated microphone with powerful loudspeakers in order to send the chanting resounding for many miles throughout the jungle countryside.

The seven designated village men and the school principal arrived in impeccable white clothes to start the chanting at 8:00 P.M. following a lamp lighting at the school's bo tree *(ficus religiosa)*. Villagers of all ages crowded into the school, taking a seat on mats on the floor. The first hour of chanting, consisting of the three main Buddhist sutras or sermons, I found quite interesting. During this time a ball of string originating in the *mandape* was unwound and passed around for all participants to take hold of and thereby receive blessings directly through it. I took hold of the string, juggling the camcorder and camera and trying to look appropriately devout while engaging in mundane photography and observation tasks.

After a pause for a vegetarian dinner, followed by a second hour of chanting through the microphone by the eight men, now chanting two-by-two *(yuga)* in the ancient Pali language, I begged off at 11:00 P.M. and retired to my house. I was utterly exhausted from the emotional intensity of the first two days.

The tremendous loudspeakers, however, were directed straight at my house, fifty yards away, with untold decibels of blessings penetrating the mud walls. Though high-tech is known to fail when really needed, the loudspeakers droned at maximum volume without faltering, appeasing the gods and honoring me. The eight men, three of them quite elderly, kept the chanting up until 5:00 A.M. as planned. Even with a pillow over my head the chants rang loud and discordant to my ears, and sleep was out of the question. At one point in this sleepless night my thoughts went to the Waco, Texas, standoff between the Branch Davidian cultists and federal agents that took place less than a year and a half before. At that time I had been indignant at the ethnocentrism of the U.S. federal agents who began so-called psychological warfare in the third week of attempts to get David Koresh and his followers to come out of their besieged compound, namely by blaring taped chants of Tibetan Buddhist monks through loudspeakers during the night. I joked to myself about the irony of the situation: The villagers saw loudly broadcasted chanting as honorific and beautiful sounding; it was their gift to me, while I came from a culture where loud Buddhist chanting was seen as a way to aggressively exhaust people and drive them to distraction.

At 5:15 A.M. I was fetched by my friend and neighbor, Leela, to return to the school to have a length of the blessed thread tied around my neck for protection (such as Sudu-Menike receives in the photograph below), and to drink a bit of the blessed water from the decorated pot in the *mandape*. Bedraggled and tired, but bestowed with many blessings to carry me through the fieldwork period, I started my third day at "home." I mustered a show of graciousness, not having the heart to tell a further irony of the situation: that one of the reasons I had longed to come back to Suduwatura Ara was for the peace and quiet of the rural setting.

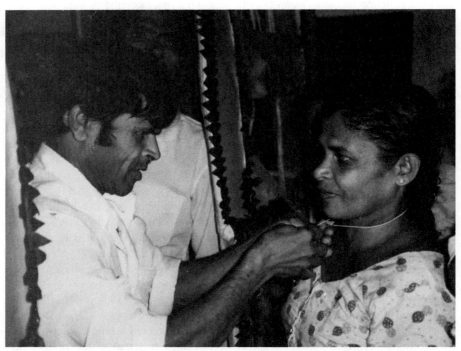

1.2 Heem Banda ties a piece of the blessed thread around Sudu-Menike's neck in the early morning after the pirith *ceremony.*

PARTICIPANT OBSERVATION AND THE POSITION OF THE FIELDWORKER

How far does—and should—the "participant" aspect of participant observation research go? To what extent is it advantageous for research purposes to live like the inhabitants do or even to start identifying somewhat with them? These were questions I mulled over from time to time.

During the first fieldwork period in Suduwatura Ara, my interaction with the inhabitants grew as the length of stay and my knowledge of the Sinhala language increased. The roles I was expected to play likewise increased: teacher, social worker, development worker, nurse, jeep-bus and ambulance driver, photographer, librarian, arbitrator, adviser, and administrator. The option of avoiding involvement did not seem feasible—nor as I saw it, desirable—after the first few months.

It was necessary to keep reminding myself that the researcher's presence and actions, along with those of other outsiders, modify the context being observed and are also influenced by it. Not only the more passive aspects of my living in the village, but particularly the active roles had considerable impact, most particularly, bringing development projects, making contacts, and inviting guests. From the other side, the village had its influence on me. Things that were originally new and unusual became normal and commonplace in my perspective. A thick pancake (roti) served with chilies and onions for breakfast started tasting delicious, and the music started to sound pleasing to the ear. My village friends were happy when I bought some Sinhala tapes and learned the words to some popular songs.

Working in the school as an English teacher in 1984–1985 and teaching adult English classes on the weekends provided a place as "participant" observer. It was also an excellent vantage point for viewing the school's functioning and for getting to know the children, parents, and teachers more closely. The lengthy period of sixteen months assisted in making the picture probably a truer one: Weaknesses came to light that could have been kept hidden during a shorter stay.

I would like to be able to say that I had started sharing the lifestyles of the villagers—for I was eating the same food they did, washing my clothes at the pond, lighting kerosene lamps at night, tilling the ground in my garden, and in the second fieldwork period, walking the 8.5 km to the nearest bus stop—but that would be pretentious and misleading. Seen on the whole, my so-called grassroots-level village life was not at all comparable to that of the farmers among whom I was living. Aside from tea or light snacks, my meals were prepared and brought on a contract basis by one of the few families with a surplus: rice and tasty but red-hot vegetable curries. I did not have to go through the laborious process of cultivating and preparing the food; and I could afford to supplement my diet with eggs or canned fish, items that were too expensive for the villagers. The possessions I had in my house, which seemed very basic to me, like an old portable typewriter, a kerosene burner for cooking, several lanterns, a tape-recorder, camera, and books, were nevertheless seen as luxuries by the villagers. And of course I could leave Suduwatura Ara whenever the desire or the necessity arose.

By the end of my second fieldwork period in 1995, my idealized and idyllic view of the jungle surroundings and the village way of life had become tempered. Perhaps it was because I was a bit older, more experienced, and a bit more spoiled by an American lifestyle (prior to my first fieldwork I had lived in the Netherlands for 17 years). While in both periods the villagers looked to me for favors, assistance, and ways that I could help facilitate development of their village, in the second period the traditional values, for example the spirit of community and cooperation, seemed to have eroded. The villagers came with rising expectations and the presumption that I had returned to help them. Still, compared to the individualistic values of the West, their hospitality and helpfulness were grand scale, and to criticize their behavior would be unfair. Thanks to their cooperation, both fieldwork periods were possible, and during the entire research a mutual feeling of respect and appreciation was shared. While I spoke of "my village" and "my villagers," they spoke of *"our* Sudu Teacher" (white teacher).

LEARNING PROPER BEHAVIOR

Adapting to proper behavior—or attempting to—can sometimes be a disconcerting enterprise, as I found upon arrival in Suduwatura Ara for the first stay. Our own automatic and socialized patterns of behavior, feeling normal to us, are not necessarily universal.

Very quickly I discovered that pleasantries such as "good morning" or a greeting like "hello" or "hi" are not part of the village repertoire. They were usually a bit taken by surprise, not knowing how to respond, when I would greet them with the classic Sinhala greeting, *"ayubowan,"* which I learned in lesson books as the proper way to say "hello" as well as "goodbye," pressing one's hands together (prayerlike) rather than shaking hands. Through experience I found that this greeting is far too formal for everyday life in Sri Lanka, especially in the villages. There you are greeted with "Where are you going?" *(Koheda yanne?)* if you are met going away from the village or your home, and "Where did you go?" *(Koheda giye?)* when returning toward the village, along with a smile and a subtle nod of the head. In the beginning I was taken aback by their seeming curiosity before learning that these are the normal questions always asked. It is really the repertoire of smiles and different facial expressions that communicate a greeting. Likewise, it is common when meeting someone to ask or state the obvious. If a person is returning from the well with wet hair, carrying a soap box and towel, he or she will probably be met with "Did you bathe?" *(Naewe da?).*

In Sri Lanka, where helpfulness, hospitality, and generosity are important values, using the expression "thank you" as regularly and automatically as Westerners do would be considered stilted and strange. Before learning this I tended to overuse the words *bohoma istuthiy* (thank you very much)—which is in fact a relatively new expression in the Sinhala language. Offering someone a chair is considered normal behavior and does not require a "thank you"; here a smile would be enough. In a way it was good to observe that expressing gratitude in words has not been inflated to a meaningless automatism, but rather is reserved for times when one is truly grateful for a personal favor or gift. My inappropriate overuse of "thank you" in the beginning led to frequent giggles and amusement. It was like our saying, "I am sincerely thankful" when offered a cup of tea. Even when I learned this and wanted to conform, it was hard to break the imprinted habit.

The matter of offering a cup of tea in this land so famous for Ceylon tea was another situation that led to some misunderstandings when I first settled in my little house. Wanting to be the hospitable hostess, I bought tea, sugar, milk powder, biscuits (cookies), even some fruit-drink syrup and bottled soft drinks to offer my guests. When they would come by for a visit, I would ask them, "Would you like a cup of tea?" (this was even a line in their third-grade English book I was teaching from), "or a cool drink?" Inevitably they would refuse. *"Epa, epa"* (No, no I don't want any) they would repeatedly say. I would then ask, "Would you like a biscuit?" thinking they surely would not turn down cookies in this place of food shortages. I felt somewhat hurt by their refusal and even wondered whether there might be a question of pollution and their not trusting the cleanliness of my kitchen. Only after relating the dilemma to my assistant some time later did the situation become clear. In Sri Lanka, *of course* the guests want a cup of tea or a soft drink and some sweets. To ask them by question if they want it is like saying, "You don't want any, do you?" A good hostess will immediately prepare the very best she has—usually extremely sweet tea, preferably with milk powder if they have it—and the best sweets to be found in the kitchen. Giving your guests the opportunity to refuse is impolite; and if you give them that choice, their proper behavior is to refuse.

It made sense. I thought back on the times that I had been a guest in village houses, remembering the cups of extremely sweet tea, sometimes with milk, put in front of me without their asking if I take milk or sugar, or even want a cup of tea at all. At those times, with my Western values—and owing to the fact that I don't like milk or sugar in my tea—I had felt disappointed but obliged to drink the tea anyway to be polite.

Thus I learned that sweet milk-tea, or very sweet "plain tea" if no milk was available, would be served if I did not quickly specify my likes when the women scurried off to the kitchen. However, the tea-preference problem was still not solved. The villagers felt a bit insulted that I would ask for the cheapest, poor-man's kind of tea, for they thought I was indirectly saying they probably could not afford to buy sugar. Usually they would put a little sugar in my tea anyway. That was from their standpoint the polite thing to do in this culture where hostesses must try to offer the best they have, and where the amount of sugar served in tea can be indicative of how much you like a person. I finally solved the problem by saying that Ceylon tea, famous the world over, is so tasty that I did not want to spoil the taste with sugar and milk. This usually worked. Most of the villagers did not know that the best Ceylon tea is exported, like many top-grade export products from diverse countries around the world, and that only the second quality is left for the natives themselves.

Taking a small gift to the hostess is the accepted practice when visiting a household, especially when invited for a meal. Unlike in the West, where a gift is opened immediately and admired, with profuse thank you's conveyed to the giver, here the gift is accepted graciously, the receiver using both hands to take it, then put aside. It is only opened after the guest has gone, and it will most probably never be mentioned again—no matter how personal or carefully selected the gift may have been. When asked about this practice, Sri Lankans will say that it is to avoid an awkward situation where some disappointment might be seen in the eyes or reaction of the receiver.

Sri Lankans are known for their hospitality. Their doors are never shut, and they always make time for visitors. This facilitated doing fieldwork and interviewing—though it made it difficult to get much work done in my own house. When a guest arrives, it is not only common to prepare a cup of tea, but also to offer them a betel chew *(bulath vita)*, a custom I never indulged in, neither as receiver nor giver (though as a dedicated participant observer, I did try it once, only to find the taste strong and unpleasant). A betel chew consists of a rolled up betel leaf together with a bit of areca nut, tobacco, chalky lime, and perhaps spices such as clove. The mildly addictive practice of chewing betel is widespread in Sri Lankan villages and is frequently seen in urban settings as well. Presenting a sheaf of betel leaves to one's teacher on the first day of classes (I received many, which I gave to people who do chew), to Buddhist monks who have come to perform an almsgiving *(dana)* ceremony, to a traditional doctor (with the contribution for his services folded in the leaves), or to some dignitary on a ceremonious occasion is a sign of respect. A few of the better-off households have a traditional brass dish on a pedestal *(ilattattuwa)* for spreading out the betel leaves when presenting them, together with a brass spittoon *(padikkama)* for guests to spit out the chewed leaves. The latter have by this time become a bright red spittle through a chemical reaction with the lime and saliva, leaving a red residue on the teeth and gums. There is no stigma attached to having betel-stained teeth in the village. Rather than finding this unattractive, some consider the redness around the mouth to even be seductive looking in young women, although they are not encouraged to start chewing.

In the presence of elders or respected people, it is not polite to sit down until the respected person asks you to sit; then you should sit on the smallest chair and keep a distance as a way of showing respect. A few of the traditionally raised villagers would never accept a chair, always standing when my assistant, the retired Education Officer, or I was in the room. When a Buddhist monk enters your house, it is impolite for anyone to sit on a chair in his presence; standing or sitting on a mat on the floor is permissible. Our local Buddhist monk, on his occasional visits to my house, could sit for an hour or more, spouting philosophical ideas, while I—understanding only small fragments here and there—nodded and pretended to be attentive, standing respectfully on tired feet until his sermon was complete. Then, as is the custom when greeting monks or when they are leaving, I would bow down in the "worshiping" posture as he departed, relieved that the demands on my conformity to custom were satisfied for at least a while.

PROBLEMS OF THE FIELDWORKER

Isolation

As a fieldworker in a remote village that had a culture very different from my own, I was often coping with the problem of isolation on several different levels.

The most obvious and perhaps easiest to deal with was the geographic isolation. Especially in the second fieldwork period, when I had decided to eliminate the headaches of a second-hand vehicle, I was daily confronted by the fact that it was a one and a half-hour walk to the nearest small town with bus stop, not to mention the nine-hour bus ride to Colombo. As Suduwatura Ara had only three tiny shops carrying a few basic items, I was compelled to ask villagers to pick me up some needed item in town, or take a day to make the long journey by foot under the scorching sun. The unavailability of so many items accented the geographic isolation—but even when goods were available in town, it was often problematic to carry them back by bus and on foot. My cane chairs, for example, were just light enough to be carried the 8.5 km on our heads. Geographic isolation was also indirectly responsible for the fact that newspapers were hard to get, the English-language radio station was hard to receive, and the cycling postman did not come every day.

More difficult than the above was the language problem and linguistic isolation. When I first came in 1984 an urban Sinhalese lady came along as my interpreter. We even planned and built a separate small room for her in my house. She had a degree in sociology and seemed to be enthusiastic about the work before we left Colombo. On our way to Moneragala District, however, as we pushed farther and farther into the less densely populated areas, her mood changed and she became more skeptical. Her shock at the primitiveness of the village was apparent on our first trip together there in April, although no secrets had been kept from her about the lack of modern conveniences. While waiting in Moneragala town for the house to be completed, her phobias about poisonous snakes and wild animals grew. Twelve days after the house-warming ceremony, my interpreter could endure no more of the hardships: the heat, and the lack of electricity, shops, newspapers, television or movies, water on tap, medical services, and so on. The fifty-meter distance to the school latrine after dark was pure anguish for her, and the imminent possibility of snakes all accumulated to make her misery complete. My anthropological paradise was to her an imprisonment in a world lacking civilization. We were both relieved when she boarded a bus back to Colombo—but I was left as the only English speaker in the village.

Pantomiming and dramatizing many concepts for which I lacked vocabulary gave rise to frequent hilarity, but also enhanced a rapid personal rapport with the villagers. A couple of older children proved to be particularly adept at deciphering my poor-quality grammar and vocabulary. They often accompanied me and served as a kind of translator, restating my pidgin Sinhala in a more understandable form for others, and rephrasing comments of my respondents using simpler words I could understand.

Much was missed due to the language barrier, however, and interviewing the households required good knowledge of the language. Mr. Senanayaka, the retired education officer, who had already provided so much assistance, offered to come out frequently from Colombo and serve as my interpreter for the interviews and formal occasions. This he also did in the second fieldwork period, together with the school's former English teacher.

In spite of the satisfactory interpreting arrangements at regular intervals, I had underestimated the need to unload my thoughts to someone in my own language without having to concentrate on forming rudimentary sentences with simple concepts in the Sinhala language. Even though my language skills improved gradually, and basic-level conversation was not a problem, the language subtleties that enrich human interaction and give it a deeper meaning were lacking, leaving a form of loneliness in spite of the many village visitors. Not having mastered reading Sinhala script reinforced my linguistic isolation. When my assistant and other English-speaking visitors occasionally came, they had to endure a flood of stories and experiences that poured out unabated until someone suggested it was time to eat or bathe.

And yet, even being able to communicate fluently with a common language did not bridge the cultural gap and the feeling of cultural isolation—the overriding fact that our respective values, perceptions, beliefs, and practices were so different. On the one hand, these observations were intriguing to the anthropologist. After all, that is what I was in the field for. On the other hand, the all-pervasive differences intensified my cultural isolation despite the respect I had for the villagers. At times I consciously knew I was in some stage of culture shock, though I was powerless to shake off mild depressions and ethnocentric feelings, covering the profound to the most trivial: How can development take place when villagers go deep in debt to pay for Buddhist almsgiving ceremonies? How nice it would be to flick on a light switch, watch the news on TV, open a fridge, and have a cold drink. How good a hamburger would taste after the same old vegetable curries every day. How incredible it is that no toilet paper can be bought in all of Moneragala District.

My escape was to listen to tapes I had brought, pour out my feelings in a letter, or read novels and other books. In the late afternoons I would often sit outside reading in my favorite place under the shady jack tree, its fruit near the trunk approaching the size of large watermelons. From here I could see the villagers returning home from their fields or the market, and I would glance up to wave as they passed. But even the pleasure of reading was often frustrated and tedious. Night falls quickly on the equator; by 6:00 P.M. it is too dark to read by daylight. Many an evening was spent reading by the light of hot kerosene lamps in sweltering temperatures, with the light attracting a multitude of night-flying insects. At the same time I strove to consciously appreciate the solitude of that remote place in the wilderness—with the intensely bright stars as if on top of the world, the exotic sounds of wildlife echoing through the valley, and the freedom from a hectic life with telephones, fax machines, e-mail, memoranda, office hours, committee meetings, and deadlines.

Specific Dilemmas

Dawn through a garden. Clarity to leaves, fruit, the dark yellow of the King Coconut. This delicate light is allowed only a brief moment of the day. In ten minutes the garden will lie in a blaze of heat, frantic with noise and butterflies.

     Half a page—and the morning is already ancient.

          —from Running in the Family by Michael Ondaatje, 1983

In addition to the more abstract problems, there were also specific dilemmas. For example, the unending claims on my time and attention as I tried to work out my notes or transcribe interview tapes could be very frustrating. Because of the many daily visitors, I was forced to hang a sign across my front door during the blocks of time set aside for writing, saying in polite Sinhala, "I would like to welcome you, but please come later." (Some people just lifted the sign and came in anyway, even though they were able to read it. And there were always resourceful villagers who assumed that the sign was not valid if they came around to the back door.) At the same time, how could a visit be refused when a guest had walked long distances and had come with some fruit, sweets, or other gifts of food? I took to directly typing observations and notes, for if the typewriter was heard outside, the hopeful visitors were more convinced the researcher was *really* working.

My Western value of privacy was also difficult for the villagers to relate to. In a society where families are big, houses are small, and the door is in principle always open, the idea that someone might like to be left undisturbed is totally foreign. Exacerbating the situation for me was the fact that I was a great curiosity: The goods that I used and the things that I did—from working at the typewriter to spreading peanut butter on crackers—were entertainment for children and adults alike. I tried to learn to accept the continual staring, rationalizing that I was meticulously scrutinizing *their* behavior, pestering them with endless questions about what they do and how they think. Still, the lack of privacy was often disconcerting: peering through the window, coming into the house without giving warning, sometimes barging right through the closed bedroom curtain.

An additional dilemma I faced shortly after arrival the second time was the constant request by villagers for me to take a formal photograph of them or their children. Knowing this may be the only photograph or one of very few they ever receive, I felt obliged in the beginning to comply; it seemed like a small thing I could do for them. After all, they, like most Sri Lankans, were graciously willing to be photographed or videotaped at almost any of their daily activities, which was a boon to my research. Quickly, however, I was spending too much of my time taking photos of villagers dressed in their best clothes, standing at attention with stiff-lipped poses. Each roll of film which I had meant to use as slides for my classes was being used up for formal portraits, which the villagers were impatient to get back. It was hard to explain that I had the camera loaded with slide film that I wanted to send back to the States for developing. After all, they probably had walked 4 km, children in their best attire in tow, bringing me a food gift.

I conceived a plan: I would hold a well-publicized "Studio Day." All families were welcome to come and sit for portraits posed in any way they chose, one or two per family depending on the size. I set aside four rolls of film and played portrait photographer for a day. The word was out that this was their chance and that later requests for portraits would likely be refused.

The people came and posed. Mothers bounced their babies and chided them to smile. It was a way for me to create goodwill and get to know the families a bit better. The exposed rolls were taken to Moneragala town and were back within a week. Of course it did not end all the requests for photos; but for a while, anyway, the villagers were pleased with the solution, and I could carry on with my work.

Problems of a Different Order

In general I felt very safe living in the village, especially when compared with the dangers of violent crime in so many U.S. cities. True, during my first stay there was a dangerous rogue elephant sighted nearby, and a leopard killed a neighbor's calf; and in the second period a herd of ten elephants tore down a villager's house to eat the grain stored there. In the interim period between my fieldwork, Tamil terrorists murdered more than twenty farmers with large machete-like knives in a village about 15 km away. But the terrorists were no longer active in the area, and dangerous incidents involving wild animals were rare. Any strangers who came to the village were eyed with suspicion by the inhabitants and were asked many questions about their intentions; and such strangers were also rare.

It was a different story with poisonous snakes. Early in my second period of fieldwork, during the rainy season, I discovered a snake crawling on the kitchen table when I returned from the latrine at night. I chased it away with a broom, but felt uneasy and reported it to some village friends. They cleared the jungle growth farther away from my house and advised me to get a cat, which would supposedly keep my house free of snakes. This information was corroborated by others: "Yes, cats won't let snakes in your house; and if they try to come in, the cat will bite them in two." It was true that I had kept a cat, as well as a dog, during my first period in Suduwatura Ara, and I had not had any trouble with snakes then. I was therefore delighted when Sudu-Menike, the village woman who advised and assisted me in so many areas, got me a young cat, which was quickly at home in my house.

A couple of months later, after I had risen early, mixed some milk-powder for the cat, and was making myself a cup of instant coffee, I happened to notice in the dawning light that a snake was sleeping on my wooden food chest. I ran to the nearest neighbors and shouted, *"Sarpayek awa!"* (A snake has come!). Piyadasa and his son Nimal did not waste a moment in coming, one bringing a small flat plank, the other breaking off and stripping a sturdy stick from a tree as he came. They quickly had the situation under control. As the snake tried to escape, one cornered it with the stick, the other killed it with the plank.

A moment later I could not help but laugh at an amusing scenario: Piyadasa was leaving the house with the dead snake draped over the plank, while the cat was sleeping contentedly on the chair. She had not been aware of the snake's presence and had even slept through all the commotion of cornering and killing it. So much for folk wisdom, I mused.

The snake was indeed a poisonous one, a *mapila* (ironically called a cat snake in English), and Piyadasa proceeded to do what all villagers would have done had they killed a *mapila* in their house. He cut it in three pieces and burned it nearby. The smoke reduces the risk of more snakes coming; the people believe it is a sign of warning to other such snakes, which will then stay away. Otherwise, seven more snakes will enter your house. In any case, it prompted me to check around my bed before getting in and never to walk into a dark room without a lantern or flashlight.

To my consternation, the snakes did not get the message, for it was not the last one I encountered in the house. I was never bitten, however. And the villagers felt assured that I was adequately protected from the maledictions, dangers, and illnesses that can afflict one in the jungle. After all, they had painstakingly carried out a host of ritual precautions on many occasions to secure my well-being. From my side I felt infinitely grateful for their efforts when I departed in good condition and health, a little older and a little wiser, after two periods of fieldwork on the Sinhalese frontier.

2 / The Village Setting and Background

The village . . . was in, and of, the jungle; the air and smell of the jungle lay heavy upon it—the smell of hot air, of dust, and of dry and powdered leaves and sticks. Its beginning and its end was in the jungle, which stretched away from it on all sides unbroken, north and south and east and west, to the blue line of the hills and to the sea. The jungle surrounded it, overhung it, continually pressed in upon it. It stood at the door of the houses, always ready to press in upon the compounds and open spaces, to break through the mud huts, and to choke up the tracks and paths. It was only by yearly clearing with axe and katty that it could be kept out. It was a living wall about the village, a wall which, if the axe were spared, would creep in and smother and blot out the village itself.

—from The Village in the Jungle *by Leonard Woolf, 1913*

Suduwatura Ara means "White Water Stream." It is a pleasant-sounding name for a village of a district located in the Dry and Semi-Dry Zones, where water is a perennial problem. In fact, it is a name the villagers chose themselves for the place where they settled some twenty years ago, preferring it to the dark and somber name formerly given to that particular frontier area: *Kalugolla Mukalana,* meaning "Black-Thicket Jungle." The former name, however, connotes more clearly the harsh environment—an environment that has changed little since young Leonard Woolf (who later married the writer Virginia Woolf) lived from 1907 to 1912 in a nearby area as a British civil servant posted in Ceylon (Sri Lanka). It is an environment that needs description in order to understand the picture of Suduwatura Ara today.

MONERAGALA DISTRICT AS SETTING

If an outsider visits Moneragala District at the end of the dry season in August-September, it is easy to see that this is part of the Dry Zone. The countryside is brown, the small streams like Suduwatura Stream are no more than sandy beds, and the farmers' highland fields are blackened by the slash-and-burn preparations for the next planting season. However, when the sojourner comes to the district in the lush months of October-December or April-May following the monsoonal rains, it is hard to understand that this is an area that suffers from water shortages. The uncultivated landscape is covered by light green, undulating *illuk* grass fields interrupted by rugged boulders here and there, some with hardy trees whose roots hug the rocks and search for earth in crevices between the picturesque formations. Patches of forest that include giant hardwood trees still dot the hills and mountainsides that are too steep to cultivate easily. Large expanses of flat terrain are filled with deep-green sugarcane fields, and the lower areas are covered by the geometric regularity of dikes and paddy fields—whose various stages of mud, seedlings, and graceful grain stalks make the region look anything but dry. It is difficult at such times to imagine that this is the Dry Zone.

That was the case for me in the second fieldwork period as I listened to the monsoon rain come down in buckets on my roof, leaving little puddles on my few belongings in spite of a recent roof repair job; or as I trudged through ankle-deep mud or rushing streams at certain points along the path; or as I struggled to insulate my camcorder and camera equipment with layers of plastic bags and handfuls of silica packets. The fact that my envelopes and stamps were always "stuck" and first had to be soaked off from whatever they were touching attested to the pervasive penetration of moisture and humidity.

It is also hard for the casual observer to imagine that Moneragala District was once the center of flourishing early civilizations dating back further than 2500 years. Today it is among the poorest and least developed areas of the island. Whenever I mentioned to urban Sri Lankans in Colombo that I was doing research in a small village in Moneragala District, they eyed me suspiciously with a combination of disbelief and pity. During my first stay, a research assistant who gathered data for me in selected Moneragala villages related that he had been asked on a few occasions if I were working for the CIA—so inexplicable was the voluntary presence of an outsider.

Despite the poverty today, there are many reminders of a glorious history. It was an exciting experience when I was first taken to the nearby Budugalge Temple hidden in rock cliffs in the mountain range that flanked Suduwatura Ara's valley, about a forty-minute walk away. A narrow footpath nearly overgrown by grass leads to the "temple" where a single resident monk lives peacefully and comfortably in a converted area of cave, enjoying a commanding view of the immediate mountainside dotted with fragrant frangipani trees planted by villagers. The climb to his secluded abode among ancient rock pillars, now standing askance among shaded roots and moss, promises more ruins to come. A much steeper climb to a higher level on the mountain over large granite-carved stone steps, many hanging at precarious angles, leads to an ancient cave that once formed part of a small temple complex. Inside lie the sad remains of a colossal reclining Buddha figure. Only the feet, the upper arm, and the outline of its form are recognizable, as the statue was destroyed by vandals—both in olden times and more recently—seeking treasure. This remote temple and probably many similar ones yet to be discovered, are nestled in the Moneragala hills, unknown to archaeologists and tourists, but attesting to the grandeur and spirituality of yesteryear.

Pilgrims and tourists who want a path laid out for them can visit the ruins of the tremendous temple complex at Maligawila (ca. 600 A.D.), about 12 km away, where the largest Buddha statue carved from a single piece of stone, and another immense bodhisattva statue, were restored in a government-sponsored cultural project in 1989–1991. Far off the track of the major tourist attraction route in Sri Lanka, it is mostly the local Sinhalese who flock there on Buddhist religious holidays, taking offerings of lotus flowers and incense to be laid at the feet of both statues.

The early civilizations with their kingdoms flourished due to a well-organized system of irrigated paddy (rice) through widespread artificial lakes made by constructing an earthen bund (dam) across a river valley; such lakes are called "tanks" in Sri Lanka and India and are still important in rice cultivation. The southern area of Moneragala was one of the main food-producing regions of the island some 2000 years ago. Its name in ancient times, Wellasse, meaning "land of a hundred thousand paddy fields," testified to its former developed status. A gradual decline, however, set in by the twelfth century, the cause of which is not well documented in history. What is certain is that this southeastern region of the island was always a safe haven of retreat from invasions from the North, a place to regroup and plan new defensive campaigns in order to drive out attackers.

The strategy of people retreating to the Moneragala area to muster their strength was used in 1818 against the British by a large army of Sinhalese rebels. In that year the British dealt the latter a crushing blow. It is reported that many tanks and permanent crops like coconut or jack trees were deliberately destroyed in order to debilitate the area's function as a place of retreat and stronghold for rebellious inhabitants. Most of the able-bodied Sinhalese men were killed. The battle survivors fled to the hills and became a timid, suspicious folk *(baiyo),* living in small pockets and doing slash-and-burn cultivation. A European passing through the town of Haputale in 1830 reported not seeing a single person (Dhammananda 1966:87).

After the battle the area was placed under martial law for three years and under military rule for twenty-three years. The British remained uninterested in developing the area; for example, roads and railways were not extended to Moneragala. The people were punished through heavier taxes. What had once been an agriculturally developed region fell into poverty and backwardness, retaining only the potential which had been proven in days gone by.

Physical Infrastructure

Regarding physical infrastructure, Moneragala has one of the lowest proportionate rates of road mileage of any district in Sri Lanka. A few trunk roads connecting the main service centers are not adequate but are in a relatively good state of repair since a governmental program in 1992. The feeder and access roads are often eroded and more pothole than paved surface, a fact which led to the ultimate demise of my old jeep in the first fieldwork period. Many villages are accessible only by a hilly footpath or a cart path that cannot be used by motor vehicles in the rainy seasons. There are no trains in Moneragala District. However, buses—both public and private—serve the trunk roads on a daily basis with routes to and from Moneragala town and the main Sri Lankan cities. Though no comforts can be expected, and I dreaded the rest stops because of the unspeakable latrines, bus transportation is reasonably priced; the fares have hardly risen in the past decade.

Telephone communication possibilities are scant, although the service has been spread to the post offices of towns on the trunk roads. Most villages do have postal delivery, albeit slow, and telegram communication is fairly efficient.

Health Facilities, Housing, and Utilities

Moneragala suffers from primitive health facilities and a great shortage of medical staff, even though the number of doctors, nurses, and clinics has increased considerably in the past decade. The largest district hospital is in Moneragala town and is inadequate. Any cases needing surgery other than the most minor stitching of a wound are sent to the Badulla hospital some 55 km away. There are two additional district hospitals, all poor in facilities, and twenty lower units for health care, including dispensaries and rural hospitals. On the several occasions when I visited villagers in such facilities, with flies swarming and hygienic conditions deplorable, the family members of patients preparing their meals on little wood fires outside the open wards—it was a great incentive to do everything possible to avoid becoming a patient there.

Electricity is limited to the town centers or larger villages on a main road. Even though there were twenty-six villages that received development benefits and subsidies under the government's Village Re-Awakening campaign of 1991–92, the housing, water supply, and sanitation facilities of the district are substandard. A large number of houses have temporary thatched roofs, cow-dung floors, and wattle-and-daub walls, obviously put up by poor farmers who have no more than the materials that nature provides. Only those people living in the towns of Moneragala, Bibile, Buttala, Wellawaya, and Kataragama have piped water possibilities for their housing units. More than a third of the houses have a pit latrine or no latrine at all. Many health problems can be traced to impure drinking water and lack of sanitation. But in spite of this somber picture of health and the primitive facilities in Moneragala, the district and the island as a whole fare quite favorably in vital statistics as compared with the rest of South Asia. The infant mortality rate per 1000 live births is low at 19, and the life expectancy at birth is high at seventy-one years. I admired the traditional naturopathic medical system that the people could combine so effortlessly with a thorough Western vaccination program.

Education

The educational opportunities in Moneragala District are comparatively poor due to lack of facilities, many isolated schools, and the difficulties in attracting and holding dedicated teachers, principals and officers. About half the teachers are outstation teachers coming from other areas. They feel unhappy, ill-adapted, and too isolated from their families. Teacher absenteeism due to personal and duty leave results in a frequent combining of classes or leaving classes without supervision, as no substitute teachers are available.

The school buildings in Moneragala District are—as they are in all of the island's rural areas—of the simplest design and construction: single, open halls with half-walls and a small office room at the end of the hall. There are no classroom partitions and a minimum of storage space. Considering the large number of outstation teachers and the lack of suitable boarding possibilities for teachers in small villages, there are far too few schools with sufficient teachers' quarters.

Not only is the situation of the schools themselves in a bad state of affairs with regard to insufficient facilities and many unsatisfied teachers, the District Education Department is also sorely lacking. The unattractiveness of Moneragala District, its remoteness, and the lack of good quarters are factors that resulted ultimately in a poorly qualified group of officers. The morale and esprit de corps as well as the efficiency in the department are low. The remote schools are rarely visited; in fact the annual school inspections have been done away with. The school principals no longer have to submit "Annual Returns," so the link of supervision and evaluation has dwindled to a minimum level, allowing school principals to shirk their duties in stagnating schools. The problems in the district on various levels are so manifold and sometimes so frustrating as to discourage even the most well-meaning and re-form-minded administrators. This has resulted in a rapid turnover with higher officers seeking transfers and a lack of continuity and direction in the Education Department as a whole. I was saddened to see how the situation had worsened in the past ten years, especially because education had been the focus of my first study and I had left the district with optimism.

A Rural Society

Moneragala District is a sparsely populated rural society, with 94 percent of the inhabitants earning their living from agriculture. Moneragala town, the capital, is the only town in the district classified as "urban" by the Department of Census and Statistics. It is a sleepy little backwater with a population of fewer than 10,000, and it still looked much the same in 1994 as it did ten years earlier. There were a few more items in the shops and the introduction of three-wheeler taxis, but for the rest it could have been yesterday that I left. There was still no movie theater, and only a few inhabitants—the wealthier merchants—could boast of a telephone. As in the first fieldwork period, I again became accustomed to the goggling stares when I went to town and the whispered questions to Leela who often accompanied me: "Who is she?" "What's she doing here?" It was unusual enough to see any white people, although occasional adventurous tourists, far off the beaten path, would turn up now and then. A lone white woman, however, was a definite curiosity. Sometimes a local inhabitant would remember me from ten years before and ask the inevitable question, "Where's your jeep?", thus belying the significance placed on a vehicle and underscoring my lower prestige now that I was among the walking masses.

Like the situation of the town dwellers, that of the farmers had also changed very little. The district is still to a large extent a region of underprivileged small agrarians, the majority of whom have holdings of fewer than three acres. The underprivileged farmers can be classified roughly as encroachers, marginalized farmers, and second-generation settlement scheme (colony) farmers, with the Indian Tamil estate workers forming a deprived group of their own. They are all coping daily with a wide range of uncertainties and risks, and each group has found its own precarious modus vivendi.

The encroachers who have migrated from another area are the largest group and are usually slash-and-burn cultivators. When they were formerly able to do shifting cultivation on virgin land, they could reap reasonably high returns. With the rapid migrant influx, however, the encroacher cultivators are forced into an increasingly uncertain subsistence life. In earlier times each year new areas of forest were felled and burned to make the land arable for farming. In recent years, however, a stop has been put to this continued deforestation as settlers have steadily advanced on the frontier, sometimes illegally felling hardwood trees such as ebony. More and more of the crown land has been made into reserves by the government, including the national parks and the buffer zones around them. The fallow periods (optimum fifteen years) have become shorter and shorter. Most farmers must now cultivate year-in-year-out on the same acreage, with the result of soil depletion.

Not only is the size of their production going down, but the encroachers face many other difficulties. Their squatter settlements have occurred spontaneously, without official planning. As a result, the areas such as the one where Suduwatura Ara is located must wait a long time before being provided with any infrastructural facilities. They lack schools nearby, health services, sanitation facilities, public transportation, and agricultural services in their frontier lifestyle.

A major problem is the uncertain position of the encroachers, for they have no title to the crown land they have encroached upon. Some have been given temporary land permits for two acres—not demarcated—but they are often cultivating more. They live with the uncertainty of whether they should put up permanent houses, with a tiled roof, a cement floor, or a permanent latrine, for example. These are large investments for cash-poor farmers, and they will not venture to make the sacrifice unless they can be sure they will not be evicted and forced to resettle elsewhere. Even the planting of permanent crops such as coconut or jack trees is prohibited if the farmers have no official deed to the land.

These squatters often lead a hand-to-mouth existence. They are not united in cooperatives and have no transportation facilities to bring their produce to market, except perhaps a bullock cart. The marketing is generally undertaken by merchant middlemen, who buy the produce at low prices. The encroachers' terms of trade are unfavorable, for they must purchase their rice at comparatively high prices. Because they have no title to land, they are not eligible for institutionalized credit. They must depend for any small investment capital on private money lenders who charge exorbitant interest rates. Also at the mercy of the whims of nature, many small farmers remain deeply in debt.

There is also a large group of marginalized farmers from very old traditional (purana) villages, especially in the northern and western parts of the district. Their difficulties mainly stem from a declining man-to-land ratio as well as from increasing landlessness. Rather than encroaching on unsettled crown land, many of these fragmented and marginalized farmers identify themselves with a particular village and are reluctant to move away. They become casual laborers on the large sugarcane plantations or sharecroppers, earning half the produce cultivated, the other half going to the landowner. If they are lucky enough to have land, many still have no access to irrigated paddyland or water. Moreover, they have little access to fertilizer and other inputs, making intensification difficult. The costs of mechanical farm power are prohibitive. Because the labor supply is ample and the work seasonal, casual laborers remain in poverty with no bargaining power. Like the encroachers, these marginalized and coolie farmers comprise a good portion of the underprivileged agricultural sector. I would see groups of such barefoot coolies, their sarongs hoisted to knee length and mamoties (large hoes) over their shoulders, walking to join a team boarding an old truck to be taken to sugarcane plantations for a long day of backbreaking, dangerous labor; and I was glad that very few of "my" villagers had to resort to this exploitative system.

Additionally, there is a large group of second- and third-generation settlement scheme farmers who are emerging in the numerous thirty- to forty-year-old planned colonies. These descendants of settlers have no land in their villages of origin, for only one successor is allowed on the settlement scheme land. There is a great deal of hidden fragmentation, with several second-generation colonists and their own families still living from their father's acreage. They suffer from unemployment, and along with the migrants, many are forced to become squatters or coolies.

Thus the new pioneers and the native farmers as well form a weak societal group in a district that has always been among the most disadvantaged regions during this century. In the center of this region lies Suduwatura Ara, my observation point for viewing with wonder—using both a wide-angle lens to gain the cultural scope, and zooming in on minute detail—how this group of human beings, my friends and helpers, coped with the impending uncertainties in their daily lives.

THE VILLAGE OF SUDUWATURA ARA

Early Years

Some thirty years ago the place where the hamlet of Suduwatura Ara lies, 14 km south of Moneragala town, was thick, impassable virgin jungle. Today it can be reached—in the dry seasons—along a dirt road from Horombuwa (7 km) or via Kumbukkana (8.5 km), or approaching from the southern direction, along a dirt road from Okkampitiya (8 km) through Galtammandiya (5 km). Farmers from the traditional village of Horombuwa had gradually pushed into the area during the 1960s, clearing forests for slash-and-burn cultivation. Here and there a temporary hut *(pela)* could be seen, some built on high poles, some in trees for safety, as elephants, wild buffaloes, and boars abounded at that time.

Forested land was plentiful, and there was no need to recultivate on abandoned chenas (shifting highland fields) where *illuk* grass with its formidable network of roots took over. By the early 1970s large forested areas, except on the mountain slopes, were replaced by *illuk* jungle on the rolling terrain, broken here and there by scattered rock knobs. A few people from the area had built semipermanent houses, but mostly there were shifting cultivators from nearby Horombuwa or Galtammandiya—here this season, gone the next—until Punchi Banda, still a respected pioneer and patriarch today, from a village near Welimada in the up-country of neighboring Badulla District, received a tip about available land from a distant relative in Moneragala. Punchi Banda:

> That was back in the days of the former government when food was scarce and expensive. We have a large family and a lot of mouths to feed. In Welimada we had no land. There it was all taken up by tea estates or divided among the descendants of the vegetable farmers. Each generation got less and less until there was none to go around.
>
> So I went to Okkampitiya to see about prospects there when I got a tip from Rathnayaka's older brother that there was an unsettled area of crown land with a tank that could possibly be repaired for paddy farming. I went out there to look over the situation and immediately took a liking to the place. The area was very remote, with dense thickets and *illuk* fields and only a few chena huts and narrow footpaths, but the land was fertile.

2.1 The cycling postman delivers the ethnographer a letter on her way to Kumbukkana, an 8.5 km walk.

I went back to Welimada and told other interested families and relatives without land. About thirty-eight men with some of our older sons came back with me. We wanted to try out the area and build houses before we brought our families. First we set up huts in camps and worked hard clearing jungle for cultivation. More than half the men decided against this kind of life and went back to Welimada. Those of us who stayed cleared a road with much difficulty and most of us built mud houses. By 1975 about twelve of us were ready to go get our families.

Thus Suduwatura Ara is a village mainly inhabited by migrant encroachers who started arriving from the Welimada area about twenty years ago. The pioneering families especially had a life of hardships, for they invested much labor in repairing the ancient tank with an earthen bund and a dam across a gorge. Jayasekara adds to the story:

> I was twenty at the time and the oldest son in the family. I helped my father build our house. We went back to Welimada, loaded our goods into a hired tractor-cart and got on the bus with our family members to come back here. We had to carry our goods the last mile or so, because the tractor couldn't make it out this far.
>
> The area was still full of wild buffaloes, leopards and elephants. We all had to be back in our houses and huts by dusk for safety.
>
> Toward mid-1975 we were ready to start building the bund of the tank. Twenty people worked for forty-five days. The tank filled with the October rains and we had plenty of water for the *maha* season paddy cultivation.
>
> In December 1976, however, the rains wouldn't stop. We saw that the dam in the narrow gorge was being gradually washed away. On the night of December 23rd, I remember it well, the dam broke. We tried cutting the bund in another place to provide a spill and save the tank. But it was no use. We were disheartened for weeks. Some families gave up and went back to Welimada after that.

The core of the encroacher-migrants who settled and stayed were the hardiest of the lot. It was symbolically suitable when they changed the name of the area from Black-Thicket Jungle to White Water Stream, for these pioneers brought with them their determination and optimism for a smoother flowing and brighter future.

The Village in 1984–85

When I arrived in 1984 the settlement was only ten years old and did not yet have the status of village in the local government system. Because the homesteads were spontaneously created by an influx of squatters and scattered over several kilometers in the length of a valley, it was hard to determine where the settlement's boundaries lay. Those families living on the borders between two hamlets would opportunistically shift their allegiance if there were any development aid and services to be gained—understandable in a hand-to-mouth subsistence economy.

After interviewing all the families in the area during my first fieldwork period, I found there was a total of forty-three households that identified strongly with Suduwatura Ara, with another seven adult children in these families who were making tentative plans for marriage, building their own house, and starting a new family. There were only 238 inhabitants—a young population with almost half the people being under fifteen years of age, three-quarters being under thirty, and a mere five elders over sixty years. Only a handful of settlers had brought their parents, for the life in a pioneering village was considered too harsh for the vulnerable older generation accustomed to a bit more luxury and the better climatic conditions of the Badulla District up-country.

Looking at the map on page 27, one sees the homesteads are concentrated in the vicinity around the tank, for that was the most attractive segment of land: low,

2.2 The old wattle-and-daub school in 1984, taken from the colossal rock across from the ethnographer's house. The frame of that house is being built on the far right.

flat, and suitable for paddy cultivation in the longer monsoonal *(maha)* season. The only community building was the schoolhouse built by the parents. A bo tree planted on the school premises, with a tiny Buddha statue in a simple wooden encasement on a platform under the tree, was the only formal place of worship in Suduwatura Ara. Many villagers, however, walked the several kilometers to the ancient Budugalge Cave Temple in the neighboring village of Horombuwa, or to the larger and more elaborate Galtammandiya Temple several kilometers southwest of Suduwatura Ara, to worship on special religious days.

A decade ago the Buddhist devotion of the people was strong. They went more regularly to the temples, and it was rare to find a farmer working in his fields on a *poya* (full moon day), the day each month on which the Buddhist precepts (such as killing no living animal) are especially important. I remember an incident that occurred shortly after my arrival in the first period.

> It was a *poya,* always a holiday in Sri Lanka, and I was glad to have a day off from working in the school. I decided to clear some of the fast-growing weeds around my house with a mamoty. Gamini, one of the neighbor children, who was always cheerfully and willingly helpful in many kinds of chores—fetching water, cleaning lamp chimneys, sweeping—came up and eyed my work.
>
> "Sudu-Teacher," he said, "I would of course help you with clearing your garden, but today is a *poya.*" He went and picked an earthworm out of the soil I had just tilled.
>
> "Lord Buddha teaches that we shouldn't kill such animals with our mamoties on a *poya,*" he said, as the earthworm wiggled in his hand.
>
> I put my mamoty down, deciding to conform to the culture and work in my garden later in the week.

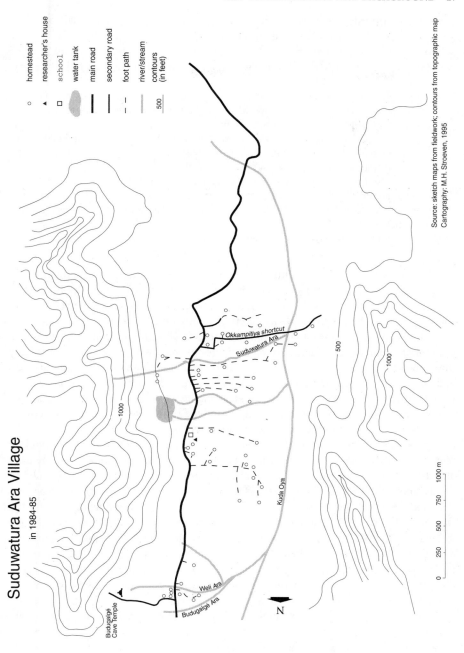

Suduwatura Ara Village

in 1984-85

Legend:
- ○ homestead
- ▲ researcher's house
- □ school
- water tank
- main road
- secondary road
- foot path
- river/stream
- 500 contours (in feet)

Okkampitiya shortcut

Suduwatura Ara

Budugalgé Cave Temple

Weli Ara

Budugalgé Ara

Kuda Oya

N

0   250   500   750   1000 m

Source: sketch maps from fieldwork; contours from topographic map
Cartography: M.H. Stroeven, 1995

By the time of the second fieldwork period, most farmers were seen working on full moon days. Buddhist traditions were on the decline, with the weather and seasonal considerations taking precedence in work decisions.

There were no permanently cemented wells during the first period until one was finally made behind the school toward the end of my stay. That well, which was completed with Education Department funding only after a long and insistent campaign by me and the villagers, had an interesting history. Because the pond near the school was always stagnant by July in the dry season, the parents decided to dig a well behind the school so the children would have water. Punchi Rala tells the story:

> Six people had been working for eight days without success. We had dug about twenty-seven feet and had not reached water. Most people were discouraged and wanted to give up because we had not even come to wet soil.
>
> I had a feeling that we were not striking water because we had started without regard to the *neketa* [astrologically auspicious time] nor with any offerings to our local god, Lord Kataragama.
>
> So I made a vow and tied a coin in a piece of cloth and put a coconut on a stand as an offering the evening before we started again. The next morning we dug one more foot and struck water. The water rushed in faster than we were able to bail it out with buckets.
>
> You must pay respect to the gods. If you do not, you will pay for it in misfortune.

In addition to the school with its small Buddhist shrine and its well dug by parents, there were also two tiny shops in the homes of enterprising families by the end of my first fieldwork. These, however, sold only the most basic of items and were forced to close when fellow villagers continued buying on credit.

The prevailing impression of Suduwatura Ara was one of wilderness in which the human element was minimally discernable. It was a wilderness that continually threatened to reclaim what the settlers cleared, aggressively taking over the dirt road and footpaths. The battle between nature and human culture could also be seen in the streams which crisscrossed the undulating terrain. Together with the heavy monsoons these streams eroded the dirt road in the rainy season, making the village inaccessible for motor vehicles without four-wheel drive.

In 1985, near the end of my first fieldwork, I was instrumental in getting funding from the Netherlands Government in order to restore the ancient tank bund, creating an artificial lake so that the village would have enough water to irrigate one acre of paddyland for each household (discussed in chapter 10). As with all important endeavors, an astrologer was consulted in order to get an astrologically auspicious time *(neketa)* for the first sod to be broken for the tank project. This was determined to be at 10:08 A.M., at which moment precisely the local member of Parliament, at a carefully chosen and decorated site near the old tank, struck a mamoty into the earth. He was thus commencing work on the project at a time when the position of the planets was favorable, thereby reducing the dangers and risks of something going wrong during construction or afterwards. It was an extremely festive occasion in the village. In his speech the member of Parliament promised the people he would see that they got a permanent school building to replace the wattle-and-daub one.

Construction of the tank bund and sluice gate were well under way by the time of my departure and completed shortly thereafter. The member of Parliament kept his promise about the school, and a few months later a new tiled-roof structure with cemented walls and floor was standing. One of the wealthier merchants of the area donated money for a separate Buddhist shrine near the sacred bo tree on the school premises. With these new additions to the public domain of the village, together with my house, which was turned into a "Learning and Development Centre" that included a small library, Suduwatura Ara was starting to look like more than a temporary encroacher settlement. The wilderness frontier was less threatening. More significantly, each of fifty households was given a ninety-nine-year lease for three acres of highland, along with plans for receiving an acre of paddyland. They were no longer squatters on crown land and could look forward to developing their homesteads without fear of eviction. I departed with much sadness at leaving behind my friends and closing a chapter in my life, but with optimism. It looked promising that the village standards of living would be on the rise and that their vulnerability to dangers and uncertainties would be lessened.

The Village Re-Awakening Program *(Gam Udawa)*

In 1991 I was pleased to receive a letter from my former assistant telling that President Ranasinghe Premadasa (of the conservative UNP, United National Party, later assassinated in 1993), after receiving a copy of my 1988 book, *The Blackboard in the Jungle,* had selected Suduwatura Ara as one of twenty-six villages in Moneragala District for his year-long village development program. This *Gam Udawa* or Village Re-Awakening was a large-scale rural-based campaign to build 150,000 houses, open new schools, clinics, water-supply schemes, and garment factories, in addition to building new villages and improving existing ones. It was touted as an experiment that would serve as a model for many regions in Sri Lanka as well as other developing countries. Each participating village would receive a prescribed package of development aid, and Suduwatura Ara started buzzing with activity as never before.

For the inhabitants the most important of the elements in the program's package were the loans they received for improving their houses. An officer from the Housing Authority came to live in the village for a year to manage and stimulate the house-building process. A committee of seven villagers met every evening with the officer and had to report on all aspects of development. Thirteen houses that existed in the lowland section in the village center, which was the command area of the tank and destined to be the paddy fields, had to relocate to highland sites. Two loops of road were cleared in the northern part of the village making these houses accessible for vehicles.

There were seventy-eight houses included in the village boundaries at that time. Each household was given loans amounting to Rs. 14,000 in three installments for construction materials such as cement. The participants agreed to work together in community labor *(shramadana)* teams to put up each others' houses. The teams made their own baked bricks and cut timber from the jungle. The second loan installment was provided in the form of roof tiles. Each family was allowed to design its own house. Those with more ambitious plans would invest some savings in the house or complete only a portion of it during the program.

The Housing Authority officer got to know all the villagers, visiting their building sites regularly. Only when good progress was being made was the household given the succeeding loan installment. Additionally, the village families received cement, a squatting pan, and a cash subsidy for a latrine.

A number of other elements were included in the Re-Awakening program: a community hall in the center of the village used for meetings and kindergarten classes; a Buddhist shrine next to the community hall; a handloom weaving center;

the clearing and extension of the road and the construction of twenty-seven culverts at low points in the road; the digging of three tube wells with hand pumps and three large traditional cement wells where twelve to fifteen people can bathe at the same time. Additionally, the bund of the tank was strengthened and extended to enlarge the tank, with the major canals being built by the program. The school was given another latrine and a urinal as well as a fence and gate.

On April 26, 1992, one year after commencement of the program, Suduwatura Ara was the first village in the district to be opened as a "Re-Awakened Village." At that time it also received the official status of "village," rather than just being a hamlet listed in a larger local government division. It was a tremendous ceremonial occasion with much fanfare and the appearance of many VIPs, including the national minister of housing, local ministers, and members of Parliament. The road had been improved to the extent that several busloads of people could arrive. Three villagers who had done exemplary work in the program received gifts, including one motorbike for the "best farmer."

While the villagers gave me credit for having focused attention on Suduwatura Ara so it could be selected for the Re-Awakening program, I had mixed and tempered enthusiasm when I was able to see the outcomes three years later. Candid chats brought to light a clearer picture of the government's propaganda activities behind the scenes. There was much public criticism that the program was an extravagant waste of government funds and that it spent far more money on publicity for the president and his party than it did on actual development. A typical comment on the lips of critics was that the government spent one million rupees on publicity for every Rs. 10,000 spent on improving the conditions of the rural poor. It is commonly believed, even in the villages that were direct beneficiaries, that the program padded the pockets of the president's political cronies, shady businessmen, dubious contractors, and the family members of public officials. In Suduwatura Ara, too, they were quick to give examples of nepotism: the local (Provincial Council) minister of textiles was the AGA's wife (assistant government agent); the contractor for the culverts in the village was the AGA's uncle.

Three years later, asking to what extent Suduwatura Ara was "re-awakened" by this expensive rural campaign, the answer might be that the village had gone back to sleep. While the tiled roofs and baked-brick walls are an improvement for the seventy-eight houses that participated, in most cases house improvement stagnated when the program ended; and the last thing on the villagers' minds is repayment of the housing loans, for which they have fifteen years. Most of the subsidized latrines remain incomplete; and there is still gossip about a village committee member, together with the public health inspector, abusing funds for latrine construction. The community hall is being used extensively, but villagers tell about the inferior way in which it was constructed, with the contractor pocketing much of the money funded for the building. The culverts are reportedly another example of contractor swindle: Those who participated in the construction tell that the proportion of cement used was far too small. Attesting to the poor quality, a number of the culverts were already broken or washed away just three years later, at the time of my second stay. Most of the six new wells are regularly used—but not as intensely as they would have been if they had been dug at more central places. The villagers were not consulted when the locations were chosen. The huge investment made in enlarging the

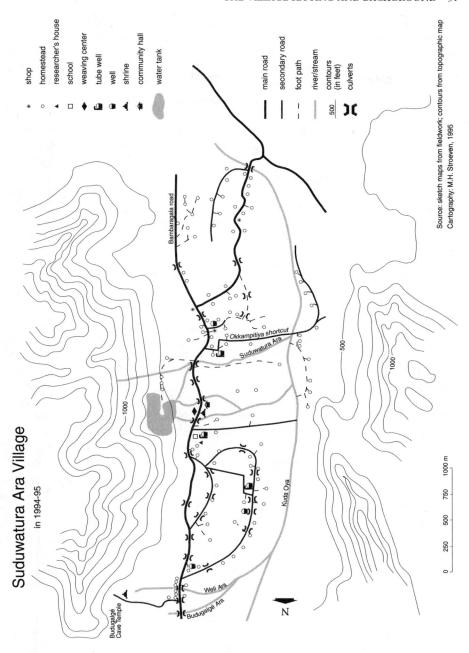

Suduwatura Ara Village
in 1994-95

shop
homestead
researcher's house
school
weaving center
tube well
well
shrine
community hall
water tank

main road
secondary road
foot path
river/stream
contours (in feet)
culverts

Source: sketch maps from fieldwork; contours from topographic map
Cartography: M.H. Stroeven, 1995

Bambaragala road

Okkampitiya shortcut
Suduwatura Ara

Kuda Oya

Well Ara

Budugalge Ara

Budugalge Cave Temple

N

0   250   500   750   1000 m

tank and building the main canals has thus far provided no benefit, as the question of paddyland distribution has not been settled.

The largest waste of investment turned out to be the construction of a building to house a handloom weaving center. The expensive looms were still standing when I left in 1995, though the class of young women who followed the weaving course had dwindled down to nothing. A government-paid weaving teacher occasionally arrived and continued to draw a salary; and the government also provided the salary of a village man who was the nighttime "watcher" at the handloom center. As cheaper and better cloth is imported from India, there is no market for the woven product, and village women feel they can spend their time more lucratively in farming. Such handloom centers, placed in many other "re-awakened" villages, have booked scant success.

After talking with the local member of Parliament in the newly elected People's Alliance government, it appeared that projects undertaken by the previous United National Party government—such as the Village Re-Awakening program— have little chance of being supported or maintained by the new officials, who were already busy designing their "own" programs and publicity stunts. Meanwhile, the spurt of development that seemed so promising for reducing risks in an uncertain world had slowed to a two-steps-forward-and-one-backward pace.

The Village in 1994–95

Looking at the map on page 31 which sketches Suduwatura Ara in 1994–95 one sees that the village had extended its boundaries and population. The 43 homesteads of 1985, which had grown in number to 78 by the time of the Re-Awakening, had increased to 108 in 1995, with the southern side experiencing great expansion. Now that Suduwatura Ara was designated as a legitimate village, it had been up to the local officials to say which houses were included in its boundaries. In fact the main area in the southern side consisting of fifteen homesteads and referred to as Kuda Oya, had formerly been included in a different village, Kahambana, separated from these houses by a forested and mountainous region. For administrative reasons they were lumped together into Suduwatura Ara in late 1992, thereby expanding its boundaries and increasing the population by eighty-four people. The residents of Kuda Oya, however, rarely attend functions or society meetings in the village, nor do their children attend the Suduwatura Ara school. They are geographically closer to Galtammandiya, an older village that has a large temple and better infrastructure and services.

With the inclusion of the Kuda Oya settlement, the population had grown to a total of 461. The increase since 1985 without the Kuda Oya inhabitants was 139, most of whom were children and grandchildren of the original settlers, or relatives of the latter who migrated from the Welimada area in the up-country. It had remained a population of young people, but the number of elderly was gradually increasing.

In twenty years' time Suduwatura Ara had moved from a crown-land jungle area with a few temporary huts to an official village with several signs of permanence, including tile-roofed houses and a community hall. However, despite a lot of hopes and high expectations, the gains were modest. The wilderness frontier had been pushed somewhat farther away, but the jungle was already taking over the roads and isolating the community again. The villagers still had to cope with the same hostile environment of the pioneering days, full of risks and uncertainties.

3 / Belief in the Supernatural

It was the days of Halley's comet . . . I turned to the Muhandiram and asked him what he thought about the comet and the planets and the stars. His answer depressed me even more profoundly than the Sinhalese villagers. . . . He told me that at a female child's birth the horoscope predicted the year, day, and hour at which her menstruation would begin, and it was always accurate. . . . Scratch the surface of his mind and you found that he believed that Halley's comet, the blazing constellations above our heads, the planets in their courses, the spiral nebulae, the infinite galaxies flaming away into space, had been created and kept going through billions of billions of years in order that a grubby little man in the Hamban-tota bazaar could calculate the exact day and hour at which the Muhandiram's infant daughter would have her first menstrual period.[1]

[1] *Of course, one must admit that he may be right, and that that is the object of the universe. (Footnote by Woolf.)*
        —*from Growing: An Autobiography of the Years 1904–1911 by Leonard Woolf, 1961*

From the first day that I went to reside in Suduwatura Ara, bouncing in my old jeep over gullies and rocks, rushing as fast as the terrain would permit to arrive in time for the astrological *neketa* that determined the lucky time for me to enter my new house, I gained my first personal insight into the significant role the supernatural plays in the village. It was a new experience to be the center of a complex house-warming ceremony that entailed a seemingly unending series of ritual prescriptions. As I lighted oil lamps and listened to *pirith* chanting before the auspicious moment to turn the key in the lock, I started to realize the seriousness with which the villagers engaged in these activities. The many ritual practices were meant to protect me as I lived in this house. It was like taking out an insurance policy against the uncertainties and dangers that lurk in dark corners and come out at unpropitious moments.

In the months that followed I was to experience and hear about innumerable customs and beliefs that crisscross diverse aspects of the supernatural: Buddhism, woven together with a myriad of other beliefs in Hindu gods, local deities, devils and evil spirits, animistic and folk beliefs, as well as an unflagging confidence in astrology—all merging to create an intricate tapestry of the supernatural world. Like Leonard Woolf (quoted above), who lived several years in a similar setting, I sometimes allowed myself to wonder at the extent that these beliefs seemed to "work" in the village; and I even had my own horoscope made at the coaxing of my assistant.

Every chapter of this book offers examples of beliefs in the supernatural, pointing to its all-pervasiveness in village life. The present chapter is an attempt to give an overview of some of the primary categories, although I am convinced that had I stayed longer, the examples would have continued to grow.

VILLAGE BUDDHISM

Buddhism plays an important role in the lives of the majority of Sinhalese people, and the inhabitants of Suduwatura Ara are no exception. Each house has a shrine dedicated to Lord Buddha. Usually this is a small shelf with a picture of the Buddha above it. On the shelf are placed simple coconut-oil lamps, a basket with fresh flowers, and some incense sticks in a container of sand—all items denoting respect for the Buddha and his teachings. A few houses have a separate tiny shrine constructed outside.

The villagers and other Sinhalese easily integrate their Buddhist religion with beliefs in diverse Hindu deities. Even major Buddhist temples have their shrines to local Hindu gods; and one may see statues or pictures of favorites such as Ganesha, Vishnu, and Pattini, who are supplicated for protection and favors. Frequently the Buddhist household shrine is shared by a picture of Kataragama, the Hindu god who is thought to reign supreme in this region of Sri Lanka. I bought what might be considered by Western taste to be a rather gaudy colored poster of Kataragama to brighten up my hut. Sitting astride his peacock, this god looked arrogant but doll-like at the same time, richly bejeweled and flanked by his two consorts. Village friends would gaze admiringly at the poster for long minutes, asking me with envy where I got it.

Suduwatura Ara has no temple of its own, but rather two small shrines with Buddha statues, one under the bo tree (*ficus religiosa,* the kind of tree under which the Buddha attained enlightenment and considered holy to Buddhists) on the school premises; and one at the Community Hall built in 1992. Nearby there is the ancient cave temple already mentioned, the Budugalge Temple, and near the southern end of the village in Galtammandiya is a large and elaborate Buddhist temple dating from the 1940s. It was constructed on the site of another ancient temple (ca. 2000 years old). The Galtammandiya Temple grew in wealth due to the lucrative paddy cultivation in that area and the original fields owned by the monks *(bhikkus)*.

During my second stay the head of the large Buddha statue in the Galtammandiya Temple's inner sanctum was broken open by vandals looking for gems or other treasure. It was the topic of gossip for many weeks, and most inhabitants were appalled and indignant. However, the number of people who are truly devout and go to one of the temples in nearby villages on a *poya* to worship had diminished in the past decade, as readily admitted by all those who discussed the matter. Formerly groups of villagers, mainly women and children, would go to a temple or the school hall on full moon days to observe *sil* (eight Buddhist precepts), dressed in white, seated on mats, and meditating or reading and listening to sermons. Such observances in recent years have mainly been on special *poya* days such as Wesak or Poson.

Wesak Poya in May is the holiest of Buddhist holidays, celebrating the birth, enlightenment, and passing away of the Buddha. Most families will make special Wesak paper lanterns *(kudu)* to hang outside; and in the evening many will join a small *perehera* (religious procession), the children crying out *"Sadu, sadu, saaaaaadu!"* (Blessings!) along the way. The procession ends at one of the shrines where coconut-oil lamps are lighted, lanterns are hung in the bo tree, and worshipers enjoy the heady fragrance of smoldering incense sticks. Buddhist stanzas are recited in Pali, and one of the elders preaches a *bana* sermon. The second most sacred full moon day is Poson Poya in June, commemorating the advent of Buddhism to Sri Lanka more than 2000 years ago. As on Wesak Poya, villagers are likely to engage in devotional activities on this day.

The school day starts with a small Buddhist ceremony in which all children recite by heart in the Pali language the Triple Gem ("I take refuge in the Buddha; I take refuge in the teachings; I take refuge in the community of monks") as well as the first five Buddhist precepts *(pan-sil)*, promising not to kill any animal, steal, engage in sexual misconduct, lie, or drink alcohol. As elsewhere in Sinhalese schools, Buddhism is taught at all levels in the curriculum.

The Budugalge Cave, forty minutes' walk away, is the temple that most villagers associate with Suduwatura Ara. This temple has one resident monk, seventy years old at the time of my second fieldwork, who has lived there for the past fifteen years. Although the temple is actually in Horombuwa, it is the people of Suduwatura Ara who take the monk his daily alms meal. Thirty households each have a day of the month on which a family member, usually the mother, takes a meal to the monk at his cave abode in the side of a mountain. After the food has been put in his containers and a bit of each item placed in his "begging bowl" to be put in front of the Buddha statue as an offering, the monk makes a sermon, asking the villager to offer him alms. He must be seated to partake of the meal before 12:00 noon, and he must fast after that until the next morning.

I accompanied several of the villagers on their long, hot walks to take the specially prepared meal to the monk. At times he was not there, and the time-consuming endeavor was for naught. Without telephones, the people were literally left holding the bag and feeling frustrated. Still they realized they had to stay in the good graces of this Budugalge monk as well as the three monks at Galtammandiya and others in the area. The monks' services are needed at funerals and at the commemorative *dana* (almsgiving) ceremonies after the death of a family member.

Death

As Buddhists the villagers believe in a cycle of rebirths after death. The form in which one will be reborn and the plane to which one will be elevated depends on the deeds done by the person—good or bad—as well as the last thoughts that come to mind at the moment of death. Such thoughts can be influenced by *pirith* chanting or reminding one of good past deeds.

When someone dies in the village, neighbors, friends, and family members immediately start dividing up the many tasks and preparations for the funeral. Neighbors clean the compound and collect money to help the family. The village's Death Donation Society, to which members have paid monthly dues of Rs. 10, pays the family Rs. 1000 (about U.S. $22), which helps defray the funeral costs but by no means covers them. Formerly people in poor villages like Suduwatura Ara would have simple coffins built by the local carpenter. The trend these days is to hire the services of a funeral parlor in a nearby town. They will embalm the body and provide the coffin, the white burial clothes, and the traditional pair of (wooden) elephant tusks to be placed around the coffin at home (costs run from Rs. 2500 to

3500). Friends and neighbors build a temporary shed adjoining the house, under which the visitors and monks will sit during the funeral.

The body is kept for two to four days, depending on how far relatives have to come; also, no funerals take place on the inauspicious days of Tuesday or Friday. At least one Buddhist monk is considered necessary for the funeral, but generally more are present. They are seated outside on chairs or cushions covered with white cloth. The coffin is placed in front of them with the people seated on mats on the ground.

The monks lead in reciting the five precepts followed by a short eulogy for the deceased. The ritual of *pansukula* is then carried out: Close relatives hold onto and pour a pitcher of water into a cup, which overflows into a basin, symbolizing the collection of merit for the spirits *(prethas)* through *dana* (just as rivers collect in an ocean, according to the chanted stanzas). The monks are given the *pansukula* gift, a minimum of four yards of cloth for a robe, according to the means of the family. They chant a funeral prayer and leave. Relatives and friends deliver more eulogies before the coffin is carried to the burial site in the village.

Along the path strips of white plastic or streamers made of young coconut fronds have been hung by the Death Donation Society, which also hangs their white banner over the path. White is traditionally the color of death and mourning, and those who have white clothes will wear them to the funeral.

Friends usually carry the coffin; and they say it gets heavier as they go along. There is a belief that an evil spirit is sitting on the coffin, weighing it down. The grave site on arrival is decorated with arching coconut fronds, and a piece of white cloth to shade the spot and show respect is suspended over it.

3.1 The funeral of a young child in 1984.

The coffin is carried around the grave three times before being lowered. Family members throw a little earth on it; the grave is covered and a small mound is built on which two young coconuts full of water are placed with a candle in each. If the water in the coconuts goes down, it is said to be a good sign, for the *prethas,* the spirits who must be appeased at the time of death, are drinking the water. Those attending the funeral return to the home of the deceased for tea and refreshments.

As Buddhists the villagers would prefer to have a cremation. But building a funeral pyre in addition to the coffin is prohibitively expensive for the family, as is buying a formal grave marker. Ahead of them are the seven-day, three-month, and one-year *dana* ceremonies, which they will organize and pay for to help the departed one. The final rites of passage are the most costly in the lives of the village people, but they will not fail to carry out the proper rituals to the extent that they are able.

I attended the funeral of a newborn infant of an especially poor young couple. At the time of the seven-day *dana* the Budugalge monk had been away from his cave temple for several days, and no one knew when he would return. The monks from the richer Galtammandiya Temple were unwilling to make the long walk for this poor couple, and the latter as unable to pay for the monks' transportation. Family members walked for many miles to find a single *silmaeni,* an elderly female monk who was not attached to a particular temple and who was willing to come and carry out the prescribed rituals for the infant's *dana.*

The suicide rate in Sri Lanka is quite high, even though Buddhism has a strong sanction against taking one's own life. Suicide victims are given a respectable funeral and *dana* ceremonies despite their sin. A common way of committing suicide is by drinking potent insecticide. Within the last four years, three villagers have committed suicide in that way. One was a young mother of two children who had an unhappy marriage. The second was a nineteen-year-old girl who had a love affair that broke up. The third was a man with a wife and four young children, who drank poison when he was swindled out of the money for his peanut crop, the main source of cash income for his family. The widow and her children were reminders of the struggle by hard-working farmers for a better way of life.

Dana (Almsgiving) Ceremonies

Following a villager's death a series of *dana* ceremonies are traditionally held on the seventh day, after three months, and on the one-year anniversary in order to convey merit and help the soul of the dead person on its way to a better place. They are extremely expensive undertakings for subsistence farmers, for they involve asking as many monks as one can afford to a large meal with varied sweets, king-coconut water, rice and many different curries, and dessert. Often the host also gives offerings to the monks, such as soap, packages of powdered milk, tea, and sugar; or saffron-colored robes, fans, umbrellas, or slippers. I was always much in demand to attend these ceremonies, and special requests were made that I photograph in detail the copious plates of food that were given to the monks as well as the gift items. The ability to display and give away such wealth conveyed a sense of status and was a kind of exchange among the families and even other villages. The *dana* gatherings reminded me vaguely of the Melanesian Big Man's feasts or the Northwest Coast Indians' potlatch. As I dutifully documented the kitchen full of food and the stacks of gift items, I could not help but marvel at this ironic development in a religious philosophy that shuns attention to material things.

If almsgivers want to convey a great deal of merit for their deceased relative, they can offer a special package of eight prescribed items (three robes, a begging bowl, a razor, a needle, a spool of thread, and a water strainer) called *ata-pirikara*. The cost of all these items can run as high as Rs. 1500, a prohibitively expensive price for most villagers. The Buddhist temple, however, commonly sells the package they received to the next almsgiver for Rs. 500, so the latter can give it back to the temple. While this dealing with money goes completely against Buddhist principles, the villagers are able to rationalize it with no problem. The new unorthodox system makes it possible for them to offer the *ata-pirikara* to the priests, something they want to do in order to obtain much merit for their loved one. Thus the very same unopened package of items can be bought at the temple and offered back several times in different *dana* ceremonies. I watched one particular wrapped *ata-pirikara* package change owners' hands several times, and together with some closer village friends, we joked that the contents might just as well be some stones and rags, as the gift package is never opened!

The monks who attend the *dana* ceremony line up at the door of the host's house, who has someone wash the monks' feet before they enter. They take their place in a specially prepared room with cushions and mats, where they do the appropriate chanting; and one offers a short sermon for the deceased. The host not only provides a sumptuous meal for the monks, but also for all the friends and family members who attend, and he arranges and pays for the transportation of the monks. Even though these *dana* ceremonies serve as important social events and family reunions, they can also put the family members deep into debt—a fact which I found troubling. It seemed that the spiritual aspects of Buddhism were diminishing while the controversial material side was gaining ground.

Sometimes, if the *dana* ceremony is an especially elaborate one—for example, commemorating the death anniversary of one's parents—it might be preceded by *bana* (Buddhist sermon) preaching or an all-night *pirith* chanting ceremony like the one offered the day after my arrival. For the latter, some invited monks or respected men from the village will go on chanting Buddhist sutras or sermons in a specially constructed and decorated enclosure or dais *(pirith-mandape)*. The *pirith* chanting is said to invoke the local deities and to convey merit or blessings on the person being commemorated or honored, or on the village itself. These are popular, well-attended events, ending by the participants drinking a bit of blessed water and having a piece of blessed thread tied around their wrist or neck. After my experience with the all-night *pirith* chanting that was offered for me—the one that left me frazzled, exhausted, and beseeching the gods for a little silence as I covered my ears with a pillow—I always begged off when chanting time came. I erroneously thought I might be able to joke with some of my closest village friends about my opinions of the "noise"; but it was no use. They were puzzled by my not wanting to

3.2 The ata-pirikara *and other gift packages are placed in front of the monks at a dana ceremony. On the right is the single resident monk of the Budugalge cave temple.*

attend. I had to say I was not feeling well, for telling them the truth would have been disappointing and somewhat insulting for them.

DEMONS, DEVILS, EVIL SPIRITS, AND MINOR DEITIES

Buddhist precepts offer guidelines for ethical behavior with an eye on the uncertain "afterlife," while the multitude of other beliefs in the supernatural are couched in fear of the uncertainties that affect one's present life—for example, how to ensure health, prosperity, good fortune, and success, and how to eliminate the opposite. Although orthodox Buddhism condemns the worship of gods, minor deities, devils, demons, and evil spirits, it does accept that these exist; and in village life much attention is given to such forms of the supernatural.

Due to the influence of Hinduism from India, together with the local indigenous beliefs, a complex of various levels of the supernatural has become intertwined in the minds of the villagers. Occupying the lower realms in the hierarchy are many categories of minor local deities, demons, and evil spirits. The inhabitants have a basic knowledge of these, but the authority in the village on how to avoid, appease, or dispel them is Punchi Rala, the ritual healer and traditional doctor.

Punchi Rala is in his element when asked to expound on evil forces. In his deep, gruff voice, holding a steady gaze and a serious air of authority that reveals his confidence, he talks about devils and demons in a manner that holds his interviewer and other listeners captive. Even those who may be jealous of him respect Punchi Rala for his knowledge and skills. He tells that in a remotely located jungle village like Suduwatura Ara, the demons to be most concerned about are the *kadawarayas,* of which there are sixty-four types. These demons mainly affect women, who are particularly vulnerable if they go to bathe between 5:30 and 6:30 P.M. They also affect men and women who eat fried dried fish or fried meat. The everyday type of small afflictions they cause are toothaches or some kind of itch or rash. Though I frequently complained of itching insect bites, Punchi Rala, with a knowing glance and decided authority, said these probably came from *kadawarayas.*

The Trinity of Devils

While the *kadawarayas* are the most commonly encountered demons or devils in Suduwatura Ara, the other main types of Sri Lankan devils are also present. For example, the awesome *tunpali* or trinity of principal devils—Mahasohona (Great Graveyard Devil), Reeriyaka (Blood-Sucker) and Kalukumaraya (Black Prince)—are sometimes encountered. Punchi Rala tells that if you are walking at night and sense that someone or something is following you, you should not twist your head back to take a look. An evil spirit or demon might take hold of your head, which will become stuck in that position; such victims may have to go to a ritual healer to get their head "unstuck." Punchi Rala advises turning around with your whole body if you must look behind. Better yet is not to look but to draw three lines across the path with your toe, thus creating a boundary so the demon can no longer follow you. Another tactic is to cut or break off the branch of a tree and place that across the path. I learned early on that it is better not to joke lightly about these matters, for even the most rational-appearing villager will cling to such beliefs when fear takes hold. Because of their sincere concern for my safety, I respected their beliefs and practices and followed them whenever it was practical.

Of the devils in the main trinity, the most ferocious is Mahasohona, who has a human body and the head of a bear, although he can take the form of any animal. His dwelling place is generally in cemeteries. Anyone can be possessed by Mahasohona and will show signs of mental illness. If the patients go into a trance, they might tell that they are possessed by this devil. If they dream of elephants it is a sure thing that they are under the influence of Mahasohona.

Reeriyaka, or Blood-Sucker, mainly influences the blood system and lives on human blood. If one is wounded and blood is flowing out of the wound, Reeriyaka comes and tries to drink it. If women are having their menstrual periods he can influence them when they go to bathe. People who eat red meat or any rare meat are especially subject to Reeriyaka's powers. Dreaming of tigers or leopards is an indication that one is under this demon's influence.

Kalukumaraya or the Black Prince is also nicknamed the "Bridegroom." He is noted for going after young women who have recently "attained age." If a girl's menstrual periods are irregular, she is thought to be under the influence of Kalukumaraya. Likewise, if she has a miscarriage, this is said to be the work of the Black Prince, who does not want a woman to have children but rather remain forever young. Punchi Rala is able to help women affected by this devil. He has mantras he chants for keeping menstrual periods regular. He also has special amulets to prevent miscarriages and tells of one woman who had numerous miscarriages until she wore the amulet; she now has four children.

Possession by all three of these devils at once, as expressed in a serious mental or physical illness, may require a large devil-dancing ceremony to exorcise the evil. These are more common in the southern part of the island and are never done in Suduwatura Ara, although Punchi Rala participated in such ceremonies in his younger years. He continues to help diagnose and cure many villagers afflicted by such demons and other evil forces, as will be seen in the chapter on healing and health.

Prethas

The *prethas* are another category of spirits or ghosts that are common in the village and elsewhere. These are thought to be the spirits of sinful people who have died in the area and have come back, or they can be the spirits of those who have died and have left something unresolved vis-à-vis someone still living. *Prethas* live everywhere; they are found, for example, at junctions where three roads meet and especially hanging around outside one's house. While most devils and demons have food, *prethas* have none and are hungry. They supposedly eat only spittle and phlegm that people have spit out.

Prethas are particularly present if someone has died. During the first seven days they are lurking around the house, and only if the family of the departed one conveys merit on that person by giving a Buddhist *dana* ceremony can the *prethas* be appeased. People who are afflicted by *prethas* may get stomach problems, become weak, lifeless, and unable to work; even their appearance might change. Only certain types of healers can get rid of *prethas* by chanting and offerings, and Punchi Rala says he is unable to do this.

Appeasing a Local Deity

The power of local gods and deities is not to be underestimated or ignored, as one will find out when some accident or misfortune occurs. I was soon to learn this, even on my first trip to Moneragala District. At various places along the dangerous, often winding mountainous road there are elaborate shrines dedicated to the local deity who has power in the particular area through which the road passes. Whether in a bus or a private car, it is common to see the driver stop briefly at such a shrine to make an offering to the deity in question, putting a one- or two-rupee coin in a slot and briefly "worshiping" with bowed head and praying hands. This is thought to ensure safety for the traveler on the dangerous journey (but still Sri Lanka has one of the highest per capita rates of fatal road accidents of any country in the world).

One of the busier shrines on the route from Colombo to Moneragala is dedicated to the local deity Ranwela, the "ferryman." Legend has it that Ranwela was a powerful man in the area who looked after the interests of the people living along the banks of the Kelani River. After his death he was apparently seen walking on water, an awe-inspiring sight that caused people to start revering his image. Later a shrine and a statue were built for this figure who had risen to the status of deity, and travelers started making their offerings—a development that decidedly helped the local Buddhist temple next to which the shrine was built. Sri Lankan passers-by of all income groups and classes make their offerings. After all, a couple of rupees is a small insurance premium for safe passage, and no one would want to raise the ire of a powerful deity on the dangerous roads through his area.

I personally found out about the wrath of local deities during a trying incident that occurred in my first fieldwork period. I was taking a jeep-load of young villagers on a picnic outing to a secluded bird sanctuary near the east coast. Everyone was in high spirits, singing along the way to the accompaniment of drums. We entered the sanctuary, a flat lowland plain with scrub brush. As we drove along the sandy road, one of the young men asked me if he could drive. He was the only person in the village with a license, which he had recently received in Colombo at great expense; but he had had little opportunity to get any driving experience. There were no other cars for miles around, the terrain was level, and there were hardly any trees in the park to run into. I decided to let him take the wheel.

All was going well. I was joining in the singing and clapping, and everyone was looking forward to observing aquatic birds and having a picnic. Then, as if drawn by a huge, demonic magnet, the young driver drove the jeep headlong into the only solid object on either side of the road for as far as the eye could see: a large driftwood log of hardwood, with pointed edges at both ends. I frantically grabbed for the wheel, but it was too late. The high-built vehicle rolled up and onto the log, whose jagged edges tore into the underside of the jeep.

No one was hurt as we came to a crashing halt on top of the log, but we were all shaken. Glancing under the jeep, it was apparent that the oil reservoir was ripped open, and the black fluid was soon covering the log and adjacent sandy ground. As the men pushed the jeep off the log, I sat in the driver's seat, only to feel, much to my dismay, that the steering wheel easily made a full revolution. The steering pin had been broken, so the jeep could not even be towed.

It took a while for the ramifications to crystallize in my mind. I have only a hazy memory of how the problem was solved: the hours of waiting while the village boys walked many miles to find a tractor with a cart; how a team of sixteen farmers pushed and pulled the jeep up a makeshift plank ramp, their sinewy legs straining; the sight of the jeep being towed in the tractor cart with the floor planks sagging under the load; the two-day wait in the small town of Pothuvil while a local mechanic went by bus to a larger town with welding facilities where new parts could be made; and the hospitable hostess' house where I was allowed to stay during the operation, but where I became covered with bedbug bites. Through some miracle of resourcefulness the jeep was "repaired." At least it would run, though the steering scope was never wide and never felt the same.

The story did the rounds in the village and surrounding countryside for months to come. What was most noteworthy was the universal explanation given by the people. Namely, we had failed to stop and put a coin in the shrine of the local deity. We had defied the power of the god who reigned over that area, and he had shown his anger. It could have been worse! Had I known about the shrine I would have gladly stopped and made my contribution. And I made it a point to do so at all roadside shrines with collection boxes in the future.

ASTROLOGY

If ever I thought that astrology had a sizable following in the United States and other Western countries, my experience in Sri Lanka—where beliefs have drifted over from India—changed all that. In the village it was clear that the impact of astrology on the lives of the people surpasses that in America by astronomical dimensions. Indeed, astrology plays a tremendous role in the lives of the villagers, as it does in the lives of most Sri Lankans. They believe that the position of the planets governs one's life from the moment of birth. For each child born the parents have an astrologer make a horoscope, which is consulted for every rite of passage or important event in the person's life, such as eating of the first rice, piercing a girl's ears, learning the first letter of the alphabet, the ritual bathing after a girl's first menstrual period, and the wedding ceremony. It is essential that the horoscopes of the couple in an arranged marriage be compatible. Conducting or beginning events at astrologically auspicious moments—whether it is the breaking of the first sod for building an important water reservoir, the entering of a newly built house, the starting of the cultivation season, or even the time of leaving the house to go take an examination—is a common practice all over Sri Lanka. It is perhaps even more important in a rural village like Suduwatura Ara, where risks and dangers are rife. Ignoring the position of the planets and thereby very possibly conducting an important event at an inauspicious time is thought to be inviting bad fortune.

An example of the integration of beliefs in Buddhism, devils, and astrology can be seen in a series of ceremonies held for an elderly woman who had been ailing for some time. Punchi Rala determined from her horoscope that she was in an astrologically bad period. This made her especially vulnerable to devils and evil spirits, so Punchi Rala did the ritual of the "charmed thread" *(nul bandinawa)* for her (see p. 70). Shortly thereafter a Buddhist *bodhi pujawa* ceremony was held for her at the school's large bo tree, which was decorated with brightly colored trian-gular pennants. Here flowers were offered, coconut-oil lamps were lighted, and two full pots *(kale)* of water were given to the bo tree, symbolically "bathing" it. Additionally, three village elders chanted stanzas for each of the nine planets. The idea is that earning merit by making an offering to the bo tree in the *bodhi pujawa* ceremony can offset some of the bad influence of the planets when a person's horoscope happens to be in an unfavorable period, thus making that person less susceptible to the powers of devils and evil spirits. I attended the ceremony and chatted with the woman shortly thereafter. The attention she received in the com-munity gathering had definitely lifted her spirits and given her some optimism. A week later, however, she was ailing again, feeling weak and troubled by aches and pains.

A *bodhi pujawa* can also be given for someone simply to show respect or ap-preciation and to bestow blessings and protection on them. Thus, toward the end of my second fieldwork period a *bodhi pujawa* was arranged in my honor—at consid-erable expense and work for the villagers. Much coconut oil had to be bought for the lamps, special baskets were woven for fresh flowers to be offered, and refresh-ments such as plantains, cookies, and local sweets had to be bought or made. I was secretly relieved that there would not be another all-night *pirith* chanting cere-mony. There were only two hours of chanting; and by this point in the fieldwork my auditory senses had become conditioned to the drone. To my surprise the chants (now without microphone and loudspeakers) even sounded soothing. The only part I had not learned to endure with equanimity was having coconut oil rubbed through my hair.

FOLK BELIEFS AND SUPERSTITIONS

I was continually learning new folk beliefs and superstitions, of which there are hundreds in the village. Many of them turn up in other sections of this book, for they transect every part of village life. Only a few will be shared below.

The small, ubiquitous lizards called geckos *(huna),* that make a sharp chirping sound, are thought to have many predictive powers, which they make known through a wide variety of signs. For example, if you are just beginning some en-deavor—whether it is leaving on a journey or writing a letter—and a gecko chirps, it is a bad omen. The villagers will put aside the task or wait a while before begin-ning. The direction from which the sound comes and the day of the week are also important. Similarly, if a gecko falls from the wall onto some part of your body, symbolism can be read into that: If it falls on your head, you can expect a quarrel; on your face, you will see relatives; falling on your hand is generally bad unless it falls on the fingers alone, which is good. The almanac found in a number of homes has a whole matrix of predictions related to geckos.

Many other animals are seen as harbingers by the villagers. A cock crowing in the middle of the night is a bad sign; at midnight it is extremely bad. The remedy to avert evil is to cut off the cock's head and throw it over the roof of the house. A crow cawing from a dead tree means one will hear of a death; cawing from a fine fruit tree, a jack tree for example, means that friends will come. The howling of dogs or jackals at night also means there will be a death in the area. Hearing owls hoot late in the night, especially at midnight, is another portent of death. I remember a villager pointing this out to me one evening in the first fieldwork period as we chatted in my hut and heard the hoot of an owl in the jungle. He reminded me the next day of what he had said when a young child suffering from a severe viral sickness died that night.

The first person you see after leaving home is said to be an omen as well. For example, a Buddhist priest is a bad sign, a beggar is good. Such omens can be controlled in very important cases. If a couple is leaving the house to get married, it might be arranged that the first person they see is a woman carrying a pot of water, which is considered auspicious. Likewise, if you notice some very bad omen or look up some sign in the almanac and it portends great evil, you can go immediately to the well without changing clothes and bathe. This is said to take the evil away.

It is not good to sleep with your head to the west side, for that is how the dead are buried. Directions are considered important in many folk beliefs. On each day of the week there is a certain direction that belongs to the devil *(maru)*, and it is advisable to consider that when leaving the house. For example, on Saturday the *maru* is on the west, so you should leave the house in the morning by going east for a while; if the *maru* is on the south, you should go to the north, and so on.

I encountered folk beliefs at unexpected turns. When I had stomach problems, villagers would tell me that it was probably because some dogs had been watching me while I was eating. One day my helpful neighbor and good friend, Leela, put some leftover rice for the cat on the kitchen floor rather than in the cat's dish. When I asked her why, she gave an interesting explanation:

> Cats kill little animals and eat them. When the cat dies and goes up to the next world, the Lord up there will ask, "Did you kill and eat animals?" The cat will respond, "No, I ate rice, and the Earth Goddess is my witness." If the rice is put in a dish, the Earth Goddess cannot see it and thus cannot testify on behalf of the cat.

The fact that I had one of the few cement floors in the village, rather than the usual earth and cow-dung floor, did not matter in this case. Neither did the fact that it is also considered sinful to lie.

This same neighbor woman had told me about her belief in a certain demon, Pattikaraya, and her dilemma some nine years ago. At that time Leela had a good milk cow, which could have brought some extra income for the family. She wanted to send two bottles of milk with her husband to sell in Okkampitiya when he went there in the very early morning to do casual labor. However, she was afraid to milk the cow before light (about 6:00 A.M.) because of Pattikaraya, the short, evil demon who is said to hang around cows in the dark hours. He carries a golden walking stick in one hand and a golden pot *(sembuwa)* in which he comes to get milk. He has an open wound on his leg with lots of worms in it. You know he has been there when you see worms on the ground. If you meet him near the cows, he will attack you on the back with his stick, giving a serious back injury; or you might even vomit blood and die. Thus mortally frightened, Leela had been unable to milk the cow before dawn and sell the milk.

BUILDING AND ENTERING A NEW HOUSE—AN EXAMPLE OF SYNCRETISM

Having lived for two lengthy periods in my little house on the school premises with no major calamities, I enjoyed thinking back on the rich complexity of prescriptions that were carried out during the building and entering of that house. The painstakingly conducted ritual practices had protected me, I mused, as I felt the urge to "knock on wood"—just as surely conditioned by my Western superstitions as the villagers were by theirs.

In any case, the building of my house in 1984 had provided me with a good example of syncretism: astrology combined with beliefs in demons, folk beliefs, and a bit of Buddhism. The same prescriptions are still followed when constructing new houses, especially by the old-timers. Younger builders are cutting a few corners and paying more attention to practicalities, such as time constraints, although the major details are still followed.

The planner and primary builder of my wattle-and-daub house was none other than Punchi Rala, the traditional doctor and ritual healer, who was for years the village carpenter. At age sixty-seven in the second fieldwork period, he was largely retired from any carpentry work or heavy work after a cycle accident a few years ago. He was pleased to share his knowledge of housebuilding with me.

When planning a house numerous things should be considered. The front of the house should face either east or south, bringing it under the influence of gods or human beings, respectively. (North would bring it under the power of demons; west belongs to the *kumbhandas,* a category of evil spirits.) The house should not be built so that it faces a slope going down. The walls should not form the shape of a cross, for this is bad luck. Outside doors should never be in the same line so that one can see straight through the house. The number of doors and windows, inside and outside, should be an odd number (in my house there are seven); and the total number of cross-beams should be an odd number as well. Moreover, when you add the units (e.g., feet) of the length and breadth, the total should also be an odd number.

From the time that the first sod for the foundation is cut, which should be done at an astrologically auspicious time *(neketa),* potentially evil spirits called *bahirawas* are present. In order to protect the house from possible evil influence, semiprecious stones, medicinal herbs, and small amulets must be deposited at the four corners of the foundation. Placing the roof beams must also be done at an auspicious time.

Most important, however, are the prescriptions around the placing of the door frame. For this an offering must be made to the *bahirawas*. The offering of fruits, sweets, and a lighted oil lamp is usually placed in a small shrine stand *(malpela)* woven out of young coconut palm fronds. For my house Punchi Rala, while chanting mantras, put the offerings on plantain leaves placed on each side of the door.

When the door frame was complete, Punchi Rala walked from the inside to the outside at the auspicious time, reciting Buddhist *pirith* stanzas. He was wearing a white cloth on his head and carrying a pot of water treated with special herbs and containing a small coin. At the very moment he passed through the door another person threw down a coconut and broke it in one dash. Symbolism can be read into how the two pieces fall. In my case both halves fell with the open side upward, still containing some water, connoting happiness and prosperity. (If only the female side with the three holes is upward, there will be prosperity for the females in the house; if the male side faces up, it is good for the males.)

Punchi Rala proceeded around the house sprinkling water from the pot. Then without looking back he went to a junction where three roads meet; there he smashed the pot down, breaking it on a rock, taking the *bahirawas* and the evil out of the new house.

While the house was being built, I was living in a boarding house in Moneragala town, waiting for its completion. I would come out to the village to visit the school periodically (it was an hour's drive in first and second gear, often getting stuck in mud bogs and having to enlist some farmers to help me out), and my visits were unannounced. Sometimes on these occasions Punchi Rala was engaged in one of the ritual practices. No person was there to observe or control him, but he sincerely followed all the prescriptions according to his knowledge of them. I was moved to learn that he was not only laying the foundation of my house, but also the foundation for my protection and safety from evil forces.

On the day of the housewarming (May 10, 1984) when I was to ceremoniously enter the house that Punchi Rala and the villagers had completed for me, more ritual practices were in store. A hearth of three stones had been laid out in the kitchen, taking care that the stones were perfectly level. This was important because the pot would later be filled with milk and heated until the milk overflowed. If the froth flows on all sides equally, it is a good sign; if the pot is not level and the milk overflows to one side, this is considered bad and could bring illness or trouble.

The *neketa* had been determined at 10:04 A.M. We came that morning with a tractor cart loaded with my goods following the jeep, heaving over rocks and gullies and breaking anything not packed to perfection. I was given the traditional pot full of water and a key to the padlock on the door. Oil lamps were lighted and placed on both sides of the entrance. At the *neketa* precisely I had to turn the key in the lock and walk through the door with the water pot, symbolizing a house full of happiness. The hearth fire, too, had to be lit at an auspicious moment. The milk boiled over on all sides. Then the remaining milk in the pot was covered by a piece of newspaper. A small bag of different grains and semiprecious stones was tied to the rim, and the pot was hung to a ceiling beam where it still hangs today—all to bring protection and good fortune to the house's inhabitants.

Reviewing these practices once again with Punchi Rala during my second fieldwork, I thanked him for his conscientious adherence to the many house-building prescriptions. He answered with pride, "You see how it paid off. Your house has always been bright and full of happiness."

I reflected on the complexity and diversity of the range of villagers' beliefs in the supernatural. Some, like Leela's account of Pattikaraya and her fear of milking the cow, or the belief that one must appease the *prethas* through expensive almsgiving ceremonies, seemed to help perpetuate the poverty of the people. Their many beliefs, however, gave them a certain feeling of security, a sense of understanding as well as being in control. They combined this kind of insurance with an intricate spirituality in their world full of dangers, risks, and uncertainties. Moreover, they used their beliefs and ritual prescriptions to help protect me in that world. I was the last one to criticize that. And as Leonard Woolf pondered in his footnote (beginning of this chapter)—perhaps with tongue in cheek—wondering about who is to say what is right or wrong regarding supernatural beliefs, I was sometimes inclined to do the same.

4 / Living Standards and Daily Subsistence

The sprouting of paddy seedlings in the field, the paddy plants that rise and bend, blowing with the lift of the light wind around the farmer when he steps into his field, like playful calves frisking around their mother, the ears of paddy that finally crown the plants, like a gift of the Earth Goddess pleased with his toil—the peasant, to whose sight and touch all these things are familiar, experiences a deeper and more intimate pleasure than the complex aesthetic enjoyment which books provide for the erudite.

—from Our Village by Martin Wickramasinghe, 1940

The rhythms of agricultural life are timeless and epitomize an unchanging cycle of agrarian practices. This I took as a given, but I also accepted that "nothing is as constant as change." At the time of my return to Suduwatura Ara in 1994 I had been away for nine years, time enough for many changes. The "Village Re-Awakening" program had taken place there, and I knew that Sri Lanka, like elsewhere in the Third World, was steadily—if slowly—moving in the direction of modernism. A professor acquaintance of mine in Colombo, whom I met ten years back when taking Sinhala lessons from his wife in the Netherlands, was able to communicate with me on e-mail. He even wrote about getting a cellular phone, which was becoming a popular item in the capital city.

Before departure various ideas about a central theme for the intended monograph passed through my mind. The obvious one, I thought, would be "tradition and change." This was going to be a revisitation of a village after a decade, and I anticipated developments and significant changes on all fronts. It did not take long to conclude that my prediction had been wrong.

LIVING STANDARDS THEN AND NOW

Although there were signs that the standard of living had risen in the past ten years (better houses, more material possessions) and that agriculture was modernizing somewhat (e.g., more farmers threshing paddy with a rented tractor rather than with bulls; some farmers affiliated with a big company for one of their cash crops like tobacco), on closer examination the improvement for most of the villagers was marginal. I was disappointed to see that the obvious changes brought by the Village Re-Awakening in 1991–92 had stymied when the program was over; and the loans given to the participants during the campaign still had to be repaid.

All of the thirty houses that had been built subsequent to the Village Re-Awakening, or had been later included in Suduwatura Ara by extending its southern boundaries, were of the type found in the village a decade earlier: wattle-and-daub walls, two small rooms and a kitchen, a grass-thatched roof, and a cow-dung floor. Glancing over the homesteads from my trusted rock and mountain perch, I could see more red-tiled roofs and white-washed walls, as well as a few houses built with fanciful decorations or arches by a ve-randa. However, this upgrading was a one-time injection by the speedily implemented development plan of former President Premadasa. Those households that had not finished building their subsidized latrine by April 1992, when the year-long structured program came to an end, still had no latrines at the time of my fieldwork. The squatting pans and bricks they had received were stacked beside their houses, sadly attesting to economic stagnation.

Only 5 of the 108 houses could boast of a cement floor in all the rooms; the rest still had cow-dung floors, which the women must replenish every one to two months. Several houses had no windows, and a couple had only door-openings without doors that could be closed. Many of the houses that participated in the Village Re-Awakening still could not afford the wood and carpentry labor for window frames nor the preferred iron lattice-work or bars across the windows. They had pro-visionally closed them with bricks or chicken wire, with bigger plans for the future.

A continual scourge for the villagers, and for me as well, was the ubiquitous presence of subterranean termites. Huge termite mounds in forms resembling tur-reted medieval castles dot the countryside. The destructive pests can turn up any-where, devouring wooden beams, window frames, roof thatching, furniture, books, paper, textiles, or shoes. Anything hanging on the wall is a target, as I found out. The insects eat the wattle lattice foundation of the mud wall and periodically make a hole in the wall's surface. If a poster or a wall hanging is on that spot, it will be in-conspicuously eaten from the back until you notice a spot of brown mud coming through the item; and it is then too late, for the object has been reduced to a fine mudlike substance.

I had to make it a point to regularly check anything termite edible that was touching the walls or lying on the floor, for they even come through tiny crevices in cement floors. During my first stay I lost clothes, shoes, the edges of many books and notes, as well as all my bank statements. The plague continued in my second stay, as termites ate my bathing enclosure, my favorite posters, and some Christmas cards I had strung around the room.

The threat is the same for all villagers, who, if they can afford it, buy old motor oil to smear on the principal beams of the house. Knowing the extent to which these "white ants" devastate the property and meager personal belongings of the farmers, I was surprised when I heard the schoolchildren singing a patriotic song that in-cluded a verse about termites: "Just as the tiny termites, working together, can build a huge termite mound, so we, the children of Sri Lanka, can build up our nation." I was also surprised at the calm way that the people reacted to termite damage. They had learned to accept the presence of white ants as a given; and the Buddhist pre-cept of not killing any living animal added to their tolerance. The tremendous ter-mite mounds in their fields, or even those in close proximity to their houses, were never destroyed. When I asked why, some answered that it is no use because termites are everywhere. Others said that the mounds are likely the homes of cobras, sacred animals in the Hindu religion; and Hinduism is intermingled with local Buddhism.

In any case, whether the mounds are home to cobras or termites, it is considered sinful to destroy any dwelling place. This is also true for mud-daubers' nests, which are left undisturbed even if located in a conspicuous place in a house. One had built a mud nest in a white blouse of mine hanging in my makeshift closet (a horizontal pole with hangers). My assistant explained that I should not destroy the nest, a warning which I disregarded. I was never able to get the mud spot from the blouse, however, which he considered to be a sign of justice.

Possessions

Furniture in most houses was still extremely sparse, usually consisting only of a bed with mat, a rough-hewn table, and a couple of wooden chairs. Some planks laid across sticks jutting from the wall serve as shelves for meager goods: a transistor radio, a kerosene-jar lamp without chimney, a flashlight, a piece of mirror, a powder tin or a few small bottles, a soap box, and a small suitcase in which valuables are kept. The latter are generally the identity cards, the marriage license, the food stamps, the land permit, miscellaneous old photographs, an old *pirith* book, and various personal treasures and mementos.

The scant collection of clothes, often threadbare, torn and soiled from days of hard labor, is thrown over a line stretched across a corner of the room. On the walls you often see a weathered picture of Lord Buddha or Lord Kataragama (the main Hindu god in the area), a few framed but cobweb-covered photographs of relatives in the native village, and maybe a calendar or some colorful pictures of singers, movie stars, light-colored Sri Lankan children, or fluffy kittens cut from a picture-newspaper.

Some of the kitchens have been improved by a built-in clay hearth. This is an addition to the traditional hearth of three stones on which a pot is placed over the wood fire. The kitchen itself is ideally a separate wattle-and-daub structure, even in the more prosperous homesteads, as the smoke from cooking fires pollutes and blackens the surroundings. In the kitchen is found an array of earthenware pots, a winnowing basket, a mortar and pestle, a coconut-scraper, a bowl for removing small stones from the rice *(nembiliya),* some jars containing various spices and condiments, serving spoons made of coconut shells, one or more water pots, maybe a grinding stone for chilies and a stone mill for millet. There is sometimes a table in the kitchen, or a home-fashioned wall rack, but many items are just placed on the floor where most of the food preparation is done, squatting or seated on stools just a few inches from the floor. After the harvesting season the kitchen and other rooms as well are crowded with bags of rice or other grains, as the compounds have no separate storage rooms or granaries.

I was humbled when women, proud of their own new hearth or newly bought dishes, would ask me about my kitchen in America. They were curious because I did not do much cooking at all, and they wondered if I could. "It's just very different in my country," is all I could bring myself to say. How could I explain my hectic life of popping food from the freezer into the microwave oven? It would be something like a science fiction story for them. "I enjoy eating Sri Lankan food while I'm here," I said, "and I won't be able to get it when I go back." They remembered that statement and prepared small packages of rice, peanuts, sesame seeds, cowpeas, and other dried grains to take with me when I returned to the States.

Material possessions that count as luxury items—while more widely distributed than a decade ago—were still sparse. Almost every house did have a transistor radio, although they could not always afford the batteries to operate it. The same was true for a battery-operated wall clock set in a heart with floral designs or a frame of cute kittens. The majority of the households (eighty-five) had a bicycle, and two had motorbikes at the time of my return; only one family had an ox-drawn cart. There were about twenty expensive Petromax lanterns, which are used only on special occasions or nighttime agricultural work such as threshing. The number of sewing machines had increased from five to eight; and there were three small television sets operated on a car battery.

One of those TVs belonged to Punchi Rala, who bought it amid much excitement toward the end of my second stay. I went to watch as some local youths worked for hours, attaching the small antenna to a long wooden pole they had cut, trying it at different places from the roof and in the yard, while a flock of children sat with eyes glued to the magical box, delighted whenever there was momentarily a discernible picture emerging from the hissing salt-and-pepper of the screen. I thought back on the village during my first stay, when there were no TVs in Suduwatura Ara—only the dream of having one. A few children had seen a television bought by a wealthy gem merchant in nearby Okkampitiya, and when asked to draw a picture of their house, they had put a TV antenna on the roof. The dream was very slowly starting to come true.

The paucity of the housing and material possessions reflects the low level of cash income earned by the villagers. With the exception of two households during my second stay, all of the inhabitants received government food stamps each month at a maximum of Rs. 50 per child under ten years of age, Rs. 40 for those ten to twelve, and Rs. 30 for those more than twelve years old. Kerosene stamps of Rs. 44 per household were also given, enough for about three liters. Being eligible for food stamps, which can be traded for food at government cooperative shops in the towns, meant the householder earned less than Rs. 700 per month (about U.S. $14). Food stamps for a month hardly covered a week's needs according to most recipients.

Recreation

What people do in their leisure time for entertainment or recreation is also molded and limited by scarcity. For example, while they enjoy listening to the radio, or watching one of the three small television sets found in the more prosperous families' houses, these activities are reduced to a few hours because batteries and recharging the car batteries are expensive. Sometimes young people, especially groups of boys, get together to sing songs and do drumming in the evening.

4.1 Two young women pose in front of a shelf that holds a typical array of household possessions.

The organized festivities that serve as the main social functions for all ages are scattered throughout the year. In Suduwatura Ara the biggest parties are held when a girl "attains age" at the occurrence of her first menstrual period, at which time the family gives a kind of "open house" that lasts from morning until late at night. It includes the consumption of much food, dancing, singing, drumming, and playing cards (see pp. 135–137). These age-attainment parties are larger than the village weddings, which are frequently no more than a small reception after an elopement. Other rites of passage, such as the first haircut, first rice, or first letter learning (chapter 7), are also attended as festive occasions where many sweets are served.

With the exception of the most elaborate annual celebration, the Sinhalese and Tamil New Year (pp. 163–168), most of the other festivities in the village serving as social functions are connected with Buddhist beliefs, namely the activities around the Wesak Full Moon in May (celebrating the birth, enlightenment, and passing away of the Buddha) and the Poson Full Moon in June (celebrating the advent of Buddhism to Sri Lanka). In addition, the nights of *pirith* chanting, the evenings of *bana* preaching of the Buddhist doctrine by a village elder, and especially the elaborate *dana* ceremonies of almsgiving to invited Buddhist monks, at which time much food is served and relatives from other villages arrive, are all occasions when the villagers get together socially.

Going on trips or pilgrimages is a favorite activity for the people, although the costs are prohibitively expensive for most to make it an annual activity. There are many inhabitants who have never seen the ocean or never traveled to the capital city of Colombo. Most of them do travel to visit relatives in their native Welimada area, although a funeral may likely be the reason. Popular pilgrimages include traveling to a monastery in nearby Buttala or going to the town of Kataragama some 60 km away to worship at the Buddhist shrine there and make offerings to the Hindu god Kataragama. It is a place where one goes to get protective blessings. For example, a trip to Kataragama is a must if you have bought a new vehicle; it is considered risky to drive the vehicle unless it has been taken to that city, where the owner makes a vow and ties a coin to the steering wheel.

I was deeply saddened to learn of a terrible accident that occurred three months after my departure. A group of Suduwatura Ara villagers went on a pilgrimage and pleasure trip to Kataragama. Ironically and tragically, the group was returning at night in a speeding bus, which crashed into a tree, severely injuring about twenty-five people. One of the respected patriarchs of the village, Sudu Banda (pictured on p. 167), died a few weeks later of his injuries.

Of all activities carried on in the villagers' leisure time, and often engaged in while doing productive work as well, the most popular is gossip. Both men and women enjoy filling each other in on the latest news of happenings and minor scandals in Suduwatura Ara and neighboring villages. Near the equator night falls early; but for many households, kerosene is too expensive for doing activities during the long evenings. Groups of people can be heard chatting in near darkness in their houses or in the huts where they guard their fields from wild animals at night. The gossip serves as recreation and social control, as newspaper and grapevine telephone.

FOOD AND CULTIVATION

Food and food procurement are the all-important topics in a subsistence village like Suduwatura Ara. Agriculture occupies the time and efforts of the inhabitants and is the most probable future of the children. A common greeting if you meet someone around the afternoon or evening mealtime is *"Bath kaewa da?"* meaning "Have you had your rice meal?" (literally: "Did you eat rice?"). Eating regularly and having enough food, especially the beloved staple food rice, is a prime value.

As the land is fertile and there are still uncultivated areas of highland that can be planted, in a year of normal rain any person who is willing and able to work hard can grow enough food to feed the family. Not all meals are well balanced, and there are times of the year that are meager, but nobody goes to bed really hungry.

Villagers eat huge, heaping quantities of rice for the afternoon and evening meals, together with two or three vegetable curries. Their diet is quite low in animal protein, however. Very few families had chickens at the time of my fieldwork; and though most households had a team of bulls for plowing, there were only about eight milk cows in the village. These few farm animals are never slaughtered for meat. Eggs, milk, and canned fish are luxuries due to their scarcity and expense. For special meals small quantities of sprats (tiny dried fish) or salted dried fish are bought at the market and fried. Additionally, boys catch the fish in the artificial lake (tank) with a fishing pole or by standing in the shallows and catching them by hand.

The villagers occasionally serve porcupine meat or the meat of the monitor lizard *(talagoya)*, reptiles that grow up to five feet long in this area. While game animals are common (deer, sambar, wild boar, and hares), there are no guns in the village for hunting. Those rifles given to twenty men in 1991 who served as "Home Guards," protecting the village from Tamil terrorists, were used for illegal hunting. But all the guns were returned to the government after the tragic accidental hunting death of a twenty-one-year-old youth in 1995 (see p. 105).

Though animal protein is low, the people eat many varieties of protein-rich pulses, such as lentils, green gram, cowpeas, and long beans *(mae)*. A new product available in the towns of the area is "soya meat," which is made into a curry.

In the ten years between my research periods, many fruit trees planted in the young frontier village grew to maturity; so the villagers were eating much more fruit such as plantains, papayas, mangoes, wood apples, passion fruit, and custard apples—samples of which they would bring to me as gifts on a regular basis.

Seen as a guest in the village, I was quite frequently honored by families inviting me to an afternoon or evening meal. Children would pester their families to extend such an invitation; and they would come to fetch me early, brothers and sisters fighting over who would carry my bag. They looked forward to the occasion, for they knew I would bring the camcorder, camera, and perhaps some balloons. More important, they knew their mother would prepare a fancier meal than the everyday one.

Usually I was served three vegetable curries, some fried bread crisps, and either some dried or canned fish or half a boiled egg. They spoiled me (and sometimes my assistant) with festive meals, ending with buffalo curd or fruit; and the children knew there would be a big meal for them, too. I never grew accustomed to being served first, served again with food piled high, and doted on by all the family members, who would eat only when I had finished and left, the mother eating last. They loved to stare amusedly at what they considered to be "dainty" eating with my fingers, as it was difficult to imitate the forceful, solid mashing of large quantities of rice and curries. While I am by no means a finicky eater, and I enjoyed the food they prepared for me, truly moved by their generosity, I had visions of certain unavailable American favorites—never to be taken for granted again.

Agriculture

There is a clear-cut division: there is first the well-known set of conditions, the natural course of growth, as well as the ordinary pests and dangers to be warded off by fencing and

weeding. On the other hand there is the domain of the unaccountable and adverse influences, as well as the great unearned increment of fortunate coincidence. The first conditions are coped with by knowledge and work, the second by magic.
        —from "Magic, Science and Religion" by Bronislaw Malinowski, 1925

In Suduwatura Ara three types of cultivation common in Moneragala District are carried out: *wee govitena* (wet rice or paddy cultivation); *goda govitena* (nonshifting highland homestead cultivation); and *hen govitena* (shifting slash-and-burn highland cultivation). These three approaches complement and compensate one another, minimizing risks in periods of unusually low or unusually high rainfall. Nevertheless, the people adhere to ritual practices (magic, in Malinowski's terms).

Paddy Cultivation. For the majority of the people in Suduwatura Ara who are upcountry Sinhalese, paddy cultivation is a matter of tradition and pride. Due to water shortage in this area on the edge of the Dry Zone, not all households can cultivate paddy. There are ten families, all of them original settlers, who have one to one and a half acres of paddyland in the command area of the village tank. Many other farmers—but not the newcomers—have fraction-acre paddy fields in the former river beds where a small stream of water still flows. If the flow of water is steady, two seasons can be cultivated. A maximum output per acre per season is sixty bushels. For almost all the households the paddy is for consumption, and they have to buy additional rice.

Having rice that you have cultivated available in your home for daily meals is of great significance to these farmers. They do not mind having three rice meals a day. Even though you can see them eating fresh bread as a snack during cooperative work campaigns, they will insist that rice is what they prefer: That is *real* food. For some it is considered a bit embarrassing and shameful to have to buy rice; and the drive to engage in paddy cultivation comes from the desire to have one's own rice for consumption, not from wanting to sell rice as a cash crop.

Rice being the mainstay of the diet, it is associated with life itself; and many respectful practices and rituals have developed around paddy cultivation. I found a few old-timers still observing all these traditions, which have diminished with each succeeding generation.

Formerly the initial activities of every new phase of cultivation required prescribed practices to be done at astrologically auspicious times. Today people tend to look more at the weather than the astrology almanac. The strongest traditions exist around the threshing floor *(kamata)* after harvesting. There it is common to see a bundle of paddy hanging from a nearby tree, even on the *kamatas* of younger farmers. This bundle consists of the first harvested paddy, which will be used to make the sweet rice offering to the local gods when the threshing is complete. Hanging it near the *kamata* is thought to protect the paddy throughout the threshing and winnowing process.

During my first research period all the farmers who cultivated rice threshed it in the traditional Sinhalese way, by driving a pair of bulls (oxen) around the circular floor on top of the paddy stalks for twelve to twenty-four hours, depending on the amount to be threshed. This was an exhausting process for humans and animals alike. However, the fact that the rice stalks were not literally threshed by beating—as done in India—is an indication of the farmers' respect for their primary source of food. These days many farmers have replaced this traditional means of threshing by hiring a tractor, which is driven and spun around on the *kamata* for three to four hours. The price for hiring the tractor is little more than hiring bulls, and the time saved is considerable. However, those with small paddy fields and their own bulls will probably opt for the traditional method.

Within two weeks after the threshing, an offering called *deva dana* is made to the local deities. This is a preparation of sweet sticky rice with sugar and cardamoms, cooked by the men right on the threshing floor (women are considered unclean for preparing food for the gods). A small elevated shrine *(malpela)* is constructed of sticks and covered with leafy branches or woven from young coconut palm fronds. In this shrine a portion of the sweet rice is placed for the gods, along with a picture of the main local Hindu god Kataragama, some flowers, oil lamps, incense sticks, and camphor cubes. Some rice for the hungry spirit-beings called *prethas* is placed on a banana leaf on the ground under the shrine platform. This ritual offering, repeated year after year, is a way to keep the gods and spirits satisfied and thus help ensure a good harvest the next year. It is a way to cope with uncertainty in a world where drought and blight can cause hunger.

While the local deities are being evoked, those who helped with the threshing and other invited villagers, many of whom are children, chant the first five Buddhist

4.2 Threshing paddy in the traditional Sinhalese way, by driving a pair of bulls around the circular floor on top of the paddy stalks for twelve to twenty-four hours.

precepts—another example of the syncretistic mixture of local beliefs and Buddhism. Each person is served a generous helping of the sweet rice, along with a piece of coconut and a plantain. At the end of the ceremony the rice that was offered to the gods is also distributed to be eaten by guests. It is considered to be very special, as the deities are believed to have partaken of it. Thus the *deva dana* is a festive occasion, a social gathering, a sweet-rice meal, and a communion with the gods in order to reduce risks.

Many other traditional practices are associated with the circular threshing floor prepared with cow dung and mud hardened in the sun—though one will see fewer of these practices today. Even a special vocabulary was traditionally used on the *kamata,* such as calling paddy *Buddha govi* (cultivated rice belonging to the Buddha), and calling a bull an *ambaruwa* instead of *gona.* It was thought that the everyday words were too vulgar for this semisacred place. Using such words might invite demons to come and take the paddy, while the respectful words would prevent this.

It is still believed by some that the amount of paddy on a *kamata* can increase or decrease due to the influence of certain demons (here, *bahirawas*). The village ritual healer Punchi Rala, for example, said you could sometimes hear a "sarrasarra-sarra-sarra" noise on a *kamata,* which was the sound of the paddy from other diminishing *kamatas* coming to a particular *kamata* that was now increasing the size of its heap. Adherence to the proper rituals is thought to reduce the risk of this occurrence. So even after a successful harvest, a farmer's paddy could diminish or disappear in a hostile world if he did not take the correct precautions.

Nonshifting Highland Cultivation. The fifty families who were living in Suduwatura Ara as migrant encroachers on crown land were each given deeds to three acres of highland shortly after my departure in 1985. This gave them the right to use that designated parcel of land for the next ninety-nine years, passing it down to their children. The land, which had originally been cleared in the area for slash-and-burn shifting cultivation, now became the permanent homestead acreage of the families. On these acres adjacent to their houses they cultivate their principal cash crops, usually corn, peanuts, cowpeas, green gram, millet, and sesame seeds. The majority of these crops are grain sorts that can be stored for long periods to be eaten or sold when the need arises. Often part of this highland acreage is also planted with chilies and onions.

Since my first stay in the village, three new cash crops were introduced to be cultivated on the villagers' highland acreage, each with the supervision of representatives from large companies: sugarcane, tobacco, and gherkins. In all three cases the farmers had to take risks, accepting large advances in the form of seeds, fertilizers, insecticides, and materials needed for the cultivation, such as the wires for drying tobacco and the ropes on which to lead the gherkin creepers. If they had bad luck, such as having wild buffaloes ruining the sugarcane field, or caterpillars eating their tobacco crop, or a dry spell killing their gherkins, the farmers could go deep in debt. Still most villagers who cultivate these new crops think the chances for making a profit are larger than with their traditional crops.

Take Leela's gherkin cultivation, for example. She started with one-eighth acre and now cultivates a half acre. The representative of a big firm comes to inspect the crops from time to time. She harvests the little cucumbers every morning and afternoon and takes them on her head in the evening to the weigh station 8 km away in Okkampitiya. There they are sorted into five grades by size, the smallest bringing the best profit per kilo. The two smallest grades are put in vinegar, the larger sizes in salt, all for export to Europe, the Middle East, and Australia.

The tiniest gherkins yield Rs. 25 per kilo (about U.S. $.50), a nice price for vegetables in this part of the world. Leela gets paid every two weeks for what she has brought in during that period—but she gets only half that amount in her hands, for half is withheld until the value of all the advanced material is paid off.

Last year Leela was unlucky enough to have a large part of her crop killed by a long dry period, so she ended up having to pay the gherkin company Rs. 3000 at the end of the season. She still owes the company Rs. 6000 for the seed, fertilizer, and insecticide this year. Knowing about the debt she owed, I was amazed that Leela was not discouraged and that she always believed she would make a profit.

Chena (Slash-and-Burn) Cultivation. Although available land is becoming more scarce, and the area has begun to suffer from deforestation, most villagers engage in shifting highland slash-and-burn cultivation (called *chena* in Sri Lanka) in addition to the above two types. Chena cultivation takes place on the distant periphery of the village, and the people often have to walk for an hour and a half or more to get to their fields.

Originally this slash-and-burn, shifting agriculture was done on virgin land. The trees were felled and burned to make the land fertile for farming. As the population grew, however, it was more difficult to spread out to unused land, and the fallow periods have become shorter and shorter. The chena cultivators of Suduwatura Ara have reached the edge of their frontier, as settlers from the village of Kahambana to the south have been moving north with their own slash-and-burn fields.

Nevertheless, these distant parcels of land allow the industrious villagers to cultivate amounts of various grain sorts (corn, cowpeas, green gram, millet, peanuts, etc.) as well as vegetables and tubers, (e.g., long beans, bitter gourds, winged beans, eggplants, pumpkins, sweet potatoes, and manioc) well above what can be grown on their two to three-acre homestead parcels. As they do for paddy and homestead highland cultivation after the harvest, an offering of sweet rice is given to the local deities, especially Lord Kataragama, in a small ceremony at the chena field itself. Also similar to paddy cultivation, a number of practices to help minimize risks and ensure a good harvest are observed by the farmers. Each major phase of chena cultivation—clearing and plowing, planting, harvesting, and bringing home the harvest—is begun at an astrologically auspicious hour. Seeds are always planted in the morning, never in the afternoon, in order to enhance their chance of growing; only yams are planted in the afternoon.

Marauding animals—hares, monkeys (grey langurs and red macaques), birds, and especially wild boars—are a continual threat to the chena fields. On occasion even wild elephants will destroy crops. Because of the danger of destruction by animals, certain additional beliefs have arisen concerning chena cultivation. For each day in the almanac an animal is listed (lion, boar, elephant, bird, tiger, or bullock). Cautious farmers should take this into consideration when building a fence around the chena. If they build the fence on the boar's day, for example, their field might be ruined by wild boars. The best time to start building the fence is at the auspicious hour on the lion's or leopard's day; the latter do not eat crops anyway, so this precautionary practice is thought to reduce the danger of wild animals eating the chena produce. Only a few of the older farmers still follow these customs, however.

By day a variety of birds must be chased away from the fields (paddy, homestead, and chena). This is usually the work of children, who shout and throw stones at the persistent creatures.

Additionally, from September through January, during the night one will hear from time to time what sounds like the loud blast of a gun reverberating across the valley. These are firecrackers set off by farmers who are watching over their fields, especially the chenas and other highland fields, sheltering in a thatched lean-to called a *pela*. Without this nightly vigilance to scare off a variety of animals, the product of hard labor in highland cultivation would be ravaged.

A *pela* can be built on the ground, with a platform where the farmers sleep and a hearth of three stones for making tea and meals; or it can also be built on stilts for better viewing. On moonlit nights the watchers can see the animals; other times they listen for rustling sounds or the cries of birds that give the animals away.

I spent some time with friends in a *pela* at night. There was a certain coziness in the atmosphere, like camping out. Songs are sung *(pel kawi)*, and there is usually a campfire burning. If the corn is ripe, people will be roasting ears. Young people especially think staying in a *pela* is more fun than staying at home, and lighting firecrackers from time to time is exciting.

Home Gardens. In addition to the three types of agriculture discussed above, most of the villagers have home gardens just outside their houses, containing coconut palms, fruit trees, and small vegetable plots. These are for household consumption as well as incidental sale at the local markets.

During my first fieldwork period I decided to cultivate my own small-scale garden. The idea was to set an example for the schoolchildren, so they could carry on with the cultivation of small plots of good cash crops on the school grounds. The profits after sale would be used for starting savings accounts.

The experiment helped me understand the frustration and weak position of the village farmers. With the help of some enterprising neighbor women, I chose eight sorts of vegetables, including red onions. The latter were recommended as a profitable cash crop, thus I bought a half kilo to plant at the expensive price of Rs. 25 per kilo. The cultivation involved much work: preparing the earth, carrying loads of water from the pond daily when the rain did not come in time, weeding, breaking the earth around the onions with a stick, and pouring a manure mixture over the plots. When the onions were ready to be harvested, all agreed that the crop looked good. We optimistically took the 2.5 kilos to a merchant in town, who would offer only Rs. 8 per kilo. My disappointment was great as he said, "I'm sorry, Madam, but the price has fallen since you bought them." I took the onions and went back home, reviewing in my mind the long labor in the sun to cultivate a few onions. I was starting to understand the difficulty of the farmers' position—caught between the fluctuating market, the middlemen, and the hard, dry earth.

TRADE

The Weekly Fairs

On any given Tuesday morning, fifteen to twenty Suduwatura Ara villagers can be seen selling produce at the Okkampitiya market. Most of them leave home at 5:30 A.M. with their goods on their heads, some taking hanging scales and weights along. They set up their tiny businesses at the same place every week, putting their vegetables down on a piece of plastic in little stacks that sell for about Rs. 3 to 6 each. Some put up a length of plastic to protect their small area from the sun or rain.

For large-scale sale of vegetables or fruits, the seller must pay Rs. 20 to the person who has leased the market grounds; for small-scale business the price is just Rs. 10 or 15. Still, on a bad day the farmers might chance bringing home less than Rs. 100 (U.S. $2). If they make more than Rs. 500 by the time the market is over at noon, it is considered a good day.

Equally important as the money to be earned, the villagers enjoy the lively atmosphere, the exchange of news, and the gossip; and they take the opportunity to do some shopping or trading for goods they need. There are a few rather elaborate stands that carry spices and simple household goods; some sell cloth, others sell fresh or dried fish. It is a bustling place full of sounds and colors and a certain excitement in the air. Having experienced my share of boredom and lack of recreation, I could attest to the fact that in a world where there is hardly any formal entertainment available, the market is a favorite place to go.

There are other fairs in nearby towns where villagers sell vegetables and fruits: Moneragala on Sundays and Buttala on Wednesdays. Only a few people sell at all three, however. It is an hour and a half walk to the nearest bus stop; and after deducting bus fares and market stand fees, the small profit makes fair hopping an exhausting and time-consuming enterprise with too few returns.

The Village Shops

Suduwatura Ara has three tiny shops located in the houses where the respective shopkeepers live. Other shops have opened and closed over the years—the opening of a new shop being a leveling mechanism for any shopkeeper who started to get ahead.

The little shops sell the most basic of goods: kerosene, soap, matches, toothpaste and tooth powder, razor blades, flashlight batteries and bulbs, coconut oil, salt; and such food items as dried fish, dried chilies, onions, lentils, coconuts, cookies, and toffees.

People tend to buy goods on credit, often forcing the shops to close down a couple of months before harvest time; only after the harvest can they collect the money villagers owe them. The shop owners are generally too cash poor to give much credit for an extended period. They go by bicycle to neighboring towns and bring back small quantities of goods they are able to buy wholesale. The price they charge is only slightly higher than the price in town. Their profits are gained in tiny increments, and the existence of the shop is always tenuous.

I was moved when "my" villagers tried to protect me from what they considered to be an unfair practice, namely, charging me more for market produce because I was a white foreigner. If I went shopping alone and bought some items, they enjoyed questioning me on what I had paid. Inevitably I would be told that I had paid too much: "You paid three rupees for a single passion fruit? I could have gotten it for one rupee!" A few friends would offer to do my fruit and vegetable shopping, knowing they were better at scrutinizing the quality of the produce as well as getting a bargain price. We would joke that white skin is expensive at the market place.

During my first stay a young village woman came by my house with a bottle of honey that she sold to me for what I considered to be a fair price. Later other village friends examined the honey and were outraged. "This is wild honey of the *bambara* wasps, not bee honey. She charged you far too much!" The young woman was chastised and was the subject of malicious gossip for a long time. "How dare she try to take advantage of our Sudu Teacher!" I felt embarrassed by the situation and tried to explain that it was not a "big deal"; but at the same time I was touched that the villagers so actively tried to defend my interests.

GEMMING AND OTHER INCIDENTAL INCOME

Income from labor is of various sorts. Many of the men and women go for casual labor (coolie) whenever the work is available—either working for some better-off farmers in Suduwatura Ara or in nearby villages. A large sugarcane company employs casual laborers in season at very low wages. A few farmers will use their bulls for plowing, mainly for people in other villages who have no bulls or plow. One local boy rents his diesel-powered winnowing machine to others for Rs. 3 per bushel of paddy.

The few village families with a son in the army or having another steady job, such as security guard or guest-house worker, will usually be given a portion of that income. One family gets a little additional cash by having two of the schoolteachers board in their house. There are a couple of men who supplement their income through incidental jobs using their carpentry and masonry skills.

One of the most sought-after occupations all over Sri Lanka is being selected to go to a country in the Middle East as a housemaid or a skilled laborer for a few years. Although no one from Suduwatura Ara has ever been abroad, one family had a relative living in neighboring Kumbukkana who went to Saudi Arabia as a housemaid. She expected to stay for a year-long contract but returned after three months because the twelve-year-old boy where she was working beat her. She went for a second time and came back early again after receiving news that her daughter was being ill-treated at home by relatives. Because she broke her contract and left in haste, she had to leave behind most of the goods she had bought, pay for her own return ticket, and forfeit a month's wages, losing considerable money on her Middle Eastern experience. I was surprised when she said that she would go again, without hesitation, if given the opportunity. And her rather typical case of booking low returns for the investment in time has not discouraged other village women from wanting to go to the Middle East. They see it as one of the few ways in which their house can be improved and an assortment of material goods collected.

Some of the more lucrative village business is illegal business. Although the brewing of homemade liquor *(kasippu)* has diminished greatly in the past ten years, there is still some illegal timber felling and the cultivation of hashish leaves *(ganja)*. Those who get ahead by selling hashish are the subject of jealousy and gossip. One conspicuously prosperous family has few friends in Suduwatura Ara, and envious inhabitants whisper that the accumulation of material goods and the high standard of living may be traced to the sale of *ganja*.

Another illegal practice is gemming on crown land in the jungle. Sri Lanka has been noted throughout history for the high quality of gemstones found on the island, particularly in the wet soil around Ratnapura. These include blue, pink, and star sapphires. In the early 1980s the jungle area near Okkampitiya was discovered to be a new location rich in gems, and the small town had a temporary boom with an influx of hopeful gem seekers. The farmers of the area, too, got wind of the new income source.

During the slower parts of the agricultural cycle, the men and older sons of many Suduwatura Ara households still often try their luck at gemming, even though the number of gems being found around Okkampitiya has diminished in the past decade. Gemming involves digging pits in the jungle, shoveling out the gem-rich soil *(illam)*, sifting and washing this in baskets, and picking out the relatively rare precious and semiprecious stones with an expert eye.

Before starting this uncertain and risky work, the men build a small shrine: a woven palm-frond enclosure on sticks, similar to the *malpela* built after a harvest. Here the gemmers place offerings of flowers, fruit, incense, and coconut-oil lamps in order to beseech the blessings of the local gods. Such a shrine is thought to help the gemmers in two ways: finding gems, and protecting them from getting caught or having accidents.

Usually a team of two to three illegal gemmers is sponsored by a merchant, who pays for the food, hoes, and gemming baskets and guarantees to bail the men out of jail if they are caught. Half the profit of the "finds"—if any—goes to the merchant after sale of the gems to local buyers, who then sell them to merchants from Thailand; the other half is divided among the team. It is a rough world where values often give way to greed, and stories of gemmers being cheated are the rule, not the exception.

Nevertheless, there are always success stories going around of "rags to riches," and getting rich quick remains the dream of many young village men. There are months when no gems are found at all; and when they are found, the profit is usually between a few hundred and a few thousand rupees, which quickly slips through the gemmer's fingers. Raja's story told ten years ago when he was twenty-five is still typical for the men I talked with during my second stay:

> I've been gemming off and on since I was sixteen. Only once was I in with a group that found a good gem, one worth Rs. 50,000. My share was Rs. 7000. I first bought this cassette-radio for Rs. 1100; then I bought clothes for Rs. 600. I gave Rs. 1000 to my mother and father and several hundred to my brothers and sisters because they're all so poor. Then I paid off my debts to the merchant-sponsor. All the money was gone before

I knew it. I can't say whether I've won or lost with all the gemming I've done. I think I've about broken even. Maybe I'll open a bank account the next time I find a good gem.

I had wondered why many families were happy when they had a son they could spare in the gemming fields—allowing their child to enter a world of ruffians and high risks. Considering the farmers' subsistence way of life, however, with the dangers of drought, insect plagues, and marauding animals, as well as the many other misfortunes that could ruin their tenuous balance in the struggle for a better lifestyle, it was more understandable. The slim possibility of finding a valuable gem provided a dream, like playing the lottery. It was not a blanket precaution against evil, as were the ritualized offerings to local deities, but it was a chance that the family might wake up one day and have a buffer against poverty or be able to buy that coveted luxury item. I resolved to count my blessings.

5 / Healing and Health

After many years of disregarding, prohibiting and deriding autochtonous solutions to health problems, it is about time to recognize the possibilities of traditional practitioners in meeting the demands of villagers. . . . Human dignity, linked with pride in the domestic culture and the possibility of integrating new achievements into that culture, are conditions for good health.

—from Changing Traditions in Health Care—Sri Lanka by Ivan Wolffers, 1987

When I moved into a remote jungle village, many hours away from anything that resembled modern medical facilities from my U.S. perspective, of course I was concerned about the health conditions in the village and the options that were available. I went armed with all the recommended shots and an ample supply of malaria tablets, vitamin pills, pain pills, diarrhea pills, antacid tablets, insect repellent, antibiotic ointment, and diverse first-aid supplies. Sri Lanka has a good reputation for health care among developing countries, but having visited a few rural clinics and hospitals in the district, I knew I did not want to do participant observation as a patient there. At the same time, I admired traditional medicine and the resourcefulness of the physicians. For example, once I took a village patient a bunch of king coconuts, the water of which is considered very healthful. To my surprise the nurse took one, cut it open, and proceeded to hook up the coconut water to be fed intravenously into the dehydrated patient—while the doctors delighted in sharing the fact that this was a sterile and superb intravenous solution.

As part of their unofficial "health insurance" in a hostile and threatening world, the villagers use four different approaches to healing or a combination of any of these: a) home remedies, b) traditional medicine (ayurveda), c) ritual healing, and d) Western medicine. The first three approaches are closely related and often difficult to divide neatly into categories, while the relatively recent Western medicine is kept separate in the minds of the villagers. Though my health remained generally good throughout both fieldwork periods, I did have occasion to observe and also experience firsthand all four approaches to healing.

HOME REMEDIES

The villagers and I had a reciprocal relationship of wanting to take good care of one another's health. Some would come to me and ask if I had some medicine *(beheth)* when they or one of their relatives were suffering and their own attempts at a cure had failed. This was particularly the case for prolonged headache and high fever or an infected wound. At the same time, if they got word that I was suffering from an upset stomach or diarrhea, for example, they were quick to offer advice and remedies.

For the most part I was happy and grateful for their attention, as when they would bring lime fruits to make a lime drink for stomach disorders and nausea. Sudu-Menike, my most loyal friend, would unfailingly make me some salty rice porridge when recovering from stomach disorders or any other illnesses. This was easily digestible and delicious; only later I found out that she first took it to Punchi Rala for him to chant the proper mantras over it and give it more healing power.

Here is one home remedy common in the village and all over Sri Lanka that I never got accustomed to: drinking strong black coffee, sometimes with garlic or lime juice in it, for diarrhea. Coffee beans are scarce and relatively expensive. Most families will save them for treating stomach disorders, for coffee is said to "shrink the intestines" and stop diarrhea. Although I am a coffee drinker, the first time my hostess in Colombo brought me the strong brew with pieces of garlic and other strong spices floating on it, I drank with secret disgust and repulsion, feeling that it would either "cure or kill," and not having the heart to tell her that this was the last thing I would have taken myself as a cure for diarrhea. Having ascertained that it did not work for me, I later did tell the villagers that we in the West never drank coffee when we had diarrhea. They were puzzled but explained the difference by saying that it probably worked in hot climates but not in cold ones. Until the end of my stay, villagers who saw me drinking my instant coffee for the first time asked if I had stomach problems.

I learned many other home remedies during my diverse periods of tropical malaise. Once during an extended headache I resorted to letting Punchi Rala rub specially prepared coconut oil into my forehead and scalp, chanting all the while, when the pain pills I had brought did not help. Rubbing coconut oil into the scalp is the first treatment for a headache and is also considered generally healthful, as opposed to letting your scalp dry out under the sun. There is no stigma attached to having very oily hair.

Sudu-Menike saw me putting cream on the deep cracks in my heels, which were the result of walking many miles in sandals on the hot village paths. She cautioned me that it was not wise to try to heal those cracks, for they served as an air vent to let heat out of your body. If the cracks healed it would cause further headaches, for heat would be trapped in and try to escape through your head. As it was a losing battle to try to heal the cracks, anyway, with all the daily walking I was doing, I decided to take her advice and wait until I was back in the States.

For a cold I was to discover that the tea made with coriander and a small ready-made package of local herbal medicine worked about as well as anything. Patients with badly congested nasal passages would breathe in the steam of boiling lime leaves with a cloth covering their head and the steaming pot. Various herbs were considered good for bringing down a fever, such as the bitter jungle plant called *bim-kohomba* boiled into a tea. A piece of wood from the *venivel-geta* creeper can also be boiled and the water taken as medicine. This same creeper is famous as a preventative for tetanus and as a source of water in the jungle (if cut, a considerable quantity of water quickly drips out).

When a small, leafy branch of margosa leaves is seen hanging above the door of the house, it is an indication that at least one of the family members is suffering from illness. The branch is thought to protect the sick person from evil spirits that might inhibit healing. If I suspected that the person had some contagious disease I would avoid visiting that house; and I could not help but think that their beliefs in an indirect way had helped protect me as well.

TRADITIONAL MEDICINE

There are two kinds of traditional medicine in Sri Lanka. One is the indigenous knowledge, especially of herbal, naturopathic medicine that has been passed down within families through generations. The other is ayurvedic medicine, which came from India through the Vedas, the earliest Brahmanic sacred verses dating from the second millennium B.C. This medical knowledge is highly respected in Sri Lanka, which has an ayurvedic hospital in Colombo and trains physicians in ayurvedic medicine. Like Sri Lanka's own indigenous medicine, it is primarily based on homeopathic and herbal treatments—whether these are drinking herbal concoctions and teas, applying herbal poultices, or rubbing various oils on the head or body. Broken bones can be successfully set in the ayurvedic way without a plaster cast, using only a simple splint.

Included in the ayurvedic tradition is the dividing of foods and drinks into the categories of "heaty," "neutral," and "cooling." These different food categories are part of every villager's common knowledge; even children are well versed. For example, they could tell you that mangoes and breadfruit are heaty, rice and lentils are neutral, and king-coconut water and milk are cooling. Depending on the illness you have, villagers know whether you should eat or avoid certain categories of foods. I often saw them turn down specific foods because it was not the right time of day to eat them, or because they had some condition that should not be combined with heaty or cooling foods. If they have a cold, for example, they will not consume cooling foods or drinks; and they would conscientiously warn me against these, even though the latter might be nutritious and rich in vitamin C.

Many of the home remedies mentioned in the previous section are couched in the ayurvedic tradition, but a sophisticated knowledge of herbal treatment is the realm of the traditional doctor. Sri Lankan villages frequently have their own traditional doctor or ayurvedic physician (vedamahatmaya). In Suduwatura Ara Punchi Rala is reputed to have a basic knowledge of such medicine, although he does not come from a family of traditional doctors, nor has he had any formal training in the field. People go to him regularly for herbal drinks and medicinal oils. When applying such oils Punchi Rala will often chant mantras as he did during my treatments, thereby linking traditional medicine with ritual healing. For more serious ailments that might require a vedamahatmaya, however, they go to a neighboring village or town where such a doctor has a practice. I had occasion to experience the treatment of a vedamahatmaya myself, as related below.

My Bout with Filariasis

During the first fieldwork period I suffered for eight months from a tropical disease commonly called filaria. It is caused by a tiny parasitic worm that is transmitted by a mosquito bite, much the way malaria is. The worm invades the lymph system, blocks the flow of lymph and causes swelling, typically in the leg or arm.

After nearly a year in the field I started to be plagued by a mildly painful red swelling that moved from place to place in my leg. I was too busy with research activities, however, to give it much attention. In Colombo my assistant said I had probably contracted filaria when visiting a coastal area. A blood test showed some filarial antibodies, and I was given the tablets that are supposed to get rid of the condition. But the problem did not go away.

After an urgent telegram from my dissertation adviser I went to one of the more reputable Western-trained physicians in the capital city. He gave me enough antibiotics to cure a horse and told me to rest the leg and stay on the antibiotics and filaria pills until the problem disappeared. I returned to the village with new hope. The pain and swelling slowly stabilized into a lump on the front of my shin.

Long weeks turned into months full of intensive activities. I was forced to try to ignore the painful leg, but it kept nagging at me. My mother sent a photocopied page on filariasis from her medical encyclopedia with a frightening picture of a patient with elephantiasis, legs swollen to shapeless, elephantine proportions. This was filariasis in its later, untreated stages. Some villagers crowded around when I read the medical article, eyes glued to the picture; yes, they said, they had once seen someone with such a disease near the coast.

By now the villagers all knew about my predicament. Punchi Rala had given me some herbal oil to rub on my leg, but to no avail. I lapsed into a mild depression. The pills I had continued taking obviously did not help. There was so much work to do. Some of the schools I had to visit were inaccessible by jeep; and after walking for miles on the painful leg I could hardly do the observation and interviewing.

In this anxious state of mind I was moved when a delegation of three villagers came to my house. They were concerned about my condition and suggested I go to a famous *vedamahatmaya* in another village who was noted throughout the region for his healing skills. I was willing to give almost anything a try at this stage.

Two village friends accompanied me as the jeep pulled up at the mud house of the traditional doctor in Gallabedde. I had difficulty hiding my surprise. Somehow I had expected this famous physician to be dressed in a white coat and have a clean clinic with waiting room and efficient assistants. We entered his humble home, which resembled those of the people of Suduwatura Ara. The doctor, with dirty fingernails and wearing an old, soiled sarong, had just come in from working in his fields. A patient with a broken arm was lying on a bed, his arm in a splint; but for the rest this was like any other poor farmer's house. My surprise was even greater when I asked to use the latrine and was told, with a bit of embarrassment, that they just went out into the bushes. Any open-minded and hopeful confidence I may have had in this *vedamahatmaya* of great repute was fading fast.

The doctor listened intently to my case, squatted down, and felt my leg for several minutes. Curious neighbors and family members gathered around. Their surprise at having a white woman there as a patient was surely as great as mine at the lack of clinical surroundings.

After some deliberation he said the condition may have been caused by an insect bite, but he would not know for three days. In the meantime I would have to use the oil and herbs that he would give. He gathered diverse fresh leaves from the bushy areas around his house. I was to apply the oil repeatedly and also prepare two small poultices with the chopped herbs, steam these thoroughly, and apply them to the swollen place at night. Like other traditional physicians, he asked no fee for his services nor for the oil and herbs. As is the custom, however, I paid him a small sum for the treatment and medicine.

I was grateful when village friends offered to help with the tedious process of steaming the herbs in a homemade poultice. Perhaps it was suggestion, but the next day my leg did seem to be better. The third day when I went back, however, it was again painful and swollen. The doctor gave new herbs that had to be boiled, spread on my leg, and then wrapped bandagelike throughout the night. It was messy and a lot of trouble, and by now my faith and hope had dwindled to nothing.

On his own initiative, the *vedamahatmaya* walked some twenty miles the next week to see me and ask about my leg. I was sorry to have to disappoint him by the fact that I was no better. He explained that if I had come sooner the cure would have been much easier; but now it would be a long and drawn-out process. He brought more herbs, and I paid him another small sum, impressed with his conscientiousness. With an uneasy sense of mild guilt and depression, I threw away the herbs. I had no more time nor patience for the traditional way.

The villagers' concern continued, however. The local Buddhist priest stopped by at their request to do two hours of chanting over some coconut oil for my leg. While chanting he tied knots in a length of string that was tied around my neck at the end of the ceremony. In case any evil forces or *prethas* were causing my leg affliction, this Buddhist ritual would turn the tide—or at least that was the consensus of opinion.

In a subsequent letter to my dissertation adviser I mentioned my experience with local ayurvedic medicine and ritual healing. I got a reprimanding telegram as reply, in which he tried to jolt me to my senses: What had gotten into me? Was I going native? Hadn't the seriousness of elephantiasis sunk in yet? I was told not to play around with "witch doctors" when it came to serious tropical illnesses and to get back to a reputable hospital in Colombo.

Not until I asked another Western-trained doctor to open and drain the lump did my bout with filaria end. I was left with only a small scar and a dent in my leg, reminders of the lurking dangers of tropical diseases and the multiple ways in which the villagers tried to protect me and to help me cope with my problems.

RITUAL HEALING

Almost all the villagers of Suduwatura Ara lay much stock in ritual healing—that is driving out or protecting oneself against evil spirits, demons, or other elements that cause afflictions or illnesses. People are commonly seen with a yellowish, knotted string tied around their neck, wrist, or upper arm; or with a *suraya*, a small metal tube on a string around the neck, containing a thin copper scroll on which a ritual healer has written and drawn protective mantras or symbols.

The local ritual healer *(kattadiya)* is Punchi Rala, who is also the traditional doctor and snakebite healer. If home remedies fail to cure an ailment, he may be called on to perform a ritual healing ceremony. The following case is a typical example:

Somapala had been feeling weak and had suffered from a headache, chest pain, and fever for quite some time. He made an appointment for Punchi Rala to come to his house to do the ritual of the "charmed thread" *(nul bandinawa)* in order to drive out the influence of some evil spirit or devil. Punchi Rala told him the things that were needed for the ritual, and Somapala and his wife prepared a tray with the prescribed items and put this on a chair *(mal-bulath putuwa)*. On the tray was first placed a banana leaf; on this they put five kinds of flowers, one betel leaf, a comb, a piece of mirror, and a small coin. A pot with burning incense was placed under the chair. Punchi Rala took a cotton string that had been rubbed with turmeric and began chanting the magical incantations. At the end of each long stanza he tied a knot in the string. During the chanting he made long, slow gestures from Somapala's body to the outside of the house, pulling the evil out and snapping his fingers at the end of each gesture.

Stanzas for each of the seven knots were chanted, the ritual taking about an hour. Then Punchi Rala tied the string around Somapala's neck, to be worn for at least three days. When I saw Somapala the day after the ritual, he said he was now feeling fine.

If the local treatment is not effective, however, the people can go to a fortune teller—either in their own village or a neighboring town—who might advise them that the affliction needs ritual treatment through the intervention of gods. The villagers of Suduwatura Ara will then go to the temple of Hindu deities *(devale)* at Kalewel Ara 10 km away. There a Tamil ritual priest *(kapurala)* of great reputation performs healing ceremonies every Tuesday and Friday. On these days people from near and far arrive early and start making offerings to various Hindu gods (including Kataragama, Pattini, and Ganesha) at the diverse small shrines on the complex: putting down flowers, lighting incense sticks and camphor cubes, and pouring water over the Shiva-lingam.

I accompanied Leela one day on the long, hot walk to Kalewel Ara, lugging my camera and camcorder. The trip was well worth the investment in time and energy, however, for the day-long spectacle of ritual healing convinced me of the villagers' devotion and their confidence in the ritual priest's diagnostic and healing powers.

We had been waiting at the complex for some three hours, a large throng of people loitering around or making offerings at the small shrines. No one complained that the ritual priest was taking his time to arrive and start the healing ceremonies, and I chatted with a few of our villagers who sat on the ground and waited patiently. Some people bathed in the nearby river. Others watched a special assistant prepare baskets of fruit, especially loved by the Hindu god Kataragama. The baskets would be sold to devotees, who would in turn offer these at a shrine. The male assistant also prepared a huge pot of sweet rice to offer the deities. No women are allowed to assist in these preparations, for women are considered too unclean for the gods.

At a given moment the *kapurala* emerged from the main shrine. To the chanting of incantations and the clanging of bells, surrounded by assistants, he walked from shrine to shrine, worshiping each Hindu god individually. The throng of people moved into a line to present him his standard fee of Rs. 15.50 (about U.S. $.35) on a sheaf of betel leaves, together with a box of incense sticks and camphor cubes. The *kapurala* positioned himself barefooted on the blades of long knives. Though he was a lightly built young man, he made an imposing impression in his white sarong with broad yellow sash. His bare chest was covered only with layers of flower garlands that his devotees presented him.

While the priest chewed on margosa *(kohomba)* leaves and rolled his eyes in trance fashion, the people came to him one by one, made their first offering, and listened to what he had to say about their ailment. An assistant translated from the Tamil language as he told them the cause of their affliction or misfortune and what they should do. I watched with fascination while people of all social classes filed up to him: government workers, businessmen, the poorest farmers, mothers carrying their infants, Tamil Hindus, and Sinhalese Buddhists of all ages and all walks of life. In some cases the priest made an appointment for them to come back for a lime-cutting ceremony *(dehi-kepima).*

In such ceremonies the *kapurala* chants mantras while cutting lime fruits in half with a sharp cutter used to slice areca nuts. In a common ceremony he will cut eight limes in front of eight places on the ailing person's body, then put the cut fruit in a basin of water; the lime halves are taken away and thrown into flowing water. The *kapurala* may then give the patient a thin copper scroll on which he has inscribed mystical symbols and mantras designed to protect the wearer. The latter inserts the rolled up scroll into a small metal tube to wear as an amulet around the neck.

The whole process is time-consuming and expensive for the villagers. Moreover, they claim to be good followers of Buddhism, a philosophy that condemns the worship of any Hindu or other deities and gods. Yet they have the greatest faith in the *kapurala's* healing powers, and most of those who have gone to him say they were cured.

A good example of a case during my second stay was that of Appuhamy, who had a long history of minor illnesses and domestic troubles. When I first talked with him he had just been to the *kapurala* for a lime-cutting ceremony. He had received an amulet (the metal tube kind called a *suraya*), which he was wearing, and he said he was feeling much better.

Three months later, however, Appuhamy was again feeling weak and ill and was suffering from more marital and financial problems. I could hear serious quarrels going on in his house at night. He returned to the *kapurala,* who told him that the amulet had lost its power and would have to be renewed. The priest also conveyed that some powerful evil *(suniyam,* literally meaning "destruction") had been effected against his household by jealous people who did not want to see the family prosper. The latter had possibly buried an amulet with evil powers in the yard or had done some chanting of black magic over fruit in the garden.

Appuhamy was instructed to take twenty-one limes, wrap them individually in pieces of white cloth, and attach them to the overhanging rafters around the perimeter of the house, in the area belonging to the spirit beings called *prethas.* Additionally, he had to hang up a large ash pumpkin outside the house. All these fruits had to first be brought to the *kapurala* for chanting before being hung, and they would then be able to neutralize the *suniyam.*

The instructions of the *kapurala* which required the most drastic actions were telling Appuhamy that he had to change the place of the door in his house. The door was typically on the east side; but this was said to be wrong for his house, which was not clean enough to face east—the direction of temples and religious

5.1 Appuhamy's daughters stand in the new doorway, that has been moved from the eastern to the southern wall of the house on the advice of the ka-purala. An ash pumpkin and limes have been hung to avert evil.

places. So Appuhamy dutifully removed the frame and filled the east-side door with bricks. He broke a new door in the south side of his house, all requiring tremendous effort and time.

The *kapurala* also prepared him a new amulet with magical symbols. The whole process, including the offerings of flowers, incense and donation fee, the fruits, the copper scroll, and travel expenses, cost Appuhamy more than Rs. 175. But he was optimistic that his illness and problems would now be relieved. In any case, the house remodeling efforts had been a good distraction amid the marital problems, and the couple appeared to have renewed intentions for a cooperative and peaceful household.

EVIL EYE—PREVENTION AND CURE

Almost every young child, from its first month to about one and a half to two years old, will be seen with a dark brown dot *(pottuwa)* on its forehead, consisting of a mixture of water and fried sago. The villagers do think the dot enhances the child's appearance, but the purpose of it is to ward off the evil eye. For example, if someone who can cast the evil eye looks at a beautiful child with envy, then the child might fall ill. If wearing a dot, however, the caster's evil eye will be drawn to the dot and thereby neutralized.

I was amazed to learn that things other than humans can be affected by the evil eye (or the evil tongue or evil thoughts)—and the ones who cast the bad influence by looking, talking, or thinking may very well be good people who do not know they have these powers. They might look at a big bunch of coconuts, for example, and the coconuts subsequently fall from the tree; or they might look enviously at some bulls plowing very well, and the bulls then get wounds. A family in the village building an especially fine house hung a large gourd to the beam in order to ward off the evil eye, much the way the *pottuwa* works on the child's forehead. I could not help but wonder if my old jeep, which was continually plagued with engine trouble and all kinds of breakdowns, was being given the evil eye. After all, I had failed to protect it by driving it to the town of Kataragama, making a vow at the Hindu temple, and tying a coin to the steering wheel.

Punchi Rala is frequently called on to cure the evil eye, manifested in a person falling ill—although there is no real way to know beforehand that the evil eye caused the illness. The cure is done with what is called *eswaha-watura* (evil-eye water). The evening before the treatment he gets a pot of water into which he puts a lime-tree twig, some cumin seeds, salt, and a bit of cotton. He chants a certain mantra above the pot 108 times. Before sunrise he goes to the house of the afflicted person and sprinkles water from the pot on the patient. This is repeated in the evening and the following early morning. If the cause of the illness is the evil eye, the evil mouth, or evil thoughts, the leaves of the lime twig will shrivel as if they had been put in boiling water; and the person will be cured. Being the subject of envy due to my relative wealth and status, it was comforting to know that we had a reputable curer of the evil eye in our village. I only wished the fix was so easy for mechanical failures of the ramshackle old jeep.

SNAKEBITES

Although there are more than eighty species of snakes identified in Sri Lanka, there are only seven highly poisonous species. The latter, however, turn up quite frequently, and poisonous snakebites are an imminent danger in a rural environment. Suduwatura Ara, like so many other villages, has its own snakebite healer—the same respected elder, Punchi Rala. He has treated forty-five poisonous snakebites in the past sixteen years, and he boasts of not losing one patient.

During my second stay in the village I attended the funeral of a thirty-five-year-old woman in neighboring Kumbukkana, who was bitten by a Russell's viper *(polanga)* when gathering firewood and died three days later under treatment by that village's snakebite healer. While the event shook me up considerably and left me with an uneasy feeling, it did not weaken the Suduwatura Ara villagers' faith in their own healer, Punchi Rala; and in the following month he treated and cured two patients.

If a snakebite victim is coming, or even a messenger bringing news of the bite, Punchi Rala claims he can tell what kind of snake is involved by the person's gestures. He can also tell by the time of day that a person is bitten or by examining the bite marks. The first thing he does is get a small branch of a "drumstick" tree *(murunga)* and wave the branch from the patient's head to toe seven times, chanting mantras. This, he says, will stop the venom from going up, and it is one of the most important steps in the treatment. He then cleans the bite area with a piece of medicinal root *(satsande)*. Sometimes he opens the wound a bit with a razor blade or a lime-tree thorn. Then he places a small (approximately one-inch long) gray, oval-shaped "snake-stone" on the bite marks. The stone immediately sticks to the wound and usually stays there from nine to twelve hours before it either falls off by itself or Punchi Rala removes it with a knife blade. According to common belief in Sri Lanka, the snake-stone sucks the poison out of the patient's body. While the victim is lying down with the snake-stone applied, Punchi Rala prepares an herbal medicine by pounding certain leaves in a mortar and mixing these with ghee and flour from the *kitul* palm. This is given to the patient to drink.

He can make his diagnosis as to the seriousness of the bite by considering such things as the sex of the victim, which side of the body (right or left) the bite is found, and the waxing or waning of the moon at the time. For example, on the third day of a waning moon, if the person is bitten on the leg, the poison goes to the neck; as the neck is considered a vital place, the person must be treated quickly. Punchi Rala also claims that if the snake that bit the patient is subsequently killed, the cure is more difficult because the venom becomes more potent.

During my first stay Punchi Rala cured one poisonous snakebite. I went to visit the young man who was recovering at Punchi Rala's house, sorry that I had missed the treatment and ritual. In my second stay a bitten woman was brought from a neighboring village; but she, too, had been treated before I heard about the incident. I went to Punchi Rala and impressed on him that I was interested in seeing his entire treatment if anyone else had the misfortune to be bitten. He agreed, and I caught myself—with a guilty feeling—hoping that the occasion would arise before my departure.

One late evening in December I was going through my own evening rituals of tucking the mosquito net around the straw mattress, peering with slight trepidation under the bed for snakes, and pouring myself some chlorinated water to start gulping down a little pile of diverse vitamin pills. I heard footsteps outside the open door and saw the darting rays of a flashlight. Punchi Rala's son appeared and brought news that I had secretly been hoping for. A snakebite victim was undergoing treatment. I quickly gathered my note pad, camera, camcorder, and lanterns, and we set off in the dark for Punchi Rala's house.

The victim's foot was painful and swollen as he slumped on a bed. The snake-stone had already been applied and was sticking to the bite while I interviewed Punchi Rala and the victim, who had been bitten by a hump-nose viper *(kunukatuwa)* that he had stepped on in an uncleared field. I returned in the early morning to watch Punchi Rala remove the stone and put it in a small glass of coconut milk (he says any kind of milk will do—cow milk, goat milk, even breast milk). The poison is said to be drawn out of the stone and into the milk within a quarter hour or so. The color of the milk is another indicator of the kind of snake involved, such as blue for a Russell's viper or pinkish for a cobra. The milk is also necessary in order to use the snake-stone again. For a hump-nose viper the stone was supposed to turn the milk black. It was hard for me to determine that the coconut milk was a blackish color, but Punchi Rala was able to see this when he took the stone out fifteen minutes later.

He applied an herbal paste he had made to the swollen area to help the swelling go down; and the patient, who said he was feeling better, was encouraged to rest some more. Later that day the man was taken home by bicycle, and he was soon completely recovered. It was Punchi Rala's forty-fifth patient. He never asks for payment or remuneration of any kind. Sometimes a grateful ex-patient will return with a small cash payment or gift. More useful for Punchi Rala, a large number of villagers show gratitude for his skills by giving labor in the planting or harvesting season.

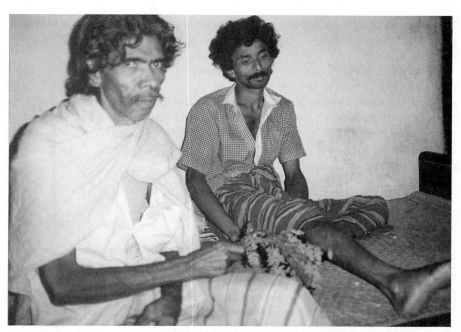

5.2 Punchi Rala holding up a murunga *branch during a snakebite treatment. The patient has the small oval snake-stone sticking to the bite wound on his foot.*

WESTERN MEDICINE

Sri Lanka has an enviable health record when compared with other developing countries. It has successfully eradicated many diseases (e.g., typhoid, diphtheria, whooping cough, polio, smallpox, measles, and tuberculosis) through its islandwide immunization program. On a set day of every month mothers in Suduwatura Ara can be seen taking their children of three months, five months, nine months, eighteen months, and five years to the clinic in a neighboring village to get their shots. The mothers take this responsibility seriously and also know that school registration requires immunization certificates. At the same clinic, those children who are underweight for their age are given two kilos of "Thriposha," a protein-rich soya cereal to supplement their diet in the coming month.

Western medicine is highly respected by the people of Suduwatura Ara, but due to the village's isolation and the long distances that must be walked to go to the dispensary or rural hospital in Okkampitiya, or to the Moneragala or Buttala hospitals, home remedies and indigenous or local ritual cures are usually the first and easiest choices for healing. Villagers will also return to these options when Western medicine has failed.

For illnesses with prolonged high fever (frequently malaria) or intense pain, many prefer to go to a clinic or hospital for Western treatment. This is also the case for serious wounds and injuries. A number have spent a few days in a rural hospital. Medical care, hospitalization, and prescription drugs are free in Sri Lanka, and in principle all citizens are eligible for any treatment they need. In practice, however, few rural villagers will ever get sophisticated Western medical treatment or surgery. No one in the village has had an operation except for the twenty women who voluntarily had a tubal ligation for sterilization, under local anesthetic, at the Moneragala hospital.

Wounds, especially on the feet and lower legs, frequently become infected and take many weeks to heal. In such cases the people will go to a government clinic in a nearby town. Sometimes they send a friend or family member to a dispensary to get pills or antibiotics that are freely distributed; and they indiscriminately take any medicine brought back to them. Likewise, anything that I took out of my medicine box or first-aid kit, usually not much more than antibiotic ointment, plastic bandages, or aspirin, they considered to be powerful cures.

DENTAL AND EYE CARE

By the time they reach their mid-thirties or forties, many villagers have lost some teeth due to lack of dental care. The fact that they drink their tea syrupy sweet or lick sugar from their hand as they drink tea contributes to early decay. They call tooth decay "teeth eaten by worms" *(dath panuwo kanawa).*

The state sponsors a dental clinic through the schools. In Suduwatura Ara the clinic is supposed to come in a van once a year to check the teeth of the second- and third-graders, although it is irregular in its visits. If a child has a bad cavity it may be filled right away with a pedal-operated drill and no painkillers. The clinic personnel give the children lessons on brushing teeth and the importance of drinking milk.

Only a couple of adults have filled teeth, and not one of the elderly who have lost all their teeth has a set of false teeth. In Sri Lanka meals are mostly soft and require little chewing. For people with or without teeth, the rice and long-boiled or finely chopped vegetables are thoroughly mashed together with the fingers before being put in the mouth.

Some people clean their teeth with a piece of charcoal. More commonly they use a twig of *endaru,* a tall plant used for fences. When a twig is broken off it exudes a milky, bitter liquid that is said to be good for teeth and gums. Another popular twig is *karanda.* Many people use an inexpensive and readily available tooth powder and their finger to clean their teeth; others use a toothbrush and toothpaste. I learned with surprise during my first stay that an acceptable practice after a meal is sloshing water around in the mouth and spitting it out the door. When they have a toothache, the remedy is usually putting a piece of tobacco on the tooth; or there are other herbal balms like cinnamon oil to ease the pain.

As eye examinations are not part of the socialized medical package, the villagers have no eye care and no prescription glasses. Three women, however, have reading glasses that they also use frequently for finding lice in the hair of friends or relatives.

Due to the scarcity of reading glasses I ordered three pairs for the people of Sudawatura to share. When I suggested that they be kept in the library and checked out when people needed them to read a book, my best friend Sudu-Menike, who looked after the library explained why, in her perception, this would not work. She was convinced that the lenses would change according to the eyes of the wearer: "If an older person uses these glasses, they can't be used by a younger person, because the glass will adjust to the older person's eyes." Another friend whose daughter had been given a pair of glasses during the Village Re-Awakening program said the doctor had put medicine in the glass to make them right for her daughter. These glasses had been subsequently broken and were never replaced.

PERCEPTIONS OF CLEANLINESS AND HYGIENE

I was constantly reminded that I had brought my Western values of cleanliness and hygiene and that these were different from those of the villagers.

Sweeping aside the leaves that have fallen from trees in the compound, or any garbage that has been thrown out the door—such as banana peels or peanut shells— is the task of the woman or any of her daughters who are available to do it. Having an unswept house or compound is considered bad housekeeping; but piles of rotting garbage in full view on the periphery of the compound, together with old plastic bags and other litter, are considered normal. As the houses are widely spaced, there is no real trash problem. My garbage pail in the kitchen, and the garbage pit that I had asked to be dug at some distance behind the house, were great curiosities for local visitors.

The fact that I insisted on drinking only boiled water was accepted but not understood by most of the people, who drink straight from the springs, streams, or wells. To make matters more difficult, the common Sinhala words used by villagers for "boiled water" are the same as for "hot water" *(unu watura);* so I usually had to make clear that I wanted my water to have bubbled as it does for making tea, not just hot in temperature.

In the village and elsewhere in Sri Lanka, water on plates, glasses, and serving bowls is a sign that they are clean and is the polite way to bring them out. The people found it bizarre that I preferred mine dry, though I soon gave up and took my chances with the wet plates, rather than trying to explain my "strange" perceptions. I was sometimes amazed, however, that they would throw away a full bucket of water they had fetched to be used for household purposes if they had seen a dog drink out of it. It was the same water from the pond where many animals come to drink, but dog saliva is considered to be especially filthy and dangerous.

Pieces of old newspaper, considered dirty from my perspective with a Western upbringing, are the acceptable and even polite thing to use to wrap food and other packages, especially homemade sweets or any kind of dry or greasy food (moist food is usually wrapped in a banana leaf). Newspaper pieces are also sometimes offered as a napkin to dry your right hand after washing it in a bowl of water before eating, although more commonly a cloth napkin is passed around to guests washing their hands.

Only the right hand is washed before eating—the hand that is used to mix and mash their rice and curries when eating. Sri Lankans are careful not to eat with their left hand, which is used with water to clean themselves after urinating or defecating. Even if a villager has a wounded right hand, a spoon will be used in the left hand, rather than eating food directly from the fingers.

Latrines

The houses in Suduwatura Ara are sparsely scattered. During my first period in the village the majority of the houses had no latrine at all, and those that existed were temporary pit latrines. As the people were encroachers on crown land at that time, they did not want to risk making the investment of a permanent latrine that they might have to abandon if evicted from their land. Another reason for seeing a latrine as a low priority item was that the villagers were not convinced of its usefulness. Why go to a smelly little house when there is lots of space between houses and plenty of bushes near water, they reasoned. Not until the Village Re-Awakening program in 1992, when all seventy-eight houses participating in the program were given cement and squatting pans, did most of the families build latrines.

Bathing

Bathing is part of the daily routine in this warm country. People bathe at a well, a stream, the pond, or the tank, wearing a bathing cloth *(diyaredda),* which they adroitly change into at the bathing place. Part of the practice of bathing is to pour many buckets of water completely over the head and body, soaping in after the first ten buckets or so. It is considered necessary to use many buckets of water; some people even count them and will not use fewer than twenty, for example, thinking they might otherwise get a chill. Wetting the head and hair is also important. In fact the verb "to bathe" *(naanawa)* includes the practice of getting the hair wet. People would often correct me if I said I had bathed and my hair was still dry. This was considered merely a "body-wash."

There are many beliefs connected with bathing, which are also connected with the uncertainties and dangers that threaten good health. The villagers do not bathe at 12:00 noon or after 6:00 P.M. because they are afraid of the influence of demons. Some people do not bathe on Sundays, for you are then more susceptible to a headache; if you get ill after bathing on a Tuesday, the duration of the illness will be long. Girls from twelve to fifteen years old should not bathe on Tuesdays, Fridays, or Sundays, because this is considered bad for their health and appearance. In all the above cases, bathing refers to the full bath that includes pouring water over the head and hair.

During my second period in the village I had a little "bathroom" constructed in back of my house, where I could bathe in private inside a cadjan (woven coconut palm fronds) enclosure. This was because the pond where I used to bathe was greatly diminished in water after the construction of the tank; also, I had never completely mastered bathing in a cloth and then adeptly changing back from the wet cloth into dry clothes. When I told several village women that I was used to taking off all my clothes to bathe, they were surprised. Nudity, even in private conditions, is an embarrassing concept for the villagers—both men and women. When I took a group of women to Colombo and we stayed in a hostel with shower stalls, they insisted on bathing with a cloth, even though they could close the shower doors, and even though it was problematic to find a place to hang all their wet bathing cloths. Said one, "I might see a reflection in the water on the floor."

LICE AND WORMS

There is no stigma attached to having head lice, but they are something you would rather get rid of because they itch. Little boys are sometimes seen with their head shaved, an effective way of attacking the problem. More commonly you will see a woman carefully going through the hair of a friend or relative with a comb, pinching dead each louse encountered. Delousing one another is considered to be a useful and relaxing pastime, even a bonding experience—as I was to find out firsthand. My visits to schools in the district sometimes required that I stay in village homes or in the dormitory of a high school, for example—a prime place for the transfer of these ubiquitous parasites. Though a bit embarrassed at first, the matter-of-fact attitude of the village women who helped rid me of the lice soon let me turn myself over to them with equanimity.

As for worms *(bade panuwo),* I had much more difficulty in relating to the villagers' attitudes and beliefs. They believe that all people have worms in their stomach (no distinction is made between stomach and intestines), and that worms—of which there is a hierarchy of some sixty-four kinds—are normal and natural. Only when the number and size of one's worms increase too much, or when the worms get disturbed, will a problem occur. Occasionally I heard the phrase, "This food is not good for your worms." At first in my naiveté I thought they might be talking about intestinal bacteria; but they graphically described the six- to eight-inch worms in question as well as the white, itching pin worms, about the size of an eyelash, that I periodically suffered from while in the field.

When I told one of the village women I had gotten rid of my worms by taking vermicide tablets, she replied, "You didn't kill all of them, or you would die yourself." Keeping the number of worms in balance, rather than eliminating them, is considered the correct approach. If children eat too much of certain kinds of food, such as cowpeas, sweet potatoes, or papayas, it is thought to increase the worms, although the worms are not believed to come from the food itself. Other kinds of foods, such as chopped *gotu-kola* (edible leaves that are cultivated but also grow wild), together with herbal medicines, are said to decrease the number and size. In extreme cases the parents of a child will buy some vermicide pills in order to get the number of worms back in balance. For children the symptoms are considered to be weight loss, vomiting, and sleeping with the eyes half open or with the face down in the pillow. For adults the symptoms are said to be nausea, increased phlegm, chest pain, or even the legs aching below the knees.

The fact that the people have learned to live in harmony with these parasites can further be seen in certain expressions and beliefs. For example, a mother might be heard saying to her children on a full moon day that they must eat their rice or they will starve their worms; and killing animals on a *poya* is especially sinful to Buddhists. A common practice after eating rice porridge *(kenda)* is to drink a little water, because there is said to be one worm that does not like porridge. Additionally, when villagers are feeling hungry and their stomach growls or makes other noises, many believe it is their worms crying out to be fed. After eating something, the worms are satisfied and keep quiet.

My health had remained in reasonably good condition throughout two fieldwork periods. I called it luck, combined with Western precautions of shots and vitamin supplements and purified water and other things we casually chalk up to common sense. My village friends, however, took some credit for themselves. They had monitored my health, teaching me diverse precautions of their own and providing me with home remedies and gifts of some of their best kinds of foods. I had eluded the serious dangers that can strike in spite of all precautions—my imported preventatives and their traditional ones—and I felt grateful.

6 / Kinship and the Family

In Sinhalese villages one often comes across dwellings in which two brothers and their children are living together, or two sisters with their children, or perhaps several brothers and sisters with their children. In such households, the children of the two brothers are categorized as brother and sister; the children of the two sisters are also brother and sister. . . . But the children of a brother and a sister, even though they live in the same household and hold property in common, are not brother and sister but find themselves in a special category . . . and they are regarded as ideal marriage partners.

—from Under the Bo Tree by Nur Yalman, 1967

Suduwatura Ara is like one big family. The majority of the people are related to one another—either by blood (consanguine kin) or by marriage (affinal kin). This stems from the fact that certain large families migrated together to this area, sent for marriage partners from their village of origin, and also gradually intermarried with the few settlers who were already doing highland cultivation on this part of the frontier. People are always referring to one another by their kinship name, a situation that left me confused and bewildered in the beginning, as I tried to sort out relationships. The puzzle was made even more complicated by the fact that common kinship terms such as "older brother" *(aiya)* are used with total strangers to get their attention or can be used as a term of friendship for non-kin relations. When I had finally figured out the system, more or less, and tried to use a kinship term for some good friends—"older sister" or "younger sister"—my friends laughed and shook their heads. I had become part of their community, their "White Teacher" or "White Lady," but my place of respect kept me in a different category. I was not part of their family.

FORMS OF ADDRESS AND TERMINOLOGY

The villagers use twenty-two different kinship terms, though for some terms there are regional variations; for example, grandmother is called *attamma* by most villagers, but a few say *kiriamma* or *achchi*. The terms by generation, eldest to youngest, are as follows:

mutta (great grandfather, or grandfather); *attamma* (great grandmother, or grandmother)

taatta (father); *amma* (mother); *loku appa* (father's older brother); *bappa* (father's younger brother); *loku amma* (mother's older sister); *punchi amma* (mother's younger sister); *maama* (uncle other than father's brothers); *nenda* (aunt other than mother's sisters)

aiya (older brother, or older male parallel cousin); *malli* (younger brother, or younger male parallel cousin); *akka* (older sister, or older female parallel cousin); *nangi* (younger sister, or younger female parallel cousin); *massina* (brother-in-law, or male cross-cousin); *naena* (sister-in-law, or female cross-cousin)

putha (son and nephew on either side); *duwa* (daughter, or niece on either side); *baena* (son-in-law, or husband of niece on either side); *leli* (daughter-in-law, or wife of nephew on either side)

munubura (grandson, or great-grandson); *minibiri* (granddaughter, or great-granddaughter)

Traditionally, marriage bonds have been important in Sinhalese society, and the diverse kinship terms reflect this. As can be seen, the more distant the generational relationship, the fewer the number of terms used—that is, the same terms are used for grandfather and great-grandfather, and for grandson and great-grandson. These are people who are either too old or too young to be considered in marriage arrangements.

In your parents' generation and in your own generation (from the point of view of "ego" when figuring the relationships), many different distinctions are made. For example, in the Sinhalese kinship system a significant distinction is made between one's paternal or maternal aunts and uncles, and between one's parallel cousins and cross-cousins. Those Sinhalese with paternal uncles and maternal aunts have more than one father and mother, at least terminologically. Your father's brothers are considered to be fathers to you; and your mother's sisters are considered to be mothers. The kinship terms corroborate this, for your father's older brothers you call *loku appa* (big father), and his younger brothers *bappa* (little father); your mother's older sisters you call *loku amma* (big mother), and her younger sisters you call *punchi amma* (little mother). The children of these paternal uncles and maternal aunts are considered to be your brothers and sisters, and those are the terms you give them: *aiya, malli, akka,* or *nangi.* (They are your parallel cousins.)

With regard to your maternal uncles and your paternal aunts, they are given different terms. Your mother's brothers are called *maama;* your father's sisters are called *nenda* (and their husbands and wives are also called *maama* and *nenda,* respectively). It is taboo to marry your *maama* or *nenda.* However, the children of *maama* and *nenda,* on either side, are not taboo as marriage partner. They are called *massina* (male cross-cousin) or *naena* (female cross-cousin).

These are the same terms that are given to your brothers-in-law or your sisters-in-law, suggesting that they are not considered to be consanguine or biological relationships. In fact, the Sinhalese villagers see their cross-cousins (father's sister's children or mother's brother's children) as the preferred marriage partner. In other words, they have preferential bilateral cross-cousin marriages, which can lead to a stable alliance between two groups.

Marrying a parallel cousin (father's brother's children or mother's sister's children) would be considered incest and is a grave social taboo. (It is not illegal, however; the legal restriction on incest applies only to the nuclear family.) The fact that you call these parallel-cousins "brother" or "sister" (e.g., *aiya, malli, akka,* or *nangi*) indicates how close the biological relationship is seen to be. When asked why the taboo exists for parallel cousins and not for cross-cousins, the villagers will tell that it leads to retardation and disabilities. Even urban Sinhalese believe that there is a close biological relationship between parallel cousins that does not hold for cross-cousins.

There are a few instances of cross-cousin marriages in the village, mainly among the older generations. One of the primary reasons for preference of such matches, namely keeping any accumulated wealth in the families, is not of relevance in a poor village with small parcels of land and no real wealth.

During my first fieldwork period a parallel-cousin couple was living in a small, open lean-to, in direst poverty, on the outskirts of the village. They had fallen in love, eloped, and were subsequently driven by both sets of parents out of their native Welimada area. They had settled tentatively on the periphery of Suduwatura Ara, where they were accepted by their more distant relatives. Ten years later, although they were still very poor, they were a respectable family with five children; but their relatives in Welimada continued to reject them for breaking the marriage taboo.

MARRIAGE

Marriages are generally patrilocal in Sinhalese society, with the bride leaving her village or compound to live in the village of her husband. In Sri Lanka as a whole, arranged marriages are still more common than a couple meeting each other, falling in love, and deciding themselves to get married. Open any Sunday edition of a newspaper and you will find lengthy classified columns titled "Marriage Proposals" with subheadings of "Brides" and "Bridegrooms," targeting young people of the middle class. Most of the advertisements mention religion, caste, education, and occupation. Sometimes the salary, property, and bank holdings are mentioned. For brides the items in the dowry are often listed; and if the woman is light skinned ("fair") and pretty, this may be included in the ad. There is usually a request for a letter with the applicant's full details and his or her horoscope, for astrological compatibility is considered essential. The successful match of a middle-class couple will usually lead to an elaborate and expensive wedding.

This is not the case for Suduwatura Ara and many rural villages, where the families are too poor for such extensive formal brokering and large weddings, though it is common that a relative in the up-country region of origin is asked to propose a potential mate for one's son or daughter. The matter of marrying within one's caste (see p. 159) remains important in the village, as elsewhere. However, the fact that all except three villagers are members of the respected *govigama* (cultivator) caste, and there are few people of other castes in the surrounding villages, make the likelihood of marrying outside one's caste remote.

Seven marriages took place in the sixteen-month period of my first fieldwork in the village. Three were arranged marriages for which a wedding ceremony was held in Welimada, after which the bride was brought back to Suduwatura Ara. In three cases the couple—each consisting of young people from Suduwatura Ara—ran away together and came back married; the girl being pregnant was the reason for elopement. The remaining case was also a love marriage, that of Sirimalini described in the next section. In this case the bride finally got her parents' approval, and the latter attended a small registration ceremony.

The trend toward elopements has persisted through today, and now about 80 percent of all the village marriages in the past ten years are comprised of couples who ran off together in a "love marriage." A number of the elopements are even with the parents' knowledge and consent. The pattern of very young partners has also continued; it is quite common that the bride is fifteen to seventeen and the groom seventeen to nineteen years old. Usually the couple will have the marriage registered in a civil ceremony after returning from the elopement. If the parents have accepted the match, a small reception and meal may be held in the bride's home. The compatibility of the couple's horoscope, which is essential in arranged marriages, has little significance in the love-marriage elopements.

Parents say that they prefer their children to have arranged or planned marriages over elopements, but the fact that most of the families are poor, thereby unable to provide a dowry for the daughter nor pay for proper dress, food, announcements, photographs, flowers, and other trappings of a formal wedding softens the disappointment of having their child elope. Families with many daughters in particular worry about getting them all successfully married, in sequence of age, without being able to offer a dowry. This can sometimes be compensated by education, beauty, and light skin—but more likely the matter will be taken out of the parents' hands by the girl running off. For the village girl of Suduwatura Ara, her "attaining age" party (see pp. 132–137) will in most cases be a bigger event than her wedding.

Sirimalini's Case

A typical case of a village wedding occurred during my first fieldwork period when Sirimalini got married. At twenty-one she was the third oldest daughter in her family. Her eldest sister was already married, but the next one in line of age, Kamala, was not. This was a reason for the family to discourage Sirimalini when it was apparent that she and a boy from nearby Kumbukkana were interested in one another.

Sirimalini's boyfriend showed up at her house off and on for a half year. When her parents realized she was probably going to elope, Sirimalini's father told her suitor that if he had serious marriage plans, he must inform his own parents and they must come to discuss the matter. Both sets of parents finally agreed to the match, with the eldest daughter's husband serving as the go-between. The couple exchanged rings, which finalized their intentions. The compatibility of the couple's horoscope—so important in arranged marriages—was not taken into consideration.

There was no dowry at stake, for the bride's family was too poor. As is the custom, the groom's family provided the bride's clothes, in this case a white sari. On the day before the wedding the groom arrived with a friend who would serve as a witness. The next morning Sirimalini's mother and sisters—starting at an astrologically auspicious time—helped her get dressed in the sari and put a garland of white flowers in her hair. The groom was dressed in the traditional Sri Lankan formal wear: a long-sleeved tailored shirt over a white sarong.

The bride and groom left the house at the next auspicious time, first offering betel leaves to the bride's parents and bowing down in front of them *(vandinawa)* as a sign of respect. It had been arranged that the first person they would see upon leaving the house was a woman (who still had a breast-feeding child) carrying a pot of water. This is considered to bring good fortune and fertility; and for such an important occasion as a wedding, fate can be manipulated by planning that the luck-bringing type of person be standing just outside the door. The woman sprinkled water on Sirimalini and playfully threw some big splashes of water on her to break the tearful mood of the bride, who is traditionally sad to leave her family home. I took some wedding pictures of the bride and groom and family members, trying to get them to smile at what I thought should be a happy occasion; but they all maintained their glum expressions, true to the idea that the bride and her family suffer a loss when the woman follows the patrilocal residence pattern and moves away.

We all piled into my old jeep—the bride and groom, her parents, and friends of both partners—to drive to Buttala for the formal registration at the office of the Registrar of Marriages, Births, and Deaths. In a small civil ceremony based on British rather than Sinhalese traditions, the registrar spoke of the solemnity of their undertaking. The groom repeated a nuptial vow, followed by the bride taking the same vow. The couple, two witnesses, and the registrar signed the registration book. In this case I was asked to be a witness for Sirimalini, which function I gladly performed—along with that of chauffeur and photographer.

We dropped the newlyweds off at the groom's house in Kumbukkana where we had some tea and sweets. There was no wedding meal, but Sirimalini's family insisted on serving me a nice meal by way of thanks when we returned. They opened a can of mackerel to complement the curries, which was a big luxury in that poor home.

It was the simplest of weddings in a culture where weddings are preferably large and extravagant affairs for those who can afford it, filled less with Buddhist religious elements than with astrology. But Sirimalini's parents were pleased that she had not eloped. They were additionally relieved when Kamala, the second daughter, got married—also with parental consent and a simple registration ceremony—within the coming year.

6.1 Sirimalini's wedding photograph, taken by the ethnographer.

Sriyani's Case

Added to the social prohibition against marrying one's parallel cousin (considered as a sibling), there are further taboos. You may not marry your grandparents' siblings' children, who are also considered by the villagers to be like fathers and mothers, aunts and uncles. Such unions are not legally considered incest, however.

One such marriage did occur in the period between my two visits. Sriyani, the bright and promising daughter of one of the more prosperous village families ran off secretly at age fifteen with Dissanayaka, the son of her mother's mother's younger brother. I had taught Sriyani in school and she was the darling of the class. It was disappointing to hear in a letter that she had married so young, and especially to hear that her choice of a partner had caused so much distress.

Prior to the elopement the high school principal in Moneragala town intercepted a love letter between the pair, which wrote of their marriage intentions. The principal threatened to inform the parents. Knowing her own parents vigorously opposed her plans, Sriyani let it be known that she would commit suicide by drinking poison (insecticide) if she were not allowed to get married. To underscore their determination, the couple even had the marriage officially registered five days after eloping.

The match between Sriyani and Dissanayaka caused much uproar and gossip in the village. Although many Sinhalese people would call Dissanayaka Sriyani's *maama* or uncle, in the village they call him her *bappa* ("little father" or father's younger brother). They reason that Dissanayaka, being Sriyani's mother's cross-cousin, would be the preferred marriage partner for her mother. If Sriyani's father had died, her mother could have married Dissanayaka, making him Sriyani's (step-) father. The whole village whispered that Sriyani had married her *bappa*.

By the time of my second fieldwork period, Sriyani was not yet eighteen and had two young children, two years and six months old, respectively. Although Dissanayaka's family had accepted the couple and gave them a modest amount of assistance, helping tend the children and providing a small bit of financial support, Sriyani's parents, who were wealthier than Dissanayaka's, still totally rejected their daughter. They did not speak to her nor to her children, and she was not allowed to enter her parental home. Her father and brother were especially vehement in their criticism, as were her mother's brothers. They saw her secretive act—running away at night and exerting her will against their wishes—as equally insulting as her marrying a person whose biological relationship constituted a taboo. The fact that Dissanayaka and his nuclear family were very poor added to their consternation.

Sriyani, from her side, tried desperately to win their approval, but the forces of poverty weighed heavily against her and her husband. They lived in the smallest and most meager hut in the village, devoid of windows and furnishings of any kind. However, Sriyani remained very proud and well mannered, and she tried to keep up appearances. She often visited me, bringing along her children who looked clean and nicely dressed, and bringing me a wood apple drink or some fruit. Once when I unexpectedly called on her with my assistant at her humble hut, she was hospitable but somewhat embarrassed that she did not have one proper chair or stool to offer (she put the baby's pillow and sheet over the mortar for me to sit on); and she did not have proper cups or glasses for tea (but rather chipped enamel bowls). Sriyani's case was a good example of how strong the forces of a love marriage can be. It is also an example of the strength of tradition. When broken, family support is lost, making the start for a young family in a subsistence village extra hard.

Shortly after my departure, Sriyani's father-in-law died of a heart attack, and a few months later her grandfather succumbed to injuries in a bus accident. These family deaths must have mellowed her mother, for Sriyani wrote that her mother had finally allowed her to visit the parental home with her children.

SORORATE, LEVIRATE, AND DIVORCE

Sororate and levirate are occasionally practiced and are encouraged when this is possible, although these are not prescribed practices with social pressure. An example is Punchi Rala's second wife. She is the younger sister of his first wife who passed away leaving six children. As the children were already quite familiar with the mother's sister, and she was in fact called "mother" by them (*punchi amma* or "little mother"), it was considered that this mother-child relationship would be stable and easy. It did prove successful, and the younger wife benefited from the deceased wife's older daughters. The second wife gave birth to an additional six children, making Punchi Rala's household one of the largest in the village.

Likewise, if the husband dies leaving a wife with children to support, the wife's family will immediately consider whether the husband has an appropriate unmarried brother (biological sibling or classificatory brother) who could take the responsibility. The chances of success are less likely, however, because the younger brothers are more apt to want a wife younger than themselves; and the older brothers will probably be already married.

Legal divorce is a concept unfamiliar to the villagers, although it occasionally occurs that a husband will abandon his wife and children, breaking the badly needed economic unit and forcing the wife to engage in casual labor or to rely on the help of family members. Suduwatura Ara has three such cases. There is also a villager among the newly arrived migrants who left his wife and came to live in Suduwatura Ara with another woman. The villagers are aware that he has a wife and four daughters in a neighboring town in addition to the new woman and their three children. He is accepted and even respected, however, because he supposedly sends some support money for his older daughters. He is also an active volunteer worker for the new ruling People's Alliance national political party, which weighs heavier for his total reputation than his moral behavior concerning his wife.

Another case of a married woman and a married man going off together for a half year, both leaving their spouses and children behind to fend for themselves, met with some village gossip but little else. The wayward partners returned home in due time and were taken in by their respective spouses, as well as being fully accepted back into the community. The forces of economic necessity that govern a nuclear family unit of husband and wife with children are considered more important than any moral indignation suffered. It is easier to carry on with a subsistence way of life when there is a division of labor: husband and wife working as a team. This matter of practicality helps hold marriages together and may help smooth over infidelities.

I was myself divorced and had a son who stayed in Holland during my field-work. After discussing the matter with my assistant, the retired education officer, I decided not to tell the villagers that I was divorced. They would have difficulty re-lating to my situation and to the frequent occurrence and acceptance of divorce in the Western world. It did give me a twinge of guilt, however, when I showed them photographs and accepted their admiration and condolences for having to "miss my husband so long" in order to come live in their village. It was a bit easier when the local Buddhist priest made an explanation, saying I was drawn to this place and able to miss my family and comforts of home with such equanimity because I surely must have lived in Sri Lanka in a previous lifetime.

The priest also gave that as the reason why the village dog, Kukka, was so loy-ally attached to me. Kukka had a family that treated him well, but he insisted on staying at my house despite my discouragement in the beginning by not giving a single scrap of food. He accompanied me everywhere I went on foot or would run after the jeep until exhaustion unless tied up, when he would cry mournfully and chew through even the strongest ropes. The villagers were amused and somewhat amazed by this behavior, but they accepted the idea that Kukka might have been my dog in a former life before I was reincarnated in my present body. I was sad to learn that he was run over by a truck when he ventured to the main road several months after my departure.

THE FAMILY

Family ties are extremely strong in Sinhalese society, and one will frequently see members of the extended family living in one household. Because Suduwatura Ara is a relatively new village of migrants from a distant area, only a few families have become extended by the arrival of the grandparents. In some cases, when the younger nuclear family's house is full, they will build an additional small wattle-and-daub house next to their own where their elderly parents sleep, although the lat-ter usually take their meals in their grown children's household.

Land on which to build a house is still relatively plentiful; and investments for the first house are mostly in labor, since the building materials of timber, mud, and thatching grass are freely obtained from the jungle. For these reasons a newly mar-ried couple (or sometimes an unmarried grown son) will build their own house near that of the young man's parents—the accepted place to settle in this patrilocal society.

There are decided advantages to living near your parents—for both the parents and the grown children. Most of these advantages are in the form of mutual care and assistance. The grandparents or any siblings still living at home are indispensable when it comes to tending infants and small children. Labor is naturally exchanged on the farms of parents and children. Luxury items, such as a sewing machine or a diesel-powered winnowing machine, will be shared among the households. As sev-eral of the parents' sons settle with their families near the parental compound, the circle of reciprocal exchange and sharing widens.

Because respect for your parents is a core family value, it is of course ex-pected that the children will care for their parents when the latter become elderly or infirm and are unable to work. Children will not hesitate to take their aging parents into their homes. This is the "social security" that the elderly have, and it is not regarded as a burden by the children. It would be unthinkable for the latter to put their relatives in a nursing home or retirement home, a concept which is totally foreign to them.

From the earliest socialization onwards, a mutual feeling of dependence is created in the family. It is not expected nor desired that the children will grow up, go away, and become independent individuals. In fact, the ponderous forces of responsibility to one's family make individualism a difficult proposition. Anyone who gets ahead financially feels the social obligation to share with his or her family. Indeed, responsibility to family members—especially parents, including the father's brothers and mother's sisters—is lifelong; and family members know they will probably one day be on the receiving end even if they are now on the giving end. It is a way of spreading risks in a harsh and uncertain world: It can be a way of gaining help when you need it; but it can also limit those who try to become more prosperous.

The above picture of the dependent and interdependent large family with many children and many extended family members is gradually changing. As the availability of land becomes tighter and the cost of living rises, particularly considering the expectations that families now have for acquiring luxury items such as a furniture set, a sewing machine, or even a small television, the average number of children in the new generation of nuclear families is decreasing. Other factors such as a lower infant mortality rate and better education also play a role. While it was common for the older generation to have eight to twelve children, the new trend is now

6.2 Family ties are marked by tremendous respect for one's elders. I was asked by Sudu-Menike and her husband to take this picture of them "worshiping" their elderly parents.

toward three to five. The largest nuclear family at present in the village has seven children (the first four were girls, and the parents wanted sons as well); and the mode is three, but many of the younger families are still growing. Raising a large family is expensive, but the chance of having some children around to look after you in your old age is greater than with a small family. In former generations your children were considered your wealth, and it was likely that returns would be reaped on the investment of raising them.

Those couples who opt for family planning after two to four children often do so to be able to offer their children more in the way of educational opportunities. This will usually mean boarding children in town during their high school years, which is an expensive sacrifice for the family. The one village family with a son who finished his Advanced Level high school examination and is presently studying at Kelaniya University, had only two children; the younger brother is now boarded in Moneragala town attending high school. In all likelihood the university-educated son will not come back to work in the village, but his responsibility to his family will remain just as strong.

Those families who have a son or daughter with a salaried job reap another kind of security from that child. A steady job with a salary, however low paid, provides a more secure existence than a subsistence farmer's, which is at the mercy of droughts and other whims of nature. When a family is in dire need, they can count on their close relative with the steady income. A few families with sons in the army or working in the city as security guards gain certain financial benefits that other farming families do not have. The son in question, however, will rarely be able to save much for his own young family.

GIVEN NAMES AND FAMILY NAMES

Village children almost always have a pet name they are called at home. For the village girls whose origins are in the up-country, a commonly heard pet name is *Menike* (meaning "precious gem"). Indeed, practically every family has at least one Menike, and sometimes descriptive words allow for more: Chuti Menike (little gem), Sudu Menike (white gem), and so on. Sometimes the personality of the child will lead to the pet name given, such as Podi Mahattaya (little gentleman), Raala-hami (officer), Nona (lady or madam), or Devi (queen).

Even though the children have pet names that are used in the family and among relatives, parents will just as frequently say *putha* (son) as a sign of affection to both their sons and daughters. Siblings will call one another by the sibling position in the family, such as *loku aiya* (big elder brother), *podi aiya* (little elder brother), *podi nangi* (little younger sister), and the like. Husbands and wives will never be heard calling each other by their first names nor referring to one another by first name, for this would be considered peculiar and somewhat disrespectful. Instead they will use pronouns or say "my wife," "my husband," or "father" and "mother" if they have children.

A child's formal given name, like so many aspects of Sinhalese culture, is in part determined by astrology. When a child is born, the exact time of birth is noted.

Shortly thereafter the father goes to an astrologer in one of the neighboring villages or towns. Rather than having a full horoscope made immediately, the father will usually ask that a preliminary chart *(wela path kade)* be made, mapping out the position of the stars at the time of birth. The astrologer determines which letter the child's name should start with according to the stars, and sometimes he will suggest a few names. The parents choose a name starting with the auspicious letter in order to give their child every chance for a good life.

The given names of most children in the village are long, multisyllabic, traditional Sinhalese names. (Only one child has the English name Desmond, but English names have been popular in some periods and places in Sri Lanka.) In front of an individual's given name are two or three initials. These are written with Latin or English letters. The initials signify the family *(ge)* name; that is the name the child gets from his or her father, as the system is patronymic. The woman keeps her own father's initials after marriage. Those who are well versed in the subject can tell a person's caste from the last initial in the family name, which usually denotes an ancestor's post in the king's retinue or a government post in the British colonial period. In Suduwatura Ara, where almost all the inhabitants are members of the *govigama* caste, a large percentage of them also have "M" as the last initial in their family name, such as R. Y. M. Leelawathie. The M stands for *mudiyanselage,* a high official under the last kings of Kandy and during the British period. Having this initial in their name is a sure indication to outsiders that they are members of the cultivator caste, which is a source of self-esteem.

It was always reassuring to see that the villagers of Suduwatura Ara, however poor they were in material surroundings and goods, always possessed something that could not be taken away: a strong sense of pride. They were proud to be Sinhalese, they were proud to have descended from up-country ancestors, and they were proud of their cultivator caste. This sense of esteem had continuity: Marriage alliances were formed, family names were bestowed on the next generation, caste membership was passed down, and cultural values were transmitted to the young. There was a positive air about these people that I had sensed from the very beginning—radiating the pride they felt in their heritage and families. This, at least, would always be theirs, as they struggled to cope with the many dangers and uncertainties that surrounded them.

7 / Childhood and Socialization

We went exploring in the jungle behind the cave. . . . We made our way very slowly, picking a
tortuous path through the trees. We seemed to be in the depths of the jungle when we came
across a small cave. We had to crawl on our knees and elbows to get in. . . . There was a lot
of this white sand and, sitting right in the middle of it, there was a human skeleton! It gave us
quite a shock to come upon it like that, but soon curiosity and amazement overcame our fear.
                                        —from Madol Doova by Martin Wickramasinghe, 1947

Growing up in Suduwatura Ara has many elements of a wholesome life for a child.
I was impressed by the loving care that parents give their children and by the simple
social fun that children engage in: climbing trees, playing with puppies, exploring
the jungle—as in the above quotation from the Sinhalese equivalent of *Tom Sawyer*.
There are always friends and siblings for amusement, and life, as seen through the
eyes of a child, is an exciting adventure.

The parents, however, know the dangers and threats that face their children in a
subsistence village: malaria, dysentery, malnutrition, accidents far from emergency
facilities, poisonous snakes, demons, and evil spirits. For this reason the parents
cling to a series of rites and prescriptions at intermittent stages of the child's development to enhance a healthy and happy life.

As I taught the schoolchildren, chatted with them on their frequent visits to my
house, and observed them playing in their compounds and throughout the village, I
was moved by their respectfulness and their unspoiled nature. It made me admire
the way the villagers brought up their children—a way that was so compatible with
village values: to be well mannered, humble, and helpful, with a deep sense of responsibility for the family.

BIRTH

There are several very young mothers in the village. Getting married at fifteen, sixteen, or seventeen (or "having to" get married as a result of pregnancy) after an
elopement is commonplace. Even if the woman is not pregnant before the wedding,
it is usual that the young couple will start a family right away. Information on family planning in addition to contraceptives have been available for the past twelve
years and can be obtained free of charge for married women (including the pill, the
coil, or a three-month injection) at a family planning clinic that is periodically held
in a neighboring village. In fact, the older girls and young women were given
lessons for several years by two family planning volunteers in Suduwatura Ara,
who followed a course themselves and then went house-to-house giving information. The usual practice, however, is to have children first until the couple decides

their family is large enough, and then for the woman to use a form of contraceptive. Twenty village women have undergone sterilization (tubal ligation) at a nearby hospital after completing their families. The government pays them Rs. 500 (about U.S. $10.50) to have this done.

There are no twins in this village and women will say they do not want twins, fearing the expense of two infants at once, as well as the possibility of not having enough milk for two. Young women will not usually eat a "double" banana with two fruits grown together, for it is believed that you will give birth to twins in the next reincarnated life. If people are very good friends, or if husband and wife love each other very much, it is said they will be reborn as fraternal twins.

These days expectant mothers can go for prenatal checkups at the rural clinic in Okkampitiya, about an hour and fifteen minutes' walk away. The trend is now to have one's baby at the hospital in Moneragala or Buttala and come home the next day by motorized three-wheeler if the road is passable. The expense for such transportation, however, makes having your baby at home still a viable option for many village women, especially if it is not the first baby and they are not anticipating any problems. There are also times when the baby comes early or too quickly for the mother to get to the hospital. In all such cases the women resort to the assistance of an experienced woman who serves as unofficial midwife, of which there are two in the village.

One of these is Gnana, or Gnanakka ("Big-Sister Gnana") as she is called. She was a close neighbor of mine in the first fieldwork period; we were also close in age and developed a bond of friendship. She learned midwifery from her mother, who had worked as a midwife in a hospital for several years. She was married herself at age fifteen and started helping her mother deliver babies when she was seventeen. I appreciated Gnana's frankness and openness when she talked about her years of midwife experiences. As I thought it might be more appropriate and easier to have the formal interview on this topic done through a woman rather than through my assistant, Mr. Senanayaka, I asked the school's female English teacher to serve as the interpreter. The latter was a young, unmarried, urban woman who disliked her remote village post. She was so embarrassed by the questions I asked and the answers Gnana gave that she could not control an incessant nervous laugh. Her extremely uncomfortable state in discussing the topic of delivering a baby made me abandon the interview until my Sinhalese was sufficient to interview Gnana directly.

Village women usually do their regular farm work up until the time that their birth contractions start; this is even considered to make the birth easier. Gnana is sent for when a woman's contractions are closely and regularly spaced. She goes to the expectant mother's house and stays there until the birth, conveying a sense of calm to the woman. If the mother is in labor for more than a day and a half, she advises her to go to the rural clinic in Okkampitiya. Even though Gnana is often awakened at night to come, and though it is frequently a time-consuming service she performs, she never asks for compensation of any kind.

The baby is usually delivered on a mat or gunny sack covered with a cloth on the floor. She has never cut the vaginal opening, but rather uses her hands to slowly stretch the tissues if necessary. In a few cases she had to extensively use her hands to help remove the baby's head when she thought it was suffocating.

The birth complete, she cuts the umbilical cord with scissors she has first sterilized in boiling water; then she ties it with a string and sprinkles it with baby powder. If the baby does not cry immediately she pours water over its back. The placenta is wrapped in an old cloth and buried in a hole by one of the family members. The father is not allowed to be present during the birth, but he is the first one to be given the baby after Gnana washes it.

Gnana has delivered more than thirty babies in Suduwatura Ara, including two of her own grandchildren. There were a few difficult births among her deliveries, including breech births; but she is proud to say she has not lost a single infant.

During the first week after the birth the mother eats only a spicy-hot mixture of chilies, garlic, and herbs made into a sauce and served with rice. It is believed that she has a wound in her stomach after the birth, and the sauce is supposed to have a healing effect. On the seventh day she is given a special curry *(hath malu)* made of any seven different kinds of vegetables. In this collection are found vegetables with different properties, such as "heaty" and "cooling." If the mother eats this curry without becoming ill, she is said to have recovered from the birth.

EARLY RITES OF PASSAGE

The birth of a child goes relatively unnoticed in the village, especially those infants who are not the couple's first child. There are no announcements, cards, eating of traditional sweets, nor celebrations of any kind. In fact, to my consternation, a newborn baby was often several weeks old before I even found out about the birth. A high infant mortality rate in earlier times probably precluded celebration until the child had passed the first few vulnerable months.

If a child is born at home it may undergo its first small rite of passage, the "first milk," called *ran-kiri katagaema.* After the newborn is bathed, the attending midwife or female relative takes a gold earring and a bit of the mother's breast milk, stirring these in a saucer with a blade of grass called *baela tana.* She then takes the blade of grass and uses it to spoon about three or four drops of the milk onto the baby's tongue. This first milk rite is carried out to ensure good health and prosperity. Subsequently, early childhood is filled with diverse rites of passage.

First Haircut

Generally a mother will cut a little of her baby's hair on the day of its birth, and then cut a little each month on the day of the month that the child was born. If she fails to cut the hair on the first day, she will have to wait until the child is around three years old to give it a haircut in a ritual ceremony, *hisa kes kepeema,* cutting the first lock at an astrologically auspicious moment.

I went to observe this rite when it was performed for Samira, just more than three years old, in the spring of 1995. Samira's mother, Geetha, had been up early that morning cooking *kiribath* (milk-rice, popular rice treats cut in diamond-shaped pieces) at the auspicious hour to serve to guests attending the ritual. The father, Nimal, had taken Samira's horoscope to an astrologer, who determined the auspicious moment for the cutting to be 6:19 A.M.

Sudu Banda, a village elder well versed in *pirith* chanting arrived around 6:00 and started preparing a basin of water, putting in fragrant jasmine blossoms, some special grains, and fried paddy seeds *(pori)*. The water was stirred and the chanting of blessings continued for about ten minutes, as the whole family watched the clock.

A few minutes before the auspicious time Samira was carried outside to the young jackfruit tree on the couple's compound. It is important that the ritual be carried out near or under a "milk tree" such as a jack. These are trees that exude a milky white substance when cut, and they play a symbolic role in rituals pertaining to women and young children. If no "milk tree" is growing nearby, a branch of one growing elsewhere should be brought and held above the child.

After applying a bit of the water in the basin to the child's head, the elder cut a lock of Samira's hair at 6:19 precisely. The father set off firecrackers, and I joined the guests who went back to eat some of the traditional sweets and plantains. I had given my friend Leela a few minutes' instruction on how to operate the camcorder before the ceremony. She was always eager to take on any new assignment, and I had wanted to get a slide as well as video coverage of the event at the auspicious

7.1 Sudu Banda cuts Samira's lock of hair at the astrologically auspicious moment during the first haircut ritual.

moment. As we sat with a cup of tea, I rewound the videotape to see what Leela had made of it. We all got some laughs when jungle trees and clouds and feet around the ceremony grounds had been recorded—but not the act of cutting Samira's hair!

The ritual basin of water was thrown into a flowing stream, and Samira's lock of hair was tied to a twig of the jackfruit tree. Later that day the boy's whole head of hair was trimmed by his father. Cutting Samira's hair without first performing this ritual is thought to be dangerous for the child's speech development. There are stories of children who started stuttering because the ritual had not been observed, and no loving parents would subject their child to that kind of risk.

First Rice

The first rice is given in a ritual ceremony *(indul katagaema)* when the baby is about four or five months old. In a poor village like Suduwatura Ara it is seldom that an elaborate first rice ceremony is given. Those who lay stock in this rite of passage, however, will consult an astrologer or almanac for an auspicious moment, at which time the child is given a bit of rice to eat. The infant is then put on a cloth with several items placed on it, such as money, a pen, toffees, or small toys. The child is encouraged to choose an item, and its future is said to be determined in part by that choice. For example, if he chooses the money, he may become a rich merchant; the pen might indicate a scholar or an office job. Relatives and guests are invited, and tea, sweets, and plantains are served. Like the other early rites of passage, giving the baby its first rice at the auspicious time is done to ensure a healthy and prosperous future.

Although this first rice ceremony is sometimes referred to as "weaning," the baby is not usually weaned from breastfeeding until the mother becomes pregnant with the next baby. As breastfeeding a child is considered to weaken the infant in the womb, the older child will be weaned by putting bitter margosa oil on the mother's nipples. The mother's last child may go on breastfeeding until four, five or even six years old.

Ear Piercing

Piercing a little girl's ears *(kan-wideema)* is usually done between her seventh and ninth month. Formerly the village midwife, Gnana, was called on to do the piercing at the auspicious moment determined by an astrologer. She would hold a small lime fruit behind the baby's ear and put a threaded needle through the earlobe. It is more common now to go to a shop in town that sells the small gold earrings for children. At the auspicious hour, there in the shop the earring itself is pushed through the lobe and fastened.

First-Letter Learning

At approximately the age of three to four, another important event is celebrated with due ritual in most families, namely the reading of the first alphabet letter by the child *(akuru-kiyaweema)*. Having the first-letter ceremony is a tradition done to ensure that the child's reading and educational progress will not be impaired. As my first fieldwork focused mainly on education and schooling, I was impressed that these subsistence farmers were carrying out a ritual to ensure literacy and scholastic success—a practice consistent with the long history of respect for education in Sri Lanka.

There is a wide range of manners in which the *akuru-kiyaweema* can be carried out—from an elaborate ceremony at the astrologically determined auspicious time, involving many sweets and offerings, to a simple letter-reading at school with several age-mates undergoing the ritual together. The person to conduct the ceremony is usually a learned, respected member of society, such as a Buddhist priest, the school principal, a traditional doctor, or the child's grandfather. A typical ceremony consists of taking the child to the school principal, who is offered betel leaves and some *kiribath,* oil cakes, or a package of cookies. At the auspicious moment the principal recites the first alphabet letter, which the child repeats.

A more extensive *akuru-kiyaweema* took place during my first fieldwork. Three-and-a-half-year-old Tilaka was taken to her grandfather, a respected elder, who had prepared a tray with a picture of the Hindu Goddess of Learning, Saraswathie, at the center. Around the picture were five varieties of sweets and five kinds of fruits as offerings to the goddess. Further the tray was arranged with flowers and betel leaves around the edge. An oil lamp was lit before the picture; and the grandfather chanted *pirith,* after which he read the first letter from an illustrated alphabet book at the auspicious time. The child repeated the letter and then bowed down to "worship" the picture of the goddess and the book. This family placed particular emphasis on education.

Ten years later, at the time of my second fieldwork, Tilaka was going to high school in Okkampitiya and doing well. She is the youngest daughter in a family whose father "disappeared" during political purges in 1988 (see p. 161). The mother has tremendous hardships in trying to maintain the family without a husband. Her elder daughter is now married and living in another village. Her elder son has epilepsy, and she must buy him expensive medicine. Her younger son, only fifteen, has to do the plowing and other heavy farm work formerly done by his father. The mother makes great sacrifices to see that Tilaka can board with relatives in Okkampitiya to attend a better high school there.

INFANT AND CHILD CARE

Although the arrival of an infant occurs without much fanfare in the village, the young women particularly are proud and immediately become doting mothers. Babies stay close to the mother for the first two to three months, sleeping next to her on her bed or mat and being given the breast every time they cry or even fret. It is very common that the young mother stays with her own mother or an older aunt during the first month or six weeks after the birth. The grandmother will advise her and also bathe the baby.

The Baby's Bath

The baby's bath is an important daily event during the first month; and it is believed that a young mother is unable to perform this function as well as the experienced grandmother. I went to the house of Bandara Menike, respected matron of the village who has raised twelve children of her own, to watch her bathe her daughter Anula's week-old baby. Anula, who lived with her husband in nearby Galtammandiya, was staying with her mother for a month after the birth, even though the baby was her second child.

A large basin of water heated to lukewarm temperature was placed on the floor of the living room. Bandara Menike was seated on a tiny stool beside the basin. Anula undressed her baby and handed him to the grandmother, who sprinkled him with water and soaped him in. She then put the baby back in the basin, holding his head with one hand and pouring water over his body and head with the other cupped hand; about sixty handfuls should be used.

When the lengthy splashing time was over, the mother handed Bandara Menike a towel and she patted the baby dry, paying attention to all the creases. She then powdered him all over with baby powder and put baby lotion on his head. Thus powdered, she proceeded to massage the baby's limbs and the features of his head and face, gently pulling and twisting, also pressing the gums. This is considered an important part of the infant's bath, one in which a young mother—perhaps not daring—will be unable to do correctly. If the baby has any small deformities on the face, arms, or legs—for example, if the feet turn inward or the nose is not straight or the ears stick out too much—it is believed that massaging will smooth out these imperfections. The baby's young mother is less adept at this. It is also considered bad for her to have to squat down for the bathing so soon after giving birth. Bandara Menike mentioned that all of her children were well formed and attractive, and this was mainly due to the careful bathing they had received.

Anula continued to fill a role more like nursemaid, handing Bandara Menike the baby's cotton shirt. The mother then mixed a bit of homeopathic medicine with a few drops of her breast milk, putting this on a spoon for the grandmother to give to the baby. Three small spoonfuls of this medicine are said to rid the infant of phlegm and prevent him from catching a cold. Thus bathed, dressed, and medically protected, the baby was handed back to the mother, who breastfed him and rocked him to sleep.

Kiriammalage Dana

If a young child falls sick and does not seem to be recovering soon enough, the parents may take special protective measures by making a fetish or having one made by a ritual priest *(kapurala)* in a neighboring village. Such a fetish might typically consist of a coin washed in turmeric water and tied in a piece of white cloth. It may be kept in a jackfruit tree, in a bo tree, or at a Buddhist shrine. The parents make a vow begging the Hindu goddess Pattini to help cure their child and promising to give a *kiriammalage dana* (offering to nursing mothers) ceremony when the child gets well.

This is a special almsgiving in which seven respected women who are past menopause and thus considered "clean" are invited to come in the earliest hours of the morning. The child's mother must prepare seven kinds of food; and no one should observe her during this preparation or the ceremony will not be a success. The guests arrive and sit on mats covered with white cloth. In front of every guest is a banana leaf with seven pieces of each of the seven food items, in addition to seven coins washed in turmeric water. In front of the group is an elevated place with a picture or statue of the Buddha and a picture of the goddess Pattini. Offerings of incense and flowers are made to these figures.

A leader among the guests reads some verses and little songs invoking blessings of Pattini. Then all the guests break off a small piece of each kind of food in front of them and give it to the goddess. The women drink some coffee but do not eat. They take home what remains on the banana leaf and depart before 5:00 A.M. When leaving it is essential that they look forward and never glance behind them, for to do so would mean the child will fall ill again.

"Toilet Training"

Village babies do not wear diapers. They are placed on a towel or cloth on a mat, usually on a bed between two cushions; and the cloth is frequently washed. When mothers take their babies out for a walk, they usually put a pair of cotton underpants on them and take an extra pair along. Toilet training starts at about four months, and by seven or eight months children are said to be able to indicate that they want to "get down." Mothers will sometimes hold them out the door; but more commonly the babies are allowed to urinate or defecate on the cow-dung floor.

INDULGING YOUNG CHILDREN

Toddlers and babies are coddled and indulged. Young mothers in particular dress their babies in expensive factory-made clothes, adding a knitted bonnet and booties. They put a dark brown dot (pottuwa) on the child's forehead—partly to ward off the evil eye (see p. 73), but also because it adds to the attractiveness of the child. The small bracelets of black beads additionally serve a protective as well as decorative purpose.

Babies of about four months and older are always being handled, bounced, and given attention by any elder sisters or other (especially female) family members who come in the vicinity. As soon as a little girl can carry a baby around on her hip, she is often seen with one. The baby serves as a doll, and the sister is a doting nursemaid. The baby is also content with this situation—never alone to amuse itself, always the center of attention, given endless stimuli, and feeding on demand. It is rare to hear an infant cry in the village.

Children grow up in the middle of their parents' own bustling household and those of their relatives. They are always amid the farm activities, among children of diverse ages to serve as playmates and role models. Though subject to strict discipline from their parents and elders, and although they are responsible for many chores and errands from an early age, village children are usually all smiles and radiate a joy in living. The children I sometimes heard crying were generally the few who recognized me as looking different from the people they were familiar with. They screamed in mortal fright when I turned up on their compound or when they were taken to my house. In order to appease or distract the child, the mother or sister would inadvertently pluck one of my hibiscus flowers in the garden—a typical gesture in a village where a child has no toys. I had to find a tactful and joking way to tell them that I liked to keep my flowers on the bush.

The idea of protecting garden flowers was hard for villagers to relate to. Picking flowers to please a small child who likes the bright colors or to offer at a Buddhist shrine is an accepted practice, no matter whose yard is being ravaged. Thus the schoolchildren were also puzzled and confused when I told them not to pick my cultivated flowers to offer to the Buddha at the school's opening ceremony.

Though some young children saw me as a ghost or goblin, most delighted in visiting my house, which was full of interesting gadgets—from a stapler to a can opener. They often brought me a bouquet of flowers, some fruit, or sweets; we would chat for a while until I told them that I had to do some writing. Unless I ushered them to the door, they could remain watching my every move, coming closer and closer as I typed a letter or transcribed notes from the tape-recorder. On the other hand, they were immediately willing to run an errand or do a small chore; and I enjoyed their visits in many ways: seeing their eyes light up in wonderment as I demonstrated the pocket calculator, or hearing their amused chatter as they thumbed through a calendar with African animals.

PLAY

There are hardly any manufactured toys in the village, and there seems to be little need for them. Even on the Sinhalese and Tamil New Year (in mid-April), when it is customary to give gifts, the children—like their elders—receive the traditional gift of clothing they need.

Children play with each other; they climb trees, swing from lianas, fish and swim in the tank, and improvise their own playthings. One will see boys running beside and rolling an old bicycle rim or car tire, or they may be pushing a crudely made hot-rod steered by a playmate. Girls might be "cooking" curries in coconut shells or carrying baskets on their heads. Discarded materials like bottle caps and flashlight batteries are used for imaginative games or noisemakers. Cricket is popular at school among the boys, who use a homemade bat. The girls often play *kotupaninawa,* a kind of hopscotch.

A popular toy made by young boys (about ages seven to ten) was a car created with an empty baby powder container, a stick for an axle, wheels cut out of the soles of old rubber sandals, and a longer stick to steer the car. Wanting to obtain such a resourcefully made toy to take back to show my students, I traded with a boy: a little manufactured car for his powder-container one. When the boy's young friends found out about the trade, several of them approached me, offering their own homemade cars for a manufactured one.

I spent several full days in village homes that had children of wide-ranging ages, observing, taking notes, and videotaping the playing children until my camcorder batteries would inevitably run out. During these long sessions the children forgot about my presence and behaved spontaneously and naturally. They played together incorporating all children: The infants were amused with pat-a-cake, the toddlers with peek-a-boo and friendly teasing; the little girls imitated the tasks of their mothers, cooking mud pies and pulling apart marigolds as vegetables to cook; the little boys took blocks of wood, pretending they were cars, running them endlessly with engine sounds over imaginary roads in the sand. Two little puppies had become completely passive as a result of continual handling, being pushed around in make-shift play trucks and propped up in coconut half-shells. The grandmother enjoyed playing with the children and was pulled around the compound seated on a gunny sack.

A typical visit to my friend Soma's compound when she and her husband were working in the fields found their twelve-year-old daughter Dinusha and her playmate Daya looking after the younger siblings. The older girls prepared tea for me and all the children, putting the one-year-old baby sister's tea in a soda bottle with a rubber nipple stretched over the top. After the bigger girls had finished playing a gambling game *(pancha),* they got all the siblings ready to go down to the well to bathe.

The daily bath is a playful and fun highlight for all the children as well as a useful time for washing clothes. On this occasion the school-aged children washed their white school uniforms. Even the little four-year-old brother washed his clothes, soaping them on the cemented area around the well and rinsing them in the small buckets drawn by the older girls. The baby splashed around in a plastic tub; and the cooling play was a welcome break on a sweltering, humid afternoon.

7.2 The daily bath is a playful and fun highlight for all children.

So much of a child's play in the village is imitating and working beside their parents or older brothers and sisters: hoeing, sweeping, bundling tobacco, pounding grain, or fetching water and firewood. Household and farming tasks are learned while playing, and responsibility toward the family is gradually and indelibly instilled.

The End-of-School Lottery

Following my departure that ended the first fieldwork period, I had several boxes of clothes and useful secondhand goods sent along with acquaintances who were going to Sri Lanka. One of these was packed with old toys that had been my son's. Mr Senanayaka, who had been my assistant, took the box to the village. There it was decided that the larger items, like the plastic jeep and ambulance, would be kept in the "Learning and Development Centre" so all the children could play with them during recess. The smaller toys would be distributed at a festive party and lottery at the end of the school year, so that each child could receive a toy of his or her own.

I was touched when I received an envelope of drawings and letters from the children in the English class, telling me what they had received and thanking me. Michael Woost, the anthropologist living in my house at that time, wrote that the toy jeep and ambulance each had at least a hundred thousand miles on it.

When I returned in 1994 it was pleasing to see that the preschoolers were still using some of the wooden puzzles I had put in the box. Even more moving was what I saw when invited as a guest in Tilaka's home. The mother took out of the family suitcase—the place where their valuables are stored for safekeeping—the toys her four children had received at the end-of-school lottery some nine years earlier: a little telephone, two cars, and a set of plastic farm animals, all familiar items that had been played with by my son.

SOCIALIZATION AT HOME

One of the most important values in Sinhalese village life, one which is taught from a very early age, is respect for your parents and your elders. Just as children in the West learn to say "thank you," the village children learn the gestures of bowing down on one's knees with head down and "worshiping" (vandinawa) their parents or other respected persons such as Buddhist monks. As soon as the small children are able to do this, the parents will coax them to bow down when they are first greeting older relatives or other elders they go to visit; the bowing is repeated when the children leave, and it is common that the parents themselves will bow down if the host in question is a well-loved relative of an older generation or a highly respected individual. The person receiving the bow might put their hand briefly on the bowed head. All this kowtowing is a sign of good upbringing and is especially typical for up-country Sinhalese. Likewise, children who answer their elders with two words, such as "Yes, Teacher" or "No, Father," are exhibiting good manners. Village youngsters are endlessly being told to do tasks or run errands by some family member or elder. I never witnessed a child refuse, complain, or even hesitate.

Socialization of village children is a combination of dependence and independence training. From its earliest months the child is taught the values of discipline, respect for parents and older relatives, sharing, a spirit of community and cooperation, and a strong commitment to the family, underscoring the value of mutual dependence.

On a more superficial level a degree of independence training takes place, for village children are taught—or learn on their own—to do many tasks without assistance from adults. First-graders can get themselves dressed and ready for school. In fact, children can do most household jobs and light agricultural work. All these independent capabilities, however, are not with a view of becoming independent individuals who can go out and "make it on their own," but rather to convey a sense of contribution to the family in a tightly woven system of interdependence.

Children learn village values early on from the many stories, verses and songs they are taught in the family or at kindergarten. These rhymes and songs are filled with examples of proper behavior, village scenarios, and the vocabulary of everyday agrarian life. Popular examples of such songs are as follows:

Wattata yannam, malak kadannam.
Saduta dennam, deela vandinnam.
Poth tika gannam, pasel yannam,
Akuru liyannam, jayak labannam.

I'll go to the garden and pick a flower.
I'll give it to the (Buddhist) priest and worship.
I'll take my books and go to school.
I'll learn to write and gain success.

Tikiri, tikiri, tikiri liya,
Kaleth aran lindata giya.
Linda watakara kabaragoya.
Kakula kapi diyabariya.

Tiny, tiny tiny maiden
Went to the well with a water pot.
The water monitor (lizard) was by the well.
The water snake bit her foot.

When parents would bring their preschool children to my house for a visit, or when I would visit their house, the parents would likely coax their four- or five-year-old into singing a song for "White Teacher." Cajoled, bribed, and mildly threatened ("White Teacher will be very unhappy if you don't sing"), the child was led through endless verses of a nursery rhyme while I indulged the family by listening admiringly. Whenever I videotaped the performing child, the proud parents were enthralled to see the recording of their child through the viewer. Thus I accumulated countless feet of singing and dancing preschoolers; and I hope that one day these young performers might be able to see themselves on screen.

VILLAGE VALUES

In addition to the above-mentioned all-pervasive values (respect for parents/ relatives/elders; discipline; sharing; cooperation/community; responsibility toward family) there are many other traditional values socialized from an early age and evident in the village. Among these are hospitality, generosity, helpfulness, resourcefulness, respect for another's property, and honesty. Prior to my first fieldwork in Suduwatura Ara, I had grown accustomed to the beggar children in the towns, who did not hesitate to hold out their hands saying "rupees," "school pens," "cigarettes," or "chewing gum." It was refreshing to find the opposite reaction from the village children. Instead of begging they delighted in bringing me things or doing favors. More than once, when I left an item somewhere—my soap dish at the pond, or a jotting notebook on a rock—a child would bring it back to me as soon as it was found. During the first fieldwork, when I once offered a neighbor boy some money to polish a few brass ornaments I had bought, the response was consistent with his upbringing and taught me a lesson about village values: "I will gladly do the polishing, but I don't want money for it."

Unfortunately, as the standard of living was gradually rising, and with this an increase in the values of materialism and individualism, the unselfishness and honesty of the village children of ten years ago seemed to have eroded to some degree. While it had never before been the case, I found in the new fieldwork period that pencils, pens, and felt markers which I left out on my desk would sometimes disappear. Knowing that I had brought some small gifts to distribute, a few children would come and ask me to give them a gift—something that had never happened in my first fieldwork period. It is also unlikely that the following incident, which occurred in 1984 with ten-year-old Sarath Bandara, a favorite village child whom I called "son," would have a chance of being replayed a decade later:

> Sarath was serving as my guide over the jungle path to Okkampitiya. Along the path I found a half-rupee coin, which I picked up without hesitation and put in his shirt pocket, saying, "Today is your lucky day, Sarath. Someone has lost the coin, and now it's yours."
>
> Trying to do so without my noticing, Sarath took the coin out of his pocket and put it back on the path. He responded to my look of surprise by saying, "Some small child might have lost it and might come back looking for it."

There is a tragic epilogue to the above tale. Sarath Bandara, that bright eyed and always helpful boy whom I had looked forward to seeing again so much, was killed at age twenty-one in a hunting accident, just three months before my arrival for the second fieldwork period in 1994. He left behind a young wife and two small children.

Like his family, I was deeply grieved. I looked back sadly at the deaths of numerous children in the short span of time I had known the village—among them Kumari's three-year-old boy who died of a chest infection while the ritual healer chanted incantations; Sirimalini's second son who fell in a well and drowned;

Manjula, whom I had taught in school and who later committed suicide, leaving behind a son and a daughter; Geetha's second infant, who died of breathing problems after only a week. And there were others. Despite their parents' loving care and all the ritual prescriptions performed to ensure a healthy and happy life, they had succumbed to the dangers prevalent in a Sinhalese jungle village.

8 / Formal Education

A teacher with fifty to eighty children in a small bare room, with no equipment but a black-board, a piece of chalk, and a few miserable dog-eared pieces of paper to go around, and another class within a yard of his, can scarcely be expected to encourage the unfolding of personalities and the emergence of creative minds. . . . While watching teachers at work under these conditions, I have often been filled with admiration that they produce any results at all, however humble, and that some youngsters struggle through this barren wilderness to real education.
—from The Quality of Education in Developing Countries by C. E. Beeby, 1966

The Suduwatura Ara School has special meaning for me. Formal education in disadvantaged rural areas was the focus of the first fieldwork period, and the choice of a village was made, in large part, because of the presence of a wattle-and-daub schoolhouse constructed by the parents. It was there on the school grounds that the villagers built my own house, giving me a close vantage point for observing the school. As a volunteer English teacher, I was brought even closer into the school's daily comings and goings, able to feel firsthand the problems so prevalent in remote rural schools. We experimented with many projects in those months—the teachers, pupils, parents, and I—and the school was the center of much activity.

Shortly after my departure in October 1985, the local member of Parliament kept his promise, and a new tile-roofed government building was erected. The children sent me pictures they had drawn of the school under construction. I was hopeful that continuing improvements would take place at the school as the number of teachers and grades increased. To my disappointment, when I returned ten years later, the quality of education seemed to be on the decline, and the school was far from a model. The urban teachers hated their remote posts, and teacher absenteeism was high. The parents were disgruntled by the lack of input, so pupils also showed poor attendance; and there was ill feeling between the school and the community. It was a typical situation found throughout the island: Signs of quality decline in Sri Lankan education were widespread. But I was especially saddened to find this school—where I had personally invested my energy and creativity at the most basic level—among the schools that were stagnating, wasting the potential of bright young minds.

THE CONTEXT

The country's education system has enjoyed an excellent reputation among developing countries. The list of glowing statistics had even improved and grown lengthier in the decade between my two research periods despite the ethnic violence in Sri

8.1 The schoolchildren tend the flower garden in front of the old school (left). The ethnographer's house is on the right.

Lanka. Public education is free from year one (age five) through university level. The total number of schools has risen along with the growing population, and primary pupils rarely have to walk farther than 4 km to school. The literacy figures are reported to have improved from an 86.5 percent overall literacy ten years ago to an estimated 90.2 percent today. The country is on the threshold of achieving universal primary education (99 percent intake), and its education flow statistics are admirable: 97 percent of grade one entrants complete primary school, and of these, 92 percent go on to secondary school. The overall teacher-pupil ratio is 23.5, one of the best in the world.

Sixty percent of the secondary school-age population attends school, and there are slightly more girls enrolled than boys. The educational expenditure as a percentage of government expenditure is 10.4 percent, with the government having financed the improvement of buildings, the construction of teachers' quarters, free textbooks, and more recently, free material for uniforms each year and free meal coupons. During the second fieldwork period there was also a dramatic increase in teachers' salaries. Sri Lanka's pride in its educational tradition and achievements is reflected in a Museum of Education recently opened at the National Institute of Education in Maharagama.

However, in spite of the superior record, there were concerns throughout the country about declining educational quality; and there was a mismatch between education and employment as seen in the high unemployment rates of educated youths. A phenomenon in the urban centers during the second fieldwork period was the proliferation of private "international schools" and private tutoring, where wealthier families could give their children an educational advantage.

Parallel to the educational profile in the nation as a whole—that is, outward indicators and statistics citing improvement, while at the same time much grumbling about quality and a cost-benefit mismatch—the village of Suduwatura Ara seemed to be in a similar situation on a local-level scale. The school staff had grown from one teacher to three during the first fieldwork, and then to a total of seven teachers when I returned in 1994. The former primary school with five grades had grown to a junior secondary school with eight grades, including kindergarten. In addition to the school now having a permanent building to replace the wattle-and-daub, thatch-roofed one, the Swedish International Development Authority (SIDA) had provided teachers' quarters, bookshelves, and teaching materials. The Village Re-Awakening program of 1991–92 provided the school with a new latrine, a urinal, a fence, and a school gate. Thus there were many indicators pointing to growth and improvement. Still the parents were disenchanted with the school; they complained about the poor educational quality and the lack of communication between school and community; and they looked back nostalgically to earlier days when they remembered more dedicated teachers.

THE VILLAGE SCHOOL HISTORY

For my first research I had enjoyed interviewing all the households about the pioneering days of the village and school, for it was something they liked to talk about. Those who had embarked on the adventure of settling a new village in the wilderness in 1976 said they had been concerned about their children's education. Some left their school-age children behind in Welimada with relatives; others said they knew that schooling would be neglected for a while, but they were forced to consider the economic side—land and food supply—first. At that time most parents considered it very dangerous to have their young children walk the 8 km distance over a jungle footpath to a school in a neighboring village. They invited the regional education director to have a look at their proposed site for a building, asking him to provide money for the roofing material and to consider their location as the place for a new government school. Shortly after he made a promise there was a change in government; the education director was transferred, and the village received no governmental support. The people were disheartened, but they put up the building with timber from the jungle, mud walls, and grass thatch—just as they built their houses—in order to start their own unofficial school and to have an assembly hall. The site had been chosen due to its proximity to water and the presence of a large tamarind tree and a mango tree planted by former chena cultivators. It has remained the central point of the village to this day.

By mid-1978 the people had given up on financial support from the government. A seventeen-year-old boy and girl, both with a tenth-grade education, were selected to be the new teachers. Each family with children in the school paid Rs. 5 per month, giving the two young volunteers a small monthly salary. Thus the parents, concerned about their children's education, took the matter of a school in their own hands. A woman who was eleven years old at that time and a pupil in the school's early years told me what she remembers:

> The school was started with a big opening ceremony. There were twenty-three children enrolled. Piyadasa and Karunawathie were our teachers, and they did a good job. Punchi Rala, the carpenter, made two long benches for us. Someone else made a blackboard on an easel. Two chairs were brought from Piyadasa's house. My mother bought the notebook for taking attendance. We started school with *pan-sil* each day. I remember those school years as an enjoyable time. Every day we had a meal supplied by the parents, such as a pancake or rice porridge. I learned to read and write and do some arithmetic there; and we learned lots of songs. After three years I had to stop school to look after my little brothers and sisters.

The next year a new circuit education officer took up the cause of the volunteer school, seeking permission from the local member of Parliament for the school to be taken over by the government and finding a principal who was willing to be posted there. A government takeover meant that the school would get a principal/teacher with a monthly government salary and some supplies and furniture. As the volunteer teachers had not completed the advanced-level high school examinations, they could not be employed at an official school, much to the regret of many parents who appreciated their services.

On June 20, 1978, a large ceremony was held for the inauguration of the new school. At this time a young bo tree provided by Punchi Rala was planted on the school grounds at an astrologically determined auspicious hour. As a bo tree is considered sacred to Buddhists, this site became the local place of worship for schoolchildren and adults alike. The school received tables and chairs as well as a bicycle and a kit with a variety of educational equipment and materials supplied by the UNICEF Small Schools Programme. The Education Department also financed the construction of a single permanent latrine—the one I would later share when I took up residence nearby in 1984.

The school struggled along during its first five years as a one-teacher/principal school with a succession of teachers who did not take their job seriously. One is reported to have spent more time having the children cultivate on the school premises than he did in teaching; and he sold the produce for himself. Another was rarely at the school and was regularly seen in the gemming fields. In 1983 a fifty-year-old woman teacher who lived in Horombuwa 8 km away was assigned to the school and took over the job of teacher/principal. Just before the start of my first fieldwork a new assistant teacher, fresh out of the university, inexperienced, and far from his native village, assumed duties. His arrival added a second teacher to the five-grade primary school of forty-seven pupils. When I moved into my mud house next to the school, it had been run by the government for five years, and I joined the staff as the (unofficial) English teacher in Suduwatura Ara's jungle setting.

HIGHLIGHTS OF THE FIRST FIELDWORK PERIOD

The Building and Premises

The wattle-and-daub school building was a sore subject with the parents and school staff. The parents felt they had been waiting too long for a permanent building, as there were only three other schools in the district with nothing but a temporary structure of mud with grass roof and cow-dung floor. There was one tiny window in the primitive and dusty rooms at the end of the open, half-walled school hall. One room served as a makeshift kitchen, the other as the lodging place of the woman principal on the days she did not return home.

Having constructed the building themselves, the parents continued to give it necessary maintenance, even though the building was officially taken over by the government. Maintenance meant monthly replenishing of the cow-dung floor by the women, putting new bundles of thatching grass on the roof twice a year to close leaking holes, and filling up part of the crumbling walls with clay daub. It is interesting that this maintenance was accepted by the parents as something they naturally should do, perhaps because they constructed the building; thus it became something they felt responsible for, as opposed to something "given" to them by the government. The following incident illustrates the difference:

> Shortly before settling in the village, when coming out to review the progress on my house, I noticed that the heavy wooden door of the school latrine (which I would be using after the move) had been torn from one of its hinges by the wind and had to be propped up with great difficulty. I asked the carpenter, who was making a minor repair on the school building, if he would mind putting the latrine door back on its hinges.
>
> "The Education Department should come out and do that," he replied, "because they built the latrine."
>
> After a short discussion we both agreed that the latrine door would still be off its hinge next year if we waited for the Education Department to do it, and I would be the main one to suffer.

As in almost all Sri Lankan rural schools, the building's main area is an open space without partitions. Having all grades in a relatively small area means that they distract one another during recitation or oral repetition exercises. In the old school (and in the new one, which had almost doubled in enrollment by 1994), it was frequent to see one or two classes being held under the large trees on the school grounds.

The government had designated five acres for the school premises. During the first fieldwork, perhaps owing to the fact that I was living on the premises and had taken an interest in the surroundings, an attractive flower garden was planted around the bo tree and several areas were planted with crops during the agriculture classes. The cultivation projects never met with a great amount of success, for vacations often fell during dry spells, and many children lived too far away to come haul water for the young farm plants. Another problem was that animals, domestic and wild, would eat the crops at night. The corn planted by the children was ruined when a bull broke his rope and wandered in. But despite the fact that the cultivation endeavors never led to a lucrative harvest, the areas around the school usually looked well maintained and put to use.

Special Activities

One of the topics I wanted to investigate was school-community interaction, so I encouraged projects that involved such interaction and also invited some of the more progressive and talented members of the Moneragala educational staff to visit the school. One of these guests launched an idea at a School Development Society meeting (similar to PTA). He suggested constructing a playground of climbing bars, swings, seesaws, merry-go-rounds, and other equipment out of jungle timber. After some drawings were displayed, the parents started gaining enthusiasm. Seven volunteered on the spot to be responsible for a particular piece of equipment, and a date was set for a *shramadana* (community work campaign) to build the playground.

I remember the day of the project as one of unusually high spirits and community cooperation. Some forty people could be seen working on the playground, digging holes, sawing logs, driving nails, and painting wood with black oil for protection against termites. Carts arrived carrying the heaviest logs. The climbing rack grew in height; the balancing bars had no sooner been finished than a line of laughing young people formed to try their skills; the merry-go-round, the most spectacular item, caused screams of delight as the children begged to be next on a ride. When the huge seesaw was finished, a battle of weight between sides added to the entertainment. At the end of the day an impressive array of equipment dotted the playground across from my front garden. I had a good feeling, having seen how the parents would rally in support of the school when sufficiently motivated.

It is uncommon for a small, remote rural school to have many special activities, and that was the case before my arrival in Suduwatura Ara. According to the school's logbook entries there were no recent music programs, plays, "sportsmeets," competitions, or special activities carried out specifically for the children. The woman principal, however, had many years of teaching experience, varied talents, and much creative potential. With a little encouragement she put together an elaborate end-of-term program, consisting of several skits dramatizing Sri Lankan folk tales. The children memorized their lines and improvised their costumes, and they learned several traditional songs with accompanying dances. An additional feature was a singing puppet performance with the puppets made during my English class. The enjoyment with which the children took part, gathering materials from the jungle for props, and the support from the parents in creating costumes and providing refreshments, refuted the notion that the parents were uninterested in what went on at school.

A positive series of activities also took place during School Week, an island-wide, nationally planned program during which a week in January was spent for maintenance and improvement of all schools through local *shramadana* efforts. The parents organized a day-by-day plan of activities, including repairing the playground equipment and fence, making a gate, putting new handles on the school mamoties, making a sign with the school's name, repairing the floor and roof of the building, clearing the road and premises of weeds, and cleaning the school. The children helped in many of these activities, also designing a garden in which the name of the school was written in letters formed by leafy plants. The parents took up a collection for the various maintenance costs and organized tea and snacks. By week's end the appearance of the school was at its best, and a festive ceremony with guest speakers was held to close School Week. I had observed the week with pride, while the school and community showed they could work together with admirable results.

THEN AND NOW—THE SCHOOL ACROSS THE YEARS

The School Day

The formal school day and curriculum was largely unchanged in the nine years I was away except for the addition of grades six and seven. The subjects taught were similar and the schedule looked much the same, requiring multiple-grade teaching, but still with relatively few pupils in each class.

Glancing back to the first fieldwork period, the school day in Suduwatura Ara officially started at 7:45 A.M., but before that time the children arrived and started cleaning the premises, sweeping the school hall, the playground, and the area around the bo tree shrine. Other children fetched water for the latrine barrel and for drinking and plucked flowers for the Buddhist ceremony. The teachers, who were not always punctual, assembled the children in the hall. The ringing of the handbell was a sign to gather around the bo tree for reciting *pan-sil* in the opening exercise. Each day a different child was called on to offer flowers in a banana-leaf basket to the small Buddha statue and to lead the Pali stanzas. Afterward, the principal gave a short lesson on some topic of morality and made announcements.

One of my favorite photographs (see p. 114) was taken at such an opening ceremony just as the early morning rays of the sun filtered through the heart-shaped leaves of the young bo tree. The two teachers and the children were standing in their usual circle around the tree, under which was the tiny Buddha statue in a homemade shrine box erected on poles. Sriyani was leading the *pan-sil*. A village dog—my dog in fact—the one that had decided to stay at my hut and remained a loyal watchdog throughout my first fieldwork period—was lying down in the circle during the quiet moment of meditation. As I examined that unstaged photo, I noticed the two pairs of slippers in the foreground that the teachers had removed, as is the custom before going into a sacred Buddhist shrine area. They were the only slippers that had to be removed, for none of the children could afford to wear any kind of shoes to school.

Back in the school building the teachers marked attendance and the formal curriculum lessons began. There were five periods (forty-five minutes each) for the kindergarten, first, and second grades, and six periods for the third, fourth, and fifth grades.

The school day is broken by a mid-morning recess, when some children eat snacks brought from home. The nutritional programs of a decade ago (CARE "biscuits"; or rice porridge made by volunteer parents) have been abandoned, as the government now issues "meal coupons" of Rs. 50 (about U.S. $1.05) per month to

8.2 The children recite pan-sil *around the young bo tree for the school's opening ceremony.*

families for each of their schoolchildren. Unfortunately, that money does not usually go directly toward the pupils' meals or snacks.

At 11:30 A.M. the kindergartners and first-graders go home, and at 12:30 the second-graders. The other children are dismissed at 1:30 P.M. after reciting Pali stanzas praising the Buddha. Hearing those verses from the hut where I was working was often my cue to go out and give one or another child an errand to run on the way home: returning a food container or dropping off a promised photograph. Always graciously willing, they departed under the relentless sun, bare feet on burning sand, some with a three-mile walk ahead of them.

Teaching Methods

The teaching methods and the course contents in 1984 were basically unchanged when I returned. The subject of Sinhala involves reading and writing. The ages and school grades of the children seem to have little bearing on their achieved levels: A few fourth- or fifth-graders can read only with difficulty and struggle to write the Sinhala letters, while a few brighter second- or third-graders are able to write simple compositions. Some of those who are far behind are children who have been kept home frequently to tend siblings or do chores.

The teachers assemble small groups around the blackboard for word drills. Individual children are called on to read simple words from the board, while the seated children may be doing a copying exercise. It is not often that the teacher walks among the children to check on their writing progress; the children who get assistance are the ones who go up to the teacher's desk and ask for help. The weaker children usually do not dare or do not bother to do this.

Typically a word is written by the beginning pupils in their exercise books along with a small drawing depicting the word, such as mango, cat, flower, sun. I became particularly attuned to the delight in the eyes of the children who were learning to read their first Sinhala words, as I was sharing again that thrill of a first-grader along with them. I clearly remember the joy of learning my first written Sinhala word, *amba* (mango), and I can still see the simple drawing of a mango beside the word.

In the first fieldwork period one of the teachers confided that he commonly "caned" the children (using a stick on the palm of the hand), although he did not do it in my presence:

> The children wouldn't do their homework if I didn't cane them for not doing it. Assignments are now coming in. I know it's negative encouragement, but it's the only thing that works—and it's the only thing we can give them free! I've told the parents of the children whom I've caned, and they don't mind, but it would of course be better if they would encourage their children at home, rather than giving them farm work or sending them on errands.

Because of my respect for this teacher, whose dedication went far beyond that of most of his colleagues who were posted in remote rural schools, I accepted the notion without a blink. At least this teacher cared about the children doing homework, while I had seen that many rural teachers (like those in the second fieldwork time) simply gave no homework, saying the pupils would not do it anyway.

The Curriculum

Arithmetic comprises counting and doing simple addition, subtraction, multiplication, and division problems—sometimes with the use of pebbles and sometimes writing sums on paper. Time is spent on elementary geometry and shapes as well as written exercises. One of the teachers during the first fieldwork focused primarily on functional arithmetic, providing many problems that dealt with the buying and selling of merchandise in market situations. He had noticed that some of the illiterate farmers were cheated at the market because of their ignorance of basic numeracy.

Buddhism is given three times a week and generally follows the Buddhism textbook, which serves as an additional reading book. The proper behavior for Buddhists is stressed and stories from the Buddha's teachings are related in informal sessions. The children enjoy these lessons, which are given reinforcement at home. They are the foundation for moral behavior and cultural identity, and such lessons play a key role in the Sinhalese socialization process.

The fifth-, sixth-, and seventh-graders take social studies, health/physical education, and agriculture, all of which are given three times a week. While the breadth of this curriculum looks good on paper, there are numerous weaknesses when the reality is examined at close range. For example, the young science and math teacher, who was undergoing "distance training" to get his teaching certificate, was transferred without a replacement during my second fieldwork, leaving a gap in the curriculum. The subject of agriculture is mostly presented in "theory" lessons. But sometimes it takes the main portion of a morning or two in school weeks already fragmented by frequent holidays and teacher absenteeism. The children are typically asked to bring mamoties (large hoes) from home, and time is spent preparing fields, planting, and weeding. There was criticism of these activities from many of the parents, who took the attitude that the children were doing activities they were already familiar with; and the harvest—if any—rarely benefits the children or school. These parents share the opinion stated by a dedicated teacher in my first stay:

> The children in our school are too weak in reading, writing and arithmetic to take prime morning time away from those subjects to work in the school garden. If the pupils cannot write two lines properly and cannot make change from a one-rupee coin, we should not be teaching them to cultivate maize and ground nuts in the morning hours.

English is in the curriculum for the third grade upward, five times a week. In my first scholastic year (1984) at the school, I taught English every day using a new experimental program designed in a joint Sri Lanka–Norway project. The children were attentive and enthusiastic, as lessons from a white woman using teaching methods that were new for them provided an extra element of interest. Songs, games, and handicraft activities to go along with the lessons contributed to a positive atmosphere among eager learners. I realized, however, that the other teachers looked on a bit skeptically, thinking I was too free with the children as I played "Simon Says" or danced the "Hokey-Pokey." They may have feared that traditional values of respect and discipline were being compromised; but from their side, they had too much respect for me to vent such feelings.

I was surprised when, during the welcoming ceremony at the time of my return in 1994, a group of children sang a song that I had taught during English lessons ten years earlier: "This is the way we wash our face . . . so early in the morning" (. . . "brush our teeth, comb our hair, eat our rice, take our books, go to school, sweep the floor," etc.; I had spun off on the words in all directions to teach vocabulary). The original tune had been modified through the years, and the pronunciation had evolved with Sinhala overtones, but the motions were unmistakable; and I was personally moved to see that my input of long ago had become a traditional local song.

For the second scholastic year in my first stay (1985) the school received its own English teacher, Sarath Perera, a young man who had learned English on his own, had passed the state examination, and did not mind being posted in a remote location. After working together with him for the first few months, he carried on alone with diligence. By the end of the field period the children could read and write simple words and had a comparatively good vocabulary.

Mr. Perera is remembered affectionately in the village. He is now a teacher in a Colombo suburb; and he returns occasionally to visit, as he married a girl in a neighboring village and now has family ties in the area. He was gracious enough to assist me as an interpreter during his holidays when I returned to the field in 1994, as well as to read over this book manuscript and give helpful comments.

In the second fieldwork period the school's young English teacher from an urban setting was unhappy and dissatisfied in the remote setting. Her lessons employing rote recitation and much seat-work booked little success in terms of pupil progress. By mid-year she had requested and received admission at a training college, leaving the Suduwatura Ara School without an English teacher—a situation common in the rural areas.

Outward Changes

On the outside it might appear that the Suduwatura Ara School has come a long way since its volunteer-teacher and mud-building days. Unfortunately, however, the situation seems to be similar to what happened in Sri Lanka's education system as a whole: A number of changes took place that look good on paper and should contribute to overall improvement; but the quality of education in terms of state examination performance (for those without extra tutoring) and parental satisfaction has declined.

The permanent building constructed just after my departure in 1985 was in a sad state of repair a decade later. There were large potholes in the cement floor, and a door was sagging and squeaking on one hinge. A comparable situation obtained for the relatively new teachers' quarters built by SIDA (Swedish International Development Authority) where two young women teachers lived. At one point a corrugated iron sheet blew off the roof, and it took months before a repair was made. The front room of the quarters was a graveyard for broken school furniture. Such maintenance arrears are a hint that there is little cooperation between the community and the school—which indeed turned out to be the case.

The little bo tree had grown to a tremendous size, its shade providing an additional place for outdoor classes; but no flowers graced the school garden, and the playground was covered with weeds. The climbing bars, swings, merry-go-round and seesaws had long disappeared. An attempt was made at cultivating peanuts, corn, and a few vegetable sorts, but these fields were neglected.

Two grades had been added to the school (it now covered kindergarten through grade seven, called year one to eight in the new system), and the enrollment had grown from forty-seven to eighty-two. In addition to the formal government primary school, the village also now had a nursery school, which used the community hall every morning on school days. An enterprising village woman— my good friend and neighbor, Leela—on her own initiative and for the mere sum of ten rupees (about U.S. $.21) per month per child, took care of about twenty-five children between ages two and four. Having only attended a five-day training course, she enthusiastically taught the children songs, dances, games, and some simple handicraft activities. It was not a question of day care for these children, as the extended families and many relatives always provide ample baby-sitters if the mother must be away. This volunteer nursery school, like the first school in 1976, attests to the fact that the parents support formal education even when it is not compulsory.

The number of teachers assigned to the Suduwatura Ara School when I returned in 1994 was impressive: seven teachers including the principal, giving a teacher-pupil ratio of twelve. However, there was not one satisfied teacher among them, even though five hailed from a nearby village or town. Only two came from urban centers, but they all still complained of the school's isolation and the lack of parental interest in the children's education.

With regard to special activities such as plays, field trips, end-of-term concerts, sportsmeets, or auctions to raise money for the school—all activities that the better functioning schools in the district regularly engage in and ones occurring in Suduwatura Ara in the first fieldwork period—these were now conspicuously absent. The only special school activity in the logbook, and one which I observed, was the annual prescribed presentation of uniform material for each child. Since 1993 the government has provided cloth—white cotton/rayon for the girls' dresses and the boys' shirts, and dark blue for the boys' short pants—free of charge for all pupils. The Ministry of Education suggests that these packages of cloth be presented in a formal ceremony on a specific day, which serves as an effective progovernment activity. There are no classes held on that day, but rather speeches by the principal and teachers, after which each child is called forward by name to receive the lengths of material (the parents must make or have the uniforms made, but such costs are small). The cloth package is formally presented like a diploma, and each child is applauded as he or she accepts it from the principal or teacher. Parents bring milk-rice, cookies and plantains as refreshments after the presentation ceremony.

This provision of free uniforms is an additional change that took place since my first fieldwork period. Although it saves the parents a bit of money and assures that all children can come to school in a uniform (an important value in Sri Lanka), it is another expensive change that has not enhanced the quality of education itself.

Quality Decline

The disenchantment by the teachers was manifested in many ways, the most blatant of which was the large amount of leave they took. During the entire second fieldwork period there was not one school day on which all teachers were present, and it was common that five or fewer were present. As I was living on the school premises and could see this firsthand, I felt it to be a painful situation. It was somewhat of an ethical dilemma: whether to broach the subject of teacher absenteeism. I wanted to remain on friendly terms with the teachers, but it was sometimes hard to hide my own disenchantment when I repeatedly saw children sitting or playing, unsupervised, wasting their school time.

Sri Lanka has many government holidays on which schools are also closed: Hindu, Muslim, Christian, and Buddhist religious holidays, for which the latter has the full moon day each month; the first of January as well as three days for the Sinhalese/Tamil New Year in April; and Independence Day. During my first fieldwork a holiday was given when Sri Lanka beat India in the cricket championship, and in the second period when the Pope visited Sri Lanka. Curfews for political and ethnic unrest also close the schools for incidental days. The teachers officially have forty-one days of leave they can take when school is in session—twenty days of personal leave and twenty-one days of sick leave, in addition to an undesignated number of duty-leave days to attend training workshops. They consider it normal to use all their sick leave days. One of the teachers was attending a course in her distant hometown of Galle and took every Friday off. It was a common complaint by the parents that the teachers took too much leave, and they also noticed that the school day usually started late and the classes were dismissed early.

One of the changes since my previous fieldwork that made leave abuses more possible and prevalent was the fact that school inspections had been discontinued as well as the requirement for principals to submit Annual Returns. In former years a district education officer visited all schools at least once a year, and the findings during this visit could have bearing on the promotion or transfer of the principal. The detailed Annual Returns filed by the principals had been replaced by a brief statistics sheet. It was as if Suduwatura Ara had become a "forgotten school," and motivation to carry out duties with commitment and accountability declined to a minimum level.

The lack of dedication on the part of the teachers and principal came from several sources. The three young, untrained university graduate teachers had not intended nor wanted to become teachers, but were forced to do so when they remained unemployed—a situation applying to many of Sri Lanka's teachers. The principal and vice principal had years of experience at larger schools with better locations. They believed their transfer to Suduwatura Ara was a punishment assignment, and they felt bitter about it. The two young women from the district, who boarded at one of the more prosperous farmer's houses during the week, were hoping to be transferred to their own village so they could live with their families.

A change occurred between the two fieldwork periods that was designed to give teachers an incentive to go to remote schools. Namely, the rural schools were classified according to their remoteness and the amount of facilities and conveniences available. For the most remote "hardship" schools, the category into which Suduwatura Ara fell, the government gave the teachers a 15 percent salary increment. Because there are fewer opportunities to spend money in remote places, and because teachers can gain additional income from cultivation, many in such schools are able to save more from their salary than would be the case elsewhere. The Suduwatura Ara teachers, however, did not see the increment as sufficient to cover their expenses nor to compensate their hardships.

While the parents complained about teachers being absent, the teachers complained about the low and sporadic attendance of the children. Particularly on Tuesdays, the day of the market in nearby Okkampitiya, many children stay home to tend siblings or accompany their parents to the fair. In the first fieldwork period the teachers also took much leave, but not an excessive amount, and the pupil attendance was much higher than in 1994–95. The parents showed that they will regularly send their children to school if convinced that serious education is taking place. When the pupils are left to amuse themselves at school, however, the parents will take more liberties in keeping them home for farm chores. Thus a cycle of absenteeism by teachers and pupils occurred in Suduwatura Ara, with both sides blaming the other for a decline in educational quality.

There was some mutual criticism between the principal and the community during my first stay, but the two other teachers had a good rapport with the villagers. The School Development Society was active, and close cooperation existed between the school and the community. The building was the focal point in the village, and some activity—from sewing lessons and literacy classes to a health workshop or a maintenance *shramadana*—was always taking place there. It was not uncommon in those days to see teachers tutoring children at the school in the evenings, free of charge, preparing them to take the primary end-of-cycle and scholarship examinations.

During the second fieldwork the School Development Society's activities had diminished to near nothing, and there was even open antagonism shown at the few meetings held, with the parents and the principal pointing at each other for the school's shortcomings. The few parents who could afford to board their children in Moneragala town during the week did so, for they were confident that the town schools were much better.

ATTITUDES TOWARD EDUCATION

That which cannot be stolen
        By thieves from where it is kept,
Or which cannot be washed away
        By the rapids to unknown depths,
Or which cannot be confiscated by kings
        Or ministers . . .
Is Learning.
Learning is all you need for the future.

                    —from Ganadevihella, much quoted verse in Sri Lanka,
                    translated from Sinhala by D. D. K. Senanayaka

During the first fieldwork I talked with all the householders at great length about education, for that was broadly the topic of my dissertation research. After the interviews I would sometimes sit for hours with my assistant, Mr. Senanayaka, the insightful retired education officer, and hash out ideas and reactions.

It was clear that the villagers all had respect for education. Most of them were literate (78 percent) and all felt that education was important for their self-esteem. The fact that they found it important to have the first-letter learning rite (*akuru-kiyaweema,* see pp. 97–98) reflected their desire for success in literacy and schooling.

All the parents interviewed who had fewer than a full five years of primary school said they regretted not getting more education. Not one said they thought education was a waste of time because their children would probably be farmers anyway. Most confided that they would be pleased if their children were able to get a salaried job, but they usually added that being a good person and leading a satisfying life were more important.

The interviewed villagers in both fieldwork periods looked back with nostalgia at the "good old days" when teachers were more dedicated and the quality of education better. "I learned more in two grades then than children know in six grades now," was a typical kind of statement. The parents were clearly disgruntled with the present school staff and concerned that their children were being put at a disadvantage. Having conducted a comprehensive study of formal education in Moneragala District in 1984–85—visiting a random sample of thirty village schools, making observations, and holding in-depth interviews with the principals—I was in a position to see that the Suduwatura Ara School, in the second fieldwork time, shared the characteristics of the stagnating and deficient schools of the district.

INFORMAL EDUCATIONAL INPUTS

One of the factors contributing to the total picture of a disadvantaged educational situation for children in remote rural areas is the lack of informal educational inputs. Aside from the socialization process through which most informal learning takes place, the more sophisticated inputs are few. There are no books or educational toys in the deprived home environments, not to mention the lack of a desk with lamp or a place to study and do homework. No films, museums, scouting clubs, and so forth are available. The radio and occasional newspapers are among the few widely distributed sources of informal education in the village.

When I sent a cash gift in 1992 on the occasion of the Village Re-Awakening festivity—to be used for a school field trip to places of interest throughout the island—it was the first time the children had gone to Colombo or to the historical sites in Anuradhapura, Polonnaruwa, or Sigiriya. The creation of the small lending library in my house provided the first supply of books with colored pictures and photographs.

In the English classes it was a pleasure to see how pupils enjoyed accounts of things of the "modern" world and the cold northern hemisphere: telephones, elevators and escalators (most children had never climbed a flight of stairs in a building); freezing food in a home freezer to preserve it; robots and computers; traveling in trains, subways, boats, and planes; ice skating, skiing, playing in the snow; and even such things as taking a shower in a bathroom kept the pupils enthusiastic and amused.

One day in 1985 the project manager arrived by car from Colombo with a cooler. In it were still some ice cubes, a new phenomenon for the village children. I called those who were playing nearby to have a look. They were curious and eager to take a piece of ice in their hand, a totally new sensation. After a moment one started screaming, "It burns! It burns!"

In the cooler were also some treats for me, among them a hunk of cheese—something I had missed for a long time, and not a food familiar in the village. I cut some small pieces for the daring ones to try; several came forward, as it is rare for these children to reject any kind of food. Not one of them liked the cheese, and two ran gagging out the door—reminding me that the foods we prefer usually have the tastes and smells we are accustomed to.

Whenever I had the tendency to lament the narrow breadth of education which the children of Suduwatura Ara received, I only had to think of how little American children—and adults as well—know about the developing world. It is not something that touches their lives, a reality that faces me anew with every introduction to anthropology course I teach. With this in mind I could accept the fact that these children, and their parents too, knew so little about the modern world from which I came. They did have a detailed knowledge of local agriculture and the many practices and processes that are needed for a well-rounded life in a Sinhalese village. They had all been socialized with the norms and values appropriate and necessary for their daily activities, including a pervasive belief in the supernatural to help them deal with the dangers in a jungle environment. The main difference was that the opportunity for expanding their scope of knowledge was limited. And today, more than in the past, the villagers are faced with uncertainties about whether their children will get the kind of formal education they need.

9 / Girls and Women

The natives of Ceylon are more continent with respect to women, than the other Asiatic nations; and their women are treated with much more attention. A Ceylonese woman almost never experiences the treatment of a slave, but is looked upon by her husband, more after the European manner, as a wife and a companion.
—from An Account of the Island of Ceylon by Robert Percival, 1803

As a woman in Sri Lanka I never felt personal discrimination. I may have caused stares of disbelief as I bounced around at the wheel of my old jeep, because most people who can afford a vehicle are expected to be able to afford and hire a driver. Indeed, any discrimination I may have felt was because I was too down-to-earth and out of place in a hierarchical society; I did not follow the role expectations of my status as Western university professor—because I lived in a mud hut, walked for miles on village paths, rode in crowded buses, and shopped at rural markets. Social discrimination works in the opposite direction for villagers—both men and women. They are expected to behave according to their down-to-earth social status as poor farmers. For Sri Lankan women on any level of the social hierarchy, the matter of class and role expectations is a more realistic issue than gender discrimination.

THE POSITION OF WOMEN

It cannot be said that women have it easy in Sri Lanka, but it is fair to say that their status is higher and their chances for improving their station in life are greater than in most developing countries. In the opinion of many, this situation can be traced in part to the Buddhist tradition, which condemns sexual discrimination. Whatever the origins, Sri Lanka can claim an impressive record. School enrollment figures and achievement scores are higher for girls than for boys. More women than men attend Sri Lanka's universities. Women are found in politics and in all the professions. In fact 48 percent of Sri Lanka's women are in the workforce, and more women have jobs than men—although the type of employment often falls in the category of casual labor or factory work. Women in both the public and private sectors get three months maternity leave. Sri Lanka boasts of having the world's first elected woman prime minister; and during the time of this case study (November 1994), a woman took office as the fourth elected president, Mrs. Chandrika Bandaranaike Kumaratunga. During this case study as well, the local elected member of Parliament for Moneragala District was a woman. It should be mentioned, however, that the latter three women leaders were elected after their husbands were assassinated (two) or otherwise died.

I was happy to see when I moved to Suduwatura Ara that the relatively equal position of women extends to the rural countryside. While village men and women agree that women work longer hours, though not necessarily harder than men, the women do not feel exploited. The Suduwatura Ara women with acquaintances or relatives who are employed in the new garment factory in Moneragala say they are not at all envious of the latter. They have a certain pride and independence as cultivators. On the many occasions that I went to a village home, it was often the mother of the household who took an active role in the conversation. Even if questions were directed at her husband, she would sometimes interject her opinions. My being a woman, however, may have given them more freedom to do this. Men and women both say that the man is considered the formal head of the household, but that important decisions are taken together.

The women of Suduwatura Ara are strong, enterprising, and hard working. They are proud to be women and proud of the contributions they make. They welcomed me in their homes with genuine hospitality as I observed them in their daily roles. Likewise, they invited me to their Women's Society meetings, where the success of their ability to work together was easily apparent.

THE WOMEN'S SOCIETY

During the Village Re-Awakening campaign (1992) a development officer who was supervising part of the program suggested that two women go to a training day held in another district town, Hambantota. There they could learn how to organize a society to benefit women. Two representatives went for training and brought back forms, brochures, and information on how to start a society. The cover of the brochure said *Duppath Ammalage Pohosath Uthsahaya* (Rich Effort of Poor Mothers).

Originally their society—which they named "Shining Stars"—was set up to help the cash-poor village women who needed money in times of illness or other crises. Similar societies were started in villages all around Sri Lanka. Now that the Shining Stars have grown prosperous, the women in Suduwatura Ara can also receive loans for cultivation or other projects and investments, such as traveling to a family function in another town or buying a sewing machine.

Meeting in the Community Hall on the 5th of every month, most of the members attend, many bringing their toddlers or infants. The secretary reads the minutes, one or two women sing a song as entertainment, and the chair leads a discussion on any matters of interest to the women. Much of the remainder of the meeting is used for collecting the Rs. 10 monthly dues (about U.S. $.21) and making loans of up to Rs. 500 on the spot, the money being taken from a cash-filled purse brought by the treasurer.

The meetings are lively and many loan transactions take place. The women are organized in groups of five, usually close friends, neighbors, or family members, who serve as each others' guarantors for the loans. The transactions are formalized on forms titled "Application for Loan," which requires not only the name, membership number, amount requested, and purpose of the loan, but also the borrower's signature across two postage stamps, signed under the statement, "I promise that I

9.1 Money changes hands at the monthly Women's Society meetings, where loans of Rs. 500 are made to women at 5 percent interest.

will repay this loan within two months at 5% interest." Two guarantors from the lender's group also sign. Although a third month is sometimes granted, up to the time of my research not one woman had failed to pay back the loan with interest.

Another transaction taking place is called *seettu.* Here a group of ten women start by each bringing two measures of rice, which is pooled in a bag. A name is then drawn to see which woman in the group gets the twenty measures that month. The winner can trade her lot with a woman who needs more rice that month—for example, if the latter is giving a *dana* ceremony or other expensive gathering. The winner can also sell the rice at a profit as long as she brings back two measures for her group the next month. No woman ever loses her two measures, and the *seettu* system helps those who must borrow money to pay for expensive obligations.

The Women's Society at the time of my stay boasted a total of Rs. 34,000 (U.S. $680), a huge sum in a small subsistence village where the average monthly cash income of a family is about Rs. 750. Only Rs. 15,000 were kept in the bank, even though it earns higher interest there. As treasurer Sudu-Menike said, "Our aim in the first place is to help our women in need, not to make the most money possible." Because the society cuts across all the village factions, differing interests are less apparent here than in the other village organizations.

This society's prosperity means that it is frequently called on for donations, and it serves as a buffer for diverse small village crises, such as if the Death Donation Society is unable to help with the costs of a funeral ceremony. Other projects are voted on by the women; for example, the woman emissary, Leela, who took the bus to Colombo to find out about my arrival time in the village was given travel expenses by the Women's Society.

The plans being made by the women at the time of my departure included the building of a storage unit so they would be able to buy and store grain and dried foodstuffs when prices are low, selling these for a profit when the prices rise. It was a good reflection of the character of the Women's Society and its members, who sought new strategies for coping with uncertainty: realistic, serious, and practical.

WOMEN'S WORK

While there is a general sexual division of labor, the trend is toward a lessening of the divisions, perhaps because Suduwatura Ara is a newly settled village and not a traditional *(purana)* village. These days one will see men helping with tasks that were traditionally relegated solely to women, such as sweeping or fetching water. A large portion of the women's and girls' work is still in the domestic sphere, mainly cooking and child care. Women also participate in much of the farm work, especially planting, transplanting, weeding, harvesting and bundling a number of crops, and tending the home garden. It is the women or their daughters of about twelve years or older who prepare the afternoon meals and take them to the people working in the fields during busy agricultural seasons. If the farm has some cows or chickens, they may also tend these.

The bulk of the housework consists of the labor-intensive job of cooking and all that it involves. Apart from that, much of the housekeeping is casual, and various chores are shared by men, women, and children. Cleaning consists mostly of sweeping the house and compound, for there are few things to be kept clean. While the women and girls wash their own clothes and those of the young children at the well, stream, or tank, the men and boys usually wash their own sarong, shirt, and other clothes when they go to bathe. Even washing dishes is a community endeavor. Family members wash their own plates when they wash their right hand (used for eating) after meals. They pour water on the plate, rub it clean with their hand, and stack it in the kitchen.

Child care is considered the responsibility of women, but in practice it is shared by all members of the extended family, as young children are coddled, carried around, dressed, and fed by doting older siblings, grandparents, aunts, and even the fathers and uncles. Children are quickly independent when it comes to getting themselves ready for school or play, and both sons and daughters help their parents with many chores.

There are a few household tasks that are exclusively the realm of women. One of these is renewing the cow-dung floor of the house every month or two. I watched my neighbor Leela engage in this process on several occasions. She would take a large plastic tub and gather the half-dry cow paddies in the adjacent fields with her hands, filling the tub until she could hardly hoist the weight of it. This she carried home on her head. Her daughters brought in a few small buckets of claylike soil, which they dumped along with the dung into the center of the floor. Containers of water were gradually mixed into the earth and dung by the women with their hands until they had an easily spreadable consistency. Starting in the far corner, they spread the dung out in fanlike motions with their flattened palms, patting it occasionally to get a smoother surface.

I was fascinated that this is never considered to be smelly or particularly dirty work. The smell of the cow dung is associated with having a clean and well-maintained house, much like floor wax might be in the West; and the smooth, newly dried surface gives little dust. Any women who happen to be around will offer to help, and any girls from about ten years upward will be given an opportunity to get some practice with the older women demonstrating and correcting them.

Although replenishing a cow-dung floor is not regarded as tedious or demeaning work, it is work that steadily recurs every month or so. The women would much prefer a cement floor. The latter gives a higher status, it is more durable, it gives less problems with dust, and it provides more protection against termites. I found it interesting that in a few households the men do help with the cow-dung application work. Putting down a cement floor (in 5 of the 108 houses) is viewed as men's work except for fetching the water to mix the cement.

The Laborious Task of Cooking

The work involved in getting a meal ready to eat in the village, or preparing the sweets for a festive occasion, can hardly be overestimated—and here we are not even talking about first cultivating the food. When it is said that women do the cooking, this means they do all the work associated directly with food preparation. They must go to the jungle to gather firewood *(dara);* they must chop it, bundle it, and carry it back in heavy loads on their heads. They must go to the well or stream to fetch water, carrying it back in large, round-bottomed earthenware or aluminum pots *(kale)* resting on one hip. They must go to the market or to their gardens to get the food to be prepared. Then begins the labor-intensive task of cooking the food itself.

Rice, the mainstay of the diet, has many steps in its preparation. Even after taking the threshed and winnowed rice to the mill, a second winnowing must be done at home to remove the remaining rice husks or other particles by throwing the rice up in a small winnowing basket *(kulla).* Then the rice must be examined by hand to take out any grains still remaining in the husks, followed by placing it together with water in a ridged bowl called a *nembiliya;* here it is swirled around to find any small stones in the rice. It is washed again before being put in the pot. For a number of traditional foods, grain must be pounded into meal with mortar and pestle, as in making green gram meal or rice flour. Millet is ground with a small stone mill.

Preparing the vegetable curries to go with the rice is also labor intensive, mainly because so many spices go into them. Chilies are ground on a grinding stone; other common spices, like turmeric, are pounded in a mortar with pestle. Many dishes require coconut milk and scraped coconut. For this the woman sits on a *hiramanaya,* a low stool with a saw-toothed coconut scraper blade attached. To make the coconut milk she must first scrape the coconut, then add a little water and squeeze this out with her hand to produce the milk.

The vegetables must be cleaned, cut in small pieces, and boiled. They are not peeled if the peel is edible. They are also not chopped on a board with a knife. Rather, the woman squats or sits on a low stool holding the upturned blade of a large knife between her feet; she then takes a handful of vegetables such as okra or string beans, lines them up, holds them with both hands and presses them down against the knife blade at short intervals. I was amazed at how quickly and efficiently large numbers of vegetables can be cut up this way.

A few women have a small clay hearth on which a pot can be placed with a wood fire underneath. Most, however, cook on an open fire with the pot propped on three stones on the kitchen floor.

Almost all the cooking is done while squatting or sitting on low stools a few inches from the ground; the atmosphere is hot and smoky, and the boiling coconut oil for *papadam* (bread crisps) or other fried foods additionally burns the eyes. The cooking pots are simple ones of clay or aluminum and must be handled when hot with a folded rag. The cooking of the morning and evening meals is done with only the light of the hearth fire and a small kerosene lamp. There is no such thing as getting ahead with the food preparation or cooking a meal far in advance, for most prepared food spoils within a few hours in the tropical heat without refrigeration. The blackened pots after cooking are usually washed and placed to dry on a simple platform rack in the compound.

The mother serves the meal to her husband and children first, who usually eat it on a plate on their lap, seated either on a bench in the kitchen or on a chair or bed in the main room. The mother eats last and in the kitchen. Anyone who has been a guest for dinner in a village home knows that the woman of the house, who has done most of the work, is usually in the background, appearing before the guests only to make sure they have been served enough food and that their wishes are satisfied. Trying to coax the hostess to eat along with you—as I often wanted to do, but restrained myself—would put her in an embarrassing situation. Women are pleased and proud to be the food preparers and servers, sacrificial in seeing that their family's nutritional needs are attended to first. This is not an area in which they would want to change or become "liberated." When asked if they think it is unfair that they have to eat the leftovers, some say that their place in the kitchen gives them access to plenty of food—as they might eat all the leftovers, rather than throwing food away.

Daughters share in the cooking tasks from an early age. By the time they are eleven or twelve they can independently prepare a meal of rice and curries if their mother is away in the fields or at the market. The men are able to cook as well if necessary, as when the women are away, or if the men are in the chenas at night guarding their crops from animals, or if they are gemming in the jungle. Some food, such as the sweet rice offered to the deities before planting and at harvest time, can be prepared only by men, as women (in the years that they are menstruating) are considered unclean for this—a tradition steming from Hinduism rather than Buddhism. The women have no problem with this restriction, however. As one told me, "It's fine for the men to cook the *deva dana;* they bring it home and we can eat it."

Sewing

The women like to sew and might spend time on sewing if they had any material, or especially if they had a sewing machine (there were still only four in the village at the time of my second stay). The women get new material for a "cloth and jacket," the traditional long wrap-around skirt and the short scoop-necked bodice, about twice a year, one time being the Sinhalese/Tamil New Year in April. These they may stitch by hand or give to one of the women more skilled at cutting and sewing. Ironing clothes is also the work of the few women who have the heavy, old-fashioned irons that are heated with smoldering coconut shells.

Some women buy inexpensive ready-made or secondhand clothes at the fair. Most of them have a sari they keep neatly folded in a suitcase, saving it for special occasions or trips. Mending torn or worn-out clothes is not a village woman's priority. Safety pins are readily available and are even the acceptable way of closing the traditional bodice-jacket in front, with the large pins on the outside in full view. A lot of torn garments are seen around the village, for clothes take a tremendous beating with the heavy agrarian work, the scorching sun, and the frequent washing by slapping the soaped-in clothes on rocks, then letting the rinsed items dry by spreading them on hot rocks, bushes, or grass. I learned how to wash my clothes the village way, but I did less slapping, saying mine were less soiled because I had not worked long hours in the fields. I also hung mine on a line with clothes pins, items which were examined with curiosity and envy.

THE "PATTERN BOOK" INCIDENT

During my first stay the lady principal organized sewing classes for the women of the village. She was an accomplished seamstress, and she received a bit of government subsidy for holding these classes. I was impressed by the seriousness with which the women and teenage girls were participating, each putting together a sampler book of different skills, such as facing an armhole, mending a tear, and making a buttonhole.

The principal herself was enthusiastic. Knowing that I occasionally asked my mother to send a box of school supplies and other items that are hard to find in the district, she requested me to have a "pattern book" sent in the next shipment. I was not quite sure what she meant, but I did mention it to my mother in a letter. The next box from home included a huge, one-season-outdated, Butterick pattern catalog with several hundred colorful pages of women's and children's spring and summer fashions.

The women were immediately enthralled by the book. They poured over it, chattering incessantly about the different styles and various sewing ideas they could get from the pictures. It quickly became one of the most coveted and popular items among the village women. The young men, too, delighted in flipping to the pages of bathing-suited ingenues. On several occasions the principal, who took in sewing at her home in the neighboring village of Horombuwa, carried the heavy book home to use some picture as inspiration for a client's dress. The women of Suduwatura Ara always became nervous when the book was borrowed by the principal. They would gossip and subtly press me to request that the book be returned to the "Library/Learning and Development Centre" in my house; and they were satisfied only when the much-loved book was safely back in its place.

Little did I know that after my departure the "pattern book" would be the source of a major feud between the lady principal and the rest of the village. When the book disappeared for a long time, the women accused the principal of taking it. She denied this, and during an emotional shouting match at a School Development Society meeting, she accused the English teacher of taking the book, as he had a key to the room where it was kept.

The English teacher, indignant and hurt, denied this countercharge and at the same time lost his respect for the principal. He felt so wronged that he was driven to take the matter even further. The English teacher asked Michael Woost, the American anthropologist staying in my house at that time, to write a letter to the local member of Parliament, complaining about the unjust accusation of stealing the pattern book.

When I returned in 1994, gossip about the lost book was still very much alive. The principal had retired in the meantime, with little fanfare, because she had become known as the pattern book thief. I was told in great detail how a delegation of village women had gone to a ritual healer/clairvoyant, asking him where the book could be found. He said it was hidden under stacks of dried thatching grass. Later one of the principal's daughters is said to have confided that her mother had indeed taken the pattern book, and it was now in the home of relatives in another district.

The retired principal had lost her husband in a tragic bicycle/car accident in 1988, but only a handful of villagers had attended the funeral. During my second stay the principal organized a major almsgiving ceremony to commemorate the seventh anniversary of her husband's death. It was hard to find one village woman to accompany me on the 8 km walk to Horombuwa to attend the large ritual meal. When I tried to coax them, it was the purloined pattern book that was on their lips. I argued that the principal is now elderly, doing heavy farm labor on her own; we might forgive her for something that happened long ago; and the styles in the pattern book are outmoded now anyway. But these words did little to change their minds.

Thinking back I pondered over all the trouble the pattern book had caused. I knew I would talk to my mother about it when I returned, and we would chuckle about how a discarded item she had obtained at a big department store could have been the focus of animosity and village dynamics for years. At the same time, the incident caused me to think seriously about scarcity in the village, the relative lack of luxury items for the women, their deeply felt values of community and fairness, and the village women's solidarity.

DRESS

I had given considerable thought to the topic of proper dress and what to wear before moving to Suduwatura Ara for my first fieldwork. Sri Lanka being a hierarchical society, there are differing dress codes for "ladies"—women of means, teachers, and women with office jobs—and village women who work on farms in the agrarian countryside or who work as servants in the homes of the middle class or wealthy.

A "lady" is generally expected to wear a sari, which consists of a tightly fitted short bodice and six yards of thin (often synthetic) cloth that is wrapped and pleated in a traditional fashion, being secured and "hung" on a tightly belted underskirt. The last couple of yards are draped diagonally across the front, with the end trailing over the left shoulder. I bought five different saris and had the matching bodices made before going to the village during my first stay. Additionally, I bought four different "cloth-and-jacket" sets traditionally worn by village women. As I was going to be teaching English in the school, and also because I would be living and doing participant observation in the village, I thought it would be good to wear a mix of the "ladies" dress and the village women's dress, interspersed with my own Western clothes.

However good my intentions were, I found it difficult to get used to wearing a sari for teaching. Just handling, pleating, and draping the six yards of cloth was a major operation for me in the morning, requiring a great deal of time and causing much frustration. Moreover, I found the tight bodice, the tight-waisted underskirt, and the synthetic material to be extremely warm and uncomfortable in the tropical climate. Adding to my misery was the awkwardness I felt when trying to move gracefully in a sari; the shoulder train was always getting in the way or falling off, and it was hard for me to anchor it properly. Also, I could not easily do the games and dances with the children that I had planned. The final psychological contributor to my anguish in a sari was the incongruence I felt—wearing this sophisticated attire, with gold earrings and chain as most lady teachers wore—in a simple mud and thatch schoolhouse.

The village women, however, loved seeing me in a sari and were truly disappointed when I soon gave up on trying to get properly dressed in one each morning. This surprised me somewhat, for I had thought they might like the egalitarian role I was playing by not wearing the sari, which all female teachers wear. They accepted, with a bit of reluctance, that I wear a Western "frock" (dress) to class—much more loose and cool and appropriate in the simple jungle surroundings to my way of thinking—but they did not approve of me teaching in the traditional cloth-and-jacket that is the daily dress of village women. This was stepping too far outside the accepted boundaries of proper dress, and it made them uncomfortable. Teachers wear saris; village women wear cloth-and-jackets; and one should not break these dress codes. As a Westerner I could get away with wearing a "frock," but I should not stretch propriety by playing the crossed roles between a lady and a village woman. Each person has his or her place.

I got the message. I saved my saris for special occasions; I used my cloth-and-jacket sets for working in the garden or doing other menial tasks, and I wore my Western clothes for daily teaching, going on trips (when village women put on their saris), or for visiting people's homes. Through trial and error I had found a compromise that kept me feeling physically comfortable, but did not disturb the village women's sensibilities of proper representation and proper behavior.

While making preparations for my second research trip to Sri Lanka, I opened the trunk where I had stored the seldom-worn saris I had bought with good intentions during the first stay. The multiple pleats of my favorite lavender sari, the one I had worn for the many hours of speech making at the farewell party in October 1985, were still pinned together with a safety pin. This is a common way of keeping the long lengths of material folded neatly in pleats for women like me, who are a bit rushed or awkward at getting dressed in a sari in the morning. As I tried to remove the pin, it crumbled in my hand, disintegrating into small pieces.

The color and texture of the sari and the crumbling safety pin hurled me back years in time. I had folded and packed the yards of cloth after the farewell party and had not examined them since that time. The front pleats, together with the pin, had been drenched in my perspiration on that long, intensely hot and emotionally exhausting day. It was my very sweat that had corroded the pin.

I decided to wash the saris, take them back to Sri Lanka, and give them away. And I resolved to wear what I considered to be cool and comfortable but appropriate dress for my position as Western observer and friend. A little worried whether the women would want my old saris, I was going to suggest they use them for decorating the walls for parties (a secondary use for saris in the village); but they received them with gratefulness, dignity, and pleasurable memories.

COMING OF AGE IN SUDUWATURA ARA

The most important event in the life of a village girl—even more important than her wedding—is the occurrence of her first menstrual period and the ensuing rituals and festivities. While a young woman's wedding ceremony in a poor village like Suduwatura Ara is frequently a minimal event or totally lacking—either the girl's parents are unable to pay for a dowry and many trappings, or the young couple elopes—the onset of the first menses provides a sure focus of attention on each individual girl. In Sri Lanka this is called "attaining age," and it is considered the rite of passage from girlhood into womanhood. The young men have no comparable rituals.

It was impressive to see the elaborate preparations, the complexity of ritual prescriptions, and most of all the favorable impact the "coming of age" had on the adolescent girl/young woman. After observing a number of these events and interviewing many young women, I came to the conclusion that this extremely important rite of passage makes a significant contribution to the positive self-image of Sri Lankan village women. The lengthy process, which involves a clear delineation of Arnold Van Gennep's three subcategories of rites of passage—separation, transition, and incorporation (1960:10-11)—gives the girl much time for reflection. It also provides for a formal reentry into her parents' home with the new status of woman, feeling deeply the change she has undergone and her new position with corresponding responsibilities.

Karuna's Case

I attended the ritual bathing and the social events surrounding attainment for several girls in Suduwatura Ara. During my 1984-85 stay I was mildly embarrassed at the idea of the girl's first period triggering so much family and village attention. It was hard for me to relate to a sequence of events that might have mortified a pubescent girl in the West. After attending a couple of ceremonies it became clear how much her own personal event meant to each girl, the extent to which this ceremony created solidarity among the women, and how central these events were to the social life of the village. Karuna's case was a memorable one and yet typical. She was fourteen years old, and she came of age during my second stay in the village.

Karuna noticed the beginning of her first menstrual period on December 19th. Her parents were working in the fields at the time, but a girl cousin of hers was at home; the latter went to tell the parents, who hurried back with thoughts of the many implications and obligations that the special event would bring. Before her father or any of her brothers entered the house, Karuna's mother ushered her to the spot of seclusion where she would remain until the ritual bathing. This was the rite of "separation" for Karuna in Van Gennep's terms. Under no circumstances was she supposed to see any men or boys—even very young brothers—during her time of seclusion, as males are considered vulnerable to the harm she could bring them in her transitional state between girlhood and womanhood. She was allowed to talk to them but not be seen by them.

Normally girls in seclusion will stay in the smallest room of the house, remaining there on a mat with a curtain across the door. As many people live in Karuna's house, and there are few rooms, her place was under the large wooden kitchen table. A mat was put on the floor for her, and a cloth was draped over the side of the table so she could not be seen. This would be her abode until the auspicious time for her bath as calculated by an astrologer.

The following morning Karuna's father took her horoscope and went to the neighboring village of Galtammandiya to consult with an astrologer. The latter was able to discern by consulting astrological charts that the time of her "attainment" was very positive; he made an astrological chart for her in which many things about her future could be foretold, including the success of her marriage and her fulfillment as a woman. The chart looked very favorable and served as a means for Karuna to cope with uncertainty she may have felt about her new status. Her lucky color was determined to be yellow, and the auspicious time (neketa) for the all-important ritual bathing ceremony was said to be ten days later, on December 29th.

Karuna's father was in a quandary, he told me later, for the event had occurred in the middle of a busy agricultural period. Moreover, the family needed more time to get together the large sum of money for the gifts, food, and arrangements for the ceremony and party that are necessary parts of this rite of passage. The father asked the astrologer to look for the successive auspicious time, and that was put at 6:30 A.M. on January 9th. While the second neketa did give the parents more time for preparations, it also meant that Karuna would have to stay in seclusion during her transition period for a full three weeks (the period is commonly five to fifteen days), lying on her mat under the table.

During this confinement Karuna was subject to many taboos. She could eat only watery foods prepared with coconut milk—no foods made with oil, no meat, fish, or sweets, and no sugar in her tea. When she left her mat to go to the latrine or have a "body-wash" (bathing, which includes getting the hair wet, must wait until the auspicious time), she had to cover her head and face and be accompanied by a

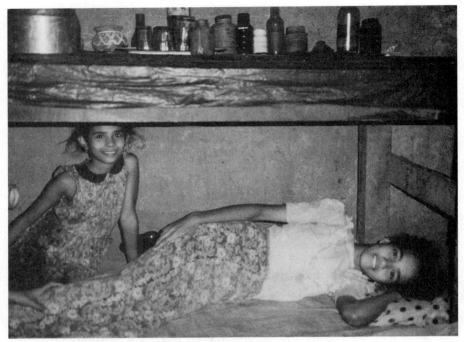

9.2 Karuna, in the separation phase of her rite of passage into womanhood. She must remain under the kitchen table, as the family has no spare room available for her seclusion.

woman. She also had to take along something metal—a large nail or an iron rod—in order to protect herself from evil spirits for which she was especially vulnerable in this period.

I went to visit Karuna in seclusion several times. She was always in high spirits, not at all appearing bored, even though it was hard to read in the dim light, and she had little else to do. But she could hear all the activity going on in the house on her behalf. Frequently girls and women came and joked or chatted with her through the curtain. A few older women also gave her advice and lessons while she was in seclusion, such as not to go out alone, especially to bathe, now that she will be a woman; not to bathe in the evening; and not to ride a bicycle anymore. Additionally, she was repeatedly advised to take her studies seriously.

With the help of friends and relations, Karuna's parents finished the intensive agricultural job of transplanting the paddy seedlings. They likewise went about the task of borrowing money from numerous relatives, knowing that many of the costs would be defrayed in the form of cash gifts given at the final party.

Next came the myriad preparations for Karuna's special day. One room in the family's new adjoining house was completed to serve as the "tea room" for guests. A temporary covered shed was constructed beside the house to accommodate a large number of guests. The female relatives collected foodstuffs to prepare the many sweets traditionally served on the ceremonial day. Additional chairs were brought in by oxcart, and arrangements were made for a photographer to come. The house was buzzing with activity for days before the party. The tea room was decorated with brightly colored saris on the ceiling and walls; crepe paper streamers and balloons were suspended.

In the meantime Karuna's mother had gone to town with an aunt to buy the traditional gifts for her daughter. The woman-to-be would get a new outfit in her lucky color, yellow, plus everything else new that a girl of her age in the village possesses: underskirt, her first bra, slippers, towel, mat, pillow, and a new party dress for the evening. Her older sister had bought her some gold earrings. Her mother carefully folded all the new gifts in a small suitcase, along with a mirror, a comb, and some talcum powder.

On January 9th I left my house well before dawn with a flashlight to walk together with Leela's twelve-year-old daughter to the distant end of the village where Karuna lived. Many women, including Leela, had been up all night helping to cook sweets for the eventful day, and the house was still alive with excitement and activity. Karuna's *loku nenda* (father's older sister) had arrived the day before and was the one designated to officiate the ritual bathing ceremony. Traditionally, a woman from the low-ranking *dobi* or laundry washer caste is called in to do the bathing, but there are few of such caste members in the region; and those who are available in neighboring towns command outlandish pay for their services.

A small earthenware pot of water with special herbs had been prepared and was covered with a piece of newspaper. Water had been warmed to fill a large plastic barrel for the bath. The household transistor radio was on to make sure that the wall clock was ticking to the right time. At 6:28 A.M. Karuna was ushered out from her place under the table with a towel hiding her head. She was taken by several women to a specified location under the jack tree in the garden. As in the first-haircut rite of passage, this "milk-tree," which exudes a white substance, is associated with womanhood and childhood. She was directed to kneel down on a flat rock under the tree. Several women chased away the young boys who were peeking around the corner. I was drawn up in the excitement, trying to manage my camcorder and camera simultaneously, and wondering whether I should video or make a slide of the exact *neketa* moment when the pot of water would be poured on Karuna. At precisely 6:30 her *loku nenda* emptied the contents of the pot over her head, then smashed the pot down on another nearby rock, breaking it and taking away all evil. This is the symbolic moment to ensure the well-being of young women who would otherwise have an uncertain future full of risks and dangers.

With a number of female relatives standing around, Karuna adroitly changed into her bathing cloth and proceeded with her ritual bath, her aunt pouring large cups of the warm water over her head and assisting with washing her hair. She was made to scrub quite thoroughly at the instructions of her female relatives. After some fifteen minutes of washing and rinsing, she was draped in a white cloth, with another over her hair and shoulders; four coins were tied in the corners of this cloth, part of the payment given to the *dobi* woman in former times. Traditionally, her clothes and anything else she might have been wearing at the time of the onset of her menses, and her personal items like mat and pillow, would go to the *dobi* washerwoman.

9.3 Karuna's ritual bathing at the precise auspicious moment. Her nenda pours a pot of specially treated herbal water over her head.

Her aunt and the other attending women then escorted her around to the front door of the family house. A large and decoratively woven mat had been put down just inside the door. On the two sides of the mat were pots of water with herbs, and on top of each was a lighted coconut-oil lamp. Some rice was strewn on the mat, and at the corner of it was a basket of vegetables. A large pestle had been laid across the threshold. (All of the items on the mat would have traditionally been given to the *dobi* woman as part of her payment). In the center of the mat was a coconut, which was sliced open by Karuna's uncle with one strong blow of a large knife just as she crossed over the threshold and entered the house with her new status as woman, the incorporation rite in Van Gennep's analysis. To everyone's joy and relief, the coconut halves fell facing upward with some water in each side, symbolizing a happy life ahead. While the other practices most probably have symbolic meanings, such as the rice symbolizing fertility and the vegetables symbolizing abundance, most of these meanings are not known by the villagers, not even by the elders and guardians of traditional knowledge like Punchi Rala.

Karuna's first deed as a new young woman was to bow down and "worship" her parents, who in turn gave her a symbolic gift of money wrapped in a betel leaf. She also bowed down at the feet of all her elder relatives present and was then led back to another room to be dressed in her new clothes.

Before getting dressed her *loku nenda* was the first to feed her some of the festive *kiribath* (milk-rice) served on a tray with several other traditional foods. She was then doted over by a bevy of female family members who dressed her in her new yellow outfit, put in her new earrings, combed her hair, and powdered her face. Karuna glanced in a mirror that was held up for her, seeing the face of a young woman—no longer a child. She was now ready to go to the decorated tea room where some twenty-four different kinds of sweets and plantains were laid out on serving dishes. As a special guest I was invited to open the tea table by taking the first sweets. I felt honored by this, but was even more privileged to have been among the inner circle of women who were allowed to observe this all-important ritual in the life of a village girl.

The rest of the day was spent finishing preparations for the party in the evening. It was raining that night when I trudged my way through the ankle-deep mud, together with a group of other villagers, clutching the camcorder bag wrapped in plastic under my umbrella, on our way to Karuna's house. There was a large turnout in spite of the rain. The continuing celebration was alive with singing, dancing, drumming, and card playing, and a great variety of food was served. Just as had been done in the morning, small groups of guests were invited into the tea room to partake of the seemingly endless supply of sweets; and guests who had not had dinner before arriving were given a rice meal as well.

Before leaving, the guests presented Karuna with a cash gift in an envelope. While the whole affair cost the family Rs. 8000, they retrieved Rs. 6000 through the gifts. The parents had a good feeling that their daughter's "age attainment" was celebrated in a worthy fashion, and the family had not lost face. Karuna had been the center of attention for many days. She had a new and respected status as "woman," and she had gained a sense of self-esteem and confidence. She would be able to build on this foundation, like other village women before her, who are strong, resourceful, and responsible.

At the next Women's Society meeting, Karuna sang a song while her mother and other women looked on with admiration and solidarity. I, too, having witnessed her entire rite of passage, observing and recording its details, felt a sense of pride for her and for all of "my" village women.

THE WOMEN OF SUDUWATURA ARA: GENUINE FRIENDS

I feel a special affinity for the women of Suduwatura Ara. So many of them were my friends and my support—concerned about my problems and trying to help me solve them. A core group of women took it upon themselves to be my assistants and protectors. They alerted me when things were going on which they thought I would like to observe; they answered my questions openly and candidly; and they allowed me to invade their domestic sphere. Without them my research would have been a shallow piece of work. Three women were particularly close and devoted friends.

Soma

R. M. Somawathie, who has five daughters and two young sons, would frequently stop by on the long walk to her highland fields, bringing me a small bottle of milk or a *roti* pancake and pausing to do some small chore around my hut. Her daughters, too, would bring me flowers and sweep my hut and check to see if I needed water.

I had the greatest admiration for Soma's determination to give her seven children the best she could. This meant attending all three markets in the area to sell her farm produce for cash. It seemed that she could never find a moment to rest, and yet she was always optimistic. Soma frequently gave me special invitations to observe the quotidian things she knew I was interested in—like the guarding of highland fields at night, the transplanting of paddy seedlings, the gathering of firewood, and the preparation of an ordinary meal. She was the first to invite me to join her family and participate in all the phases of the Sinhalese/Tamil New Year. I felt like I was on a true woman-to-woman plane of communication with Soma. We respected one another; and I knew I could learn much from her—not only about village customs and lifestyles, but also about what it meant to be the mother of a large family, tirelessly working from sunup long past sundown to provide for their needs.

Leela

R. Y. M. Leelawathie was one of my nearest neighbors. She was not a typical village woman, and fate was not on her side when she was born with a rural village destiny. Leela was dynamic, impulsive, emancipated, and adventurous, always wanting to be where the action was. She was the first person present on the school grounds when I discovered Suduwatura Ara in 1984; she quickly outlined the village situation and gave an invitation for me to come live there.

As a younger woman Leela was a born flirt, flashing her eyes and smile at male visitors to the village, both Sri Lankans and Western foreigners. Her marital problems had still not been solved by the time of my second stay. Most village men sympathized with her husband, Appuhamy, who had never been able to "tame" his high-spirited wife.

Leela had tireless energy, and she was always present as one of the hardest working participants at any community endeavor. She was not good at managing her household's finances, however. If she saw a piece of cloth she wanted for a new blouse, and she had money in her pocket, the temptation was irresistible for her. Her family was usually in debt.

The schoolteachers said she could work as hard as any man, and no one doubted it. She could have a sharp tongue and a piercing voice that would be heard across the valley—but at the same time she was a good mother to her four children and a generous contributor to the community. For example, she taught the nursery school and kindergarten class with great dedication, creativity, and love for the children—and for this she received only a small sum donated by the parents.

I greatly admired Leela's determination. During my first fieldwork, when we organized evening literacy classes at the school for those villagers who were illiterate, Leela persisted the longest in taking these classes. She had gone through only second grade as a girl, but by the time the classes were over, she could read books and write letters.

Leela's unabashed emotionality was moving. She cried piteously and held my leg and begged me not to go at the end of my first fieldwork. And it was she who made the long bus trip alone to Colombo to find out my time of arrival in the village for the second fieldwork; she embraced me with tearful emotion and sincerity when we met.

I was sad to see that this beautiful woman looked worn and thin in my second fieldwork period. She had lost some teeth and confided that she often had abdominal pains and was worried that she would die because of the tubal ligation she had undergone years earlier in a family planning program; but I could not convince her to go to the doctor.

In spite of her diminishing health she was still the vibrant woman I had known, always ready for action, always ready to go. She was the one who accompanied me to town on my long hikes; and it was she who volunteered for any risky deed—like going to Colombo to pick up my suitcase that arrived on a later plane and bringing it back on the night bus. When the bus was stopped at a random police control point, and she was accused of stealing a tourist's bag, she resourcefully went into hysterics, screaming, and crying until she attracted the attention of someone who could vouch for her bizarre story of a white woman living in a remote Moneragala village. She then carried the suitcase from the bus stop for 9 km on her head.

Leela is the person of Suduwatura Ara that all my visitors remember most vividly: her vivacious personality and her unflagging energy. She was always ready to help me, and she did it with exuberance. I loved her for her irrepressible spirit and her uniqueness in a rural subsistence village.

Sudu-Menike

My dearest and most loyal friend, a person who served as a model for me—not just as a Sinhalese village woman, but also as a human being—was H. M. Sudu-Menike (pronounced Sudu-Mani-Kay). She remains in my mind as the epitome of wisdom, modesty, and grace. We were approximately the same age, but I always felt a sense of deference for her, the feeling that her insights into human nature run far deeper than mine.

Sudu-Menike was a faithful and devoted support for me in both field research periods; and during the decade of interim time she ran the small lending library with impeccable accuracy and care, keeping charge over the door key and maintaining the house with all its contents. Her own house had been moved to the north side of the village during my nine-year absence, following the highland distribution of land deeds. It was a half-hour walk to my house from hers, but she appeared quietly every evening after her long hours of agricultural work and started sweeping my compound. She fetched me several buckets of water from the tube well behind the school, checked to see that everything was all right—for example, whether I had enough kerosene for my lamps and some fresh fruit on my table— and then she silently left. I never asked her to do this work and regularly insisted that she must be tired and that I could take care of it myself—but she persisted with a sense of duty. She was a person of principle, exemplifying the ideal characteristics of the up-country Kandyan women: generosity, hospitality, and unobtrusive service for one's guests.

She understood and anticipated my needs with uncanny intuition—keeping children away so I could get some writing done; protecting me from too many well-wishing visitors when I was ill (she would put the padlock on the front door so it would look like I was not home), bringing me specially prepared porridge and herbal teas; designing fanciful flower beds and planting many flowers in my garden because she knew I loved them. When I casually mentioned I wanted a small bathing enclosure behind the house, Sudu-Menike brought the palm fronds, the wood, and the tools the very next day. Recruiting several women, among them Leela, the enclosure was woven and built within a few hours.

She was also a well-educated and respected leader among the village women, having served as family-planning counselor and as an officer in the Women's Society. An excellent organizer and manager, she was efficient, pragmatic, and thrifty. If children were hanging around my compound, she would cleverly put them to work: "Don't just be standing around, my son. Can't you do some weeding?" She was herself an excellent mother, whose three well-mannered children reflected a caring and stable home life.

Whatever my needs, Sudu-Menike was one jump ahead of me. When she knew I was going on a trip, she would arrange that some boy would take my suitcase to the bus stop by bicycle, and she would appear early, bringing breakfast, to see me off. She checked the house regularly for termites, dug my garbage pit, and kept a wide area around my compound cleared to protect me from snakes. If she was in the vicinity when my guests came, she would immediately start boiling water to make tea; and she was generally the person who took on the responsibility of planning the large meals served to whole delegations of visitors.

It was also Sudu-Menike who organized my farewell party in late April of 1995. As I bid her a sad goodbye, I realized all too well that it was doubtful I would ever find a more faithful and supportive helper. It was also unlikely that I would ever find a person whom I admire so much for her quiet dignity and her exemplary character. Sudu-Menike is truly a genuine friend.

The time for my farewell party rolled around far faster than I had expected, considering the seemingly slow pace of agrarian life. As I sat listening to the obligatory speeches in Sinhalese, my mind wandered. I thought of the "liberated" women in my own country, and I could not help but muse that we could learn a thing or two from these village women—about solidarity, mutual help, and giving self-esteem to our daughters. I watched in appreciation as numerous women, and even young teenage girls, gave a speech or sang a song on my behalf. Most moving of all was when the Women's Society presented me with a beautiful framed *istuthiy pattara* or "thank you letter," printed in two languages and decorated with a hand-painted border—a considerable investment for these poor women. It read in Sinhala and in English: "Presented to Prof. Victoria J. Baker by the members of the Shining Stars Women's Organisation and villagers of Suduwatura Ara in the Moneragala District, Sri Lanka, in recognition of great service rendered by her, 1984–1995." It is one of my most prized possessions.

10 / Polity, Factionalism, and Social Control

Rice lands are one of the chief indices of wealth in the community. . . . The shrewd person with means always acquires land if possible. The psychology of this attitude is significant. In the villages it was felt that no other undertaking could compare to the acquisition of rice land, in terms of productivity and prestige. All other investments were considered risky, and unless one succeeded in becoming very rich they did not enhance one's social position.
—from Under the Bo Tree by Nur Yalman, 1967

Suduwatura Ara is a village of factions. This is something I wanted to deny or ignore as much as possible during my first fieldwork period, perhaps out of my idealistic view of village community life and cooperation. By the end of my first stay I was still optimistic, especially since I had helped launch a small development project in which all villagers were supposed to benefit equally from irrigated rice land. During the long interim, when the projections never materialized, when the paddyland was never distributed, and when old factions shifted and grew, my optimism faded. By the end of the second fieldwork period the realism of rivalries and jealousies had overshadowed all hopes of a simple solution to paddyland problems. I had learned a general lesson about the universality of such jealousies in human society. I had learned a specific lesson about the sensitivity of land issues. And I had learned a hard lesson on how the best intentions of outsiders can go awry and lead to unintended results.

LEADERSHIP

If a stranger should come to Suduwatura Ara and ask to speak to a representative or some kind of village leader, the inquiries would cause disagreement and confusion. There is no consensus in the village about leadership—except that there is a dearth of leadership. Neither was there a single pronounced leader in the first fieldwork period, but at that time there was more agreement about who filled leadership roles and who was given respect and authority for these roles. By the time of the second fieldwork, the answers to the question of who were the village leaders were widely divergent if any answer was given at all. The inhabitants even looked back nostalgically at the bygone incipient years of settlement where there was more sense of community and when a few respected persons could be counted on to act for the common good of the people. It should be noted here that it never crossed anyone's mind to put forward a woman's name as village representative or leader. Even though I felt that many of the women had good leadership qualities, it was not in the Sinhalese tradition to consider a woman as head of a village; and the women who had become prime minister or president of Sri Lanka did so after their high-positioned husbands had been assassinated.

In the earliest days of Suduwatura Ara the pioneer Punchi Banda, who encouraged friends and relations from Welimada to come and settle in the new surroundings, was regarded by the settlers as their leader. At that time he also took an active role in arranging marriages between local men and girls in Welimada, who would come and thus increase the size of the settlement. Punchi Banda gradually fell into the background, however, perhaps partly because he was illiterate and therefore reluctant to head a formal society or to be a representative link with district-level government, which might involve posting notices, keeping records, or reading and writing letters. His large and once prominent family was living in relative poverty by the time of the second fieldwork. Growing elderly and in poor health, Punchi Banda and his wife Bandara Menike were still taking care of their own aged parents who had come from Welimada. More significantly, they were devastated by the accidental death of their favorite son, Sarath (see p. 105), who was also one of my favorite village children; and they had gone into debt spending large sums on the funeral and almsgiving ceremonies. They were supporting Sarath's wife and two children, who lived in their home. Bandara Menike, the strong and proud matron of the village, could still not mention her son without her eyes welling with tears. Despite their increasing poverty, she and her husband were striving to add small increments of savings to their fatherless grandchildren's bank accounts. The latter had been opened, at the advice of the judge who presided over the case, by the young man who had committed the accidental shooting. This man had been a friend of Sarath's from a neighboring village and was also greatly shocked by his deed. Punchi Banda bore him no malice, but neither could he bear to see the young man.

Punchi Banda's early leadership position was taken over by another of the pioneering settlers, Punchi Rala, the carpenter, traditional doctor, and snakebite healer. Even during my first fieldwork, when he was fifty-eight, Punchi Rala was counted as one of the "elders" in this settlement of relatively young inhabitants. In addition to being a pioneer and an elder with a seventh-grade education, he had a number of skills that were useful in a frontier village. Carpentry he learned from his cousin; while he made little money from the cash-poor inhabitants with this skill, the people respected him for it. Many of the frames, doors, windows, tables, and chairs in the houses were made by him.

Throughout the years he has usually had a couple of requests per week for making herbal medicines, chanting mantras, dispelling demons, and determining auspicious times for ritual ceremonies. He never charged the people for these services; and in spite of his age and skills, Punchi Rala was not among the better-off of the villagers in terms of income, surplus, and possessions until recently. His large family with many mouths to feed made it difficult for him to get ahead materially. Only in the past few years has he been able to improve his house substantially, accumulating such goods as a manufactured furniture set and a small television. He attributes his new wealth to the tobacco he now cultivates and dries as a cash crop under the direction of the Ceylon Tobacco Board. With his declining health after a serious bicycle accident, he can no longer take an active leadership role. Moreover, he is the

10.1 Punchi Rala (P.R. Rathnayaka)—traditional doctor, snakebite healer and carpenter—working in his house/carpentry shop in 1985. The ethnographer is interviewing him while he works. A poster of former UNP President Jayawardana hangs on the wall.

only villager who openly claims to still support the former UNP (United National Party) government, which was defeated by the new PA (People's Alliance) during the second case-study period. In a country where the wrong political color of a village can mean missing out on possible government development aid, Punchi Rala's loyalty to the UNP would not make him an effective village link to the outside.

I was selfishly relieved to learn that Punchi Rala had not succumbed to his bicycle accident injuries before my return for the second fieldwork. As an anthropologist I was drawn to him and felt the urge to document the wealth of ritual knowledge he possessed. His appearance, voice, and demeanor made him the epitome of the ritual healer. Both he and I were disappointed that none of his twelve children was interested in learning the skills and lore to carry on in their father's tradition of ritual healer, snakebite curer, and *vedamahatmaya* making herbal medicines. I could not help but lament that much valuable and intriguing traditional knowledge would meet another dead end, suffer another loss, with the passing of Punchi Rala.

There are a number of other respected elder men who are called on to do *pirith* chanting and to perform ritual functions. None of these has sufficient authority, respect, or leadership qualities to unite the village, however, partially due to the factionalism and jealousies present. One was Sudu Banda, the gentle, white-haired elder who chanted the mantras for the ritual haircut of Samira during my second fieldwork, who anointed the heads of a long line of villagers during the Sinhalese and Tamil New Year celebrations, and who chanted Buddhist verses in Pali during the *pirith* and *bodhi pujawa* services in my honor.

In addition to the elders, there are a number of men in their thirties who have a relatively high education level; that is, they have passed their high school examinations—either GCE-OL or GCE-AL (General Certificate of Education, Ordinary or Advanced Level). They seem little motivated, however, to assume any leadership roles or work for the benefit of a united village. One who has become relatively prosperous is the target of much gossip about the swindling of community funds in the treasury of the local Rural Development Society and the abuse of subsidy money for latrines during the Village Re-Awakening program. The reciprocal community work parties that villagers engage in to help one another during planting and harvesting are conspicuously absent on his fields. Another young man who has attempted to be a village representative is accused of ignoring the interests of the newcomers to Suduwatura Ara.

Also among the newer generation of better educated youths is a young man who was accepted at Kelaniya University and was just finishing his Bachelor's Degree in Social Geography in 1995. I remember teaching Tikiri, as we called him, and his brother, now a high school graduate, in the little wattle-and-daub schoolhouse, and I felt proud of both boys. My assistant, Mr. Senanayaka, related how Tikiri's father had deposited a sum of money with him in Colombo, to be used for Tikiri when he needed it or in emergency situations. But the boy rarely tapped this source, living a frugal life near the university. Completing a university degree was a considerable accomplishment for a student from a remote village like Suduwatura Ara. Tikiri still felt obligated to support his family in any way he could—for he was fully aware of the extent they sacrificed for him—but it was unlikely that he would return to live in the village after his university graduation.

Time and again the interviewed villagers remained silent on the question of leadership or suggested a number of people who sometimes assumed leadership roles under different circumstances. Almost all agreed that Suduwatura Ara suffered from a lack of unity and a lack of leaders. Several voiced their opinion with a show of regret, that the educated young people today are interested only in bettering their own position, not in community service.

LOCAL LEVEL GOVERNMENT

Moneragala District is divided into six voting electorates headed by a member of Parliament, eight Assistant Government Agent Divisions headed by a divisional secretary (formerly called the AGA), and eighty-four *grama seva* divisions. The latter are the smallest administrative units in Sri Lanka. In every *grama seva* division there are a number of villages, hamlets and settlement areas. Suduwatura Ara belongs to the Horombuwa *grama seva* division in which there are eight small villages and hamlets: Horombuwa village itself, Suduwatura Ara, Talawa, Bambaragala Yaya, Kuda-Oya Yaya, Peramandiya, Galwala Para, and Polgas Yaya. The formal head of a *grama seva* division is the *grama niladhari,* the village officer (formerly the *grama seveka*), who keeps the records and should serve as a link with the higher levels of district government.

The village officer of Suduwatura Ara's *grama seva* division lives in a different village and rarely visits or shows interest, although the people say he did work hard some six years ago. They now complain that he has made few efforts to help solve the paddyland distribution problems, that he does not inform them of available opportunities (such as training programs for unemployed youth), and that he is more concerned with his personal interests. It was the common type of story, which the people related with a sense of resignation. Officials with personal interests in mind were the norm, and the villagers had long since abandoned any high expectations.

VILLAGE ORGANIZATIONS

Although Suduwatura Ara has a number of organizations, many of these have weakened in their effectiveness due to the absence of leadership and cooperation. The Women's Society, however, does not fall in this category (see pp. 124–126). I was impressed to see that the village men will openly admit that the Women's Society is the strongest and most successful organization in Suduwatura Ara, saying it is because the women are able to work together, while the men are engaged in quarrels and jealousies.

A society that still meets on a regular basis but is not supported by all villagers is the Death Donation Society. Families who choose to be members contribute Rs. 10 per month as a kind of insurance in the event of a death in the family. If a death occurs the Society pays the family Rs. 1000 (about U.S. $20.50) to help defray a portion of the funeral and *dana* ceremony costs. It also helps with the funeral arrangements and puts up the white flags on the way to the grave site. Not all village families make their contributions, however, and when a death occurs in these families, a collection is taken.

Another organization is the Youth League. It also suffers from the fact that some of the more ambitious and able young people have left the village—if only temporarily—to look for jobs in cities. While the Youth League used to meet regularly every month together with the Horombuwa young people, those meetings are now less frequent. They organized the all-night *pirith* chanting evening held at the time of my arrival; and they distributed application forms and information about training programs to become motorbike mechanics. Aside from these activities, the Youth League remained inactive. The School Development Society, too, had lost its effectiveness due to squabbles and differing opinions between the parents and the school staff.

The Rural Development Society, an organization promoted by the former government and one that was active during my first fieldwork period, was defunct in the second period, having been replaced by the Farmers' Organization. This was supposed to be the largest and most powerful organization in the village, for its membership extends to all the adult villagers. However, due to factionalism and lack of cooperation it had been rendered impotent. A unified organization with dedicated leaders would be in a stronger position to engage in activities that would benefit the village, such as approaching the government's Cooperative Development Board for setting up a cooperative shop, a rice mill, cottage industries, or a storage unit;

applying for loans to buy a tractor for village use; getting bus service to the village and having the road tarred; and having electricity extended to the village. More important, they could have been instrumental in getting the paddyland distributed so that the water in the artificial lake could be used. But the Farmers' Organization meetings were poorly attended and the officers took few initiatives. I sadly had to observe that Suduwatura Ara was stagnating due to factionalism and the fear that one group would get ahead of another.

An additional consequence of the ineffective organizations was a reduction in the number of *shramadanas* (free community labor campaigns) that went on. I had been fascinated by this concept and pleased to see it in action during the first fieldwork. Such projects might include clearing the road, maintaining the school and its premises, and maintaining community property. The refurbishing of my house before my arrival for the second fieldwork, for example, was done in a *shramadana* organized and carried out by the Women's Society. Aside from a couple of sparsely attended road-clearance *shramadanas,* however, the project to repair my house was the only one held during the time I was in the field. There was no maintenance of the wells, culverts, school, or community hall. In earlier days such community projects were more common, even though there was not as much common property to be maintained. It was all too apparent that the spirit of cooperation had dwindled.

FACTIONALISM

The Early Factions

In both research periods there were a number of factions existing in Suduwatura Ara. The people tried to put up a front to hide this fact; however, minor feuds and derogatory comments belied their true feelings. The population during the 1984–85 period consisted of four factions:

1. The Geelon Tea Estate families (1967–72). These first chena cultivators in the area had been working on a tea estate near Moneragala town, which was forced to close down during the JVP (*Janatha Vimukthi Peramuna,* People's Liberation Front) socialist uprisings in the early 1970s. Though they were the first in the area, they built no permanent houses but put up temporary small huts. Most members of this group were brothers and sisters born of a single large family.
2. The Horombuwa families (1972). This was the first group of chena cultivators to build permanent houses. They moved from the neighboring village of Horombuwa when new homestead sites in close proximity to a good water source were no longer available near their village.
3. The Welimada *Yaya* (1974). This was the largest group of settlers in Suduwatura Ara. They migrated from villages around Welimada in the up-country due to a land shortage, bringing with them a great deal of pride in their origins and a tradition of wet paddy cultivation. They often referred to their group of families as the Welimada *Yaya,* the latter being an expanse of paddy fields.
4. The Galtammandiya migrants (1975). This group arrived from an area around Badulla or Passara in the up-country through the southern side of the village via

Galtammandiya and Okkampitiya. They first settled in the latter two communities before pushing into the jungle to find better sites with water.

When I arrived in 1984 there were still numerous animosities and jealousies among the above groups. The Welimada settlers looked down on the chena cultivators of the area: "Until we came they didn't even know how to make paddy fields." Especially the former Geelon Tea Estate workers were criticized as being lazy and ignorant. Some suspected that they were Indian Tamils who were trying to pass as Sinhalese. The Geelon families resented the prejudice: "When the Welimada people moved out here we welcomed them and even gave them manioc sticks to plant; but now they don't want anything to do with us and won't inform us of activities in the village." The Horombuwa settlers were also viewed with some disdain by the Welimada families because the latter said they originally did not know how to cultivate paddy (other than highland rice). The Horombuwa people, on the other hand, claimed to have been cultivating wet paddy for many years.

As a researcher in the village I tried to remain as neutral as possible. It was difficult, however, as my meals were brought by one of the better-off families from the Welimada group. There were more families in this group who were forthcoming in offering me information, assistance, and invitations to their family functions. For these reasons it was almost impossible to appear to be treating all groups on an equal and neutral basis, and I was aware there were some grumblings that I favored the Welimada group and protected their interests.

By the end of my first stay the animosities among the different factions had begun to smooth themselves out, as evidenced in a number of intergroup marriages. Only the Geelon people remained the target of explicit prejudice. When I returned ten years later, however, the factionalism was more intense than ever. Suduwatura Ara had grown into a village of factions cutting across factions, with new ones having emerged since my first stay. I realized regretfully that the new lines of enmity had resulted, at least in part, from the 1985 "tank project"—the restoration of an ancient water reservoir or artificial lake *(waewa)* through outside development funds. What I had embarked on with hope and pride a decade earlier had gone astray, as some of our best laid plans are inclined to do.

The Tank Project

Background and Preliminaries. From my first visit to the village, I was taken to the site of the early tank—a low valley area in the center portion of the village. It was the place where an ancient artificial lake had been restored by the Suduwatura Ara settlers through the construction of an earthen bund or dam; the bund had been broken and washed away in 1976 during the *maha* monsoon. It was clear from the beginning of my stay that a lack of water was a major problem of the farmers—at least in their own minds—for they wanted to produce paddy for their daily rice meals.

During the in-depth interviews with the householders I asked them all what they considered to be most important for development of their village. A number of the respondents told me they considered water to be important, but that restoration of the present tank would benefit only twelve families living in the command area of the tank. "A tank will make a few families rich and the rest of us will remain paupers," explained one farmer who lived north of the tank. Others said they would not put a tank as development item number one unless all the families were able to get paddyland.

In mid-June 1984 we called a first informal gathering of interested members of the Rural Development Society to discuss village views on tank restoration. It was obvious that more people were interested when I said I would not try to help with the seeking of funds unless the whole village would benefit from the tank, and not just twelve families.

I was delighted that the idea met with an optimistic response when I discussed it as a possibility for the "Netherlands Embassy Small Projects" fund, a program for one-time projects to help "the poorest of the poor," costing not more than 15,000 Dutch guilders (about U.S. $7000 at that time). The idea found support with the AGA (Assistant Government Agent) and the planning director. An Agrarian Services engineer promised to make a construction design and a cost estimate that could be submitted to the Dutch Embassy along with a project proposal. The AGA stated that he would in principle be willing to have the land surveyed and an equitable (re-)distribution of land made if the families in the command area were agreeable.

In the preliminary village meetings everyone seemed enthusiastic. They would shake their head in positive affirmation when there was talk of cooperation and all families benefiting. After the meeting, however, some individuals would come to my house. We would start with pleasantries and chitchat, but I began to learn the pattern: The individual farmers had misgivings which they did not dare to vent in a public meeting. "Our family came long ago and worked many years to develop this land," they would say, for example. "It wouldn't be fair if these newcomers, who don't even know how to make a paddy field, got land that we already cleared."

Though the tell-tale signs were there, I did not fully recognize that the farmers would be reluctant to cooperate when it got down to the line of land distribution. I had likewise not realized how much work was involved in such an undertaking. A thick file of the many letters, informal village discussions, meetings with officials, visits to the embassy, drawings, estimates, and proposals continued to grow, documenting construction preliminaries. My own research on rural schooling threatened to be compromised. And little did I know that the complex social implications of the tank project had only begun.

The Netherlands Embassy promised to approve and fund the project on condition that the AGA be instrumental in distributing the crown paddylands so that all village families would benefit. Thus began the sensitive question of land allocation. After eight months of discussions in open participatory gatherings, the four groups or factions of villagers—despite the differences in background and levels of prosperity—had at least put up a convincing front of unity and desire for cooperation for the good of developing the village. This was especially reflected in their apparent agreement with regard to the redistribution of paddyland after the tank restoration. The district Director of Plan Implementation prepared a list on which the fifty-one surveyed command-area paddy acres were to be allocated to members of the forty-three households. Every household was to receive a deed for one acre of paddyland; and seven adult children of the pioneering families, who had not yet married and built their own houses, would also receive one acre each. All of the participants claimed to be satisfied with this arrangement, which they agreed was an equitable distribution of potential irrigated paddyland. The land in question, part of which was already under cultivation, was still crown land on which the villagers were encroachers without legal rights.

The same applied to all the highland fields being cultivated at that time: The people had no land permits and thus no legal rights. A great boon to the villagers' position came when the AGA also promised to allocate three acres of highland to every household, leasing the land to them with deeds valid for ninety-nine years. To a group of squatter farmers with an imminent threat of being evicted—a situation faced by many encroachers as land was made available to international sugarcane plantations—the receipt of land permits was a significant advancement in their security.

Hopeful Beginning. A local contractor from a neighboring village was selected, a person involved in the government's rural development participation scheme at that time. The beneficiaries of the tank project, here the villagers of Suduwatura Ara, were to provide the labor—some of it free community labor *(shramadana)* and some paid labor—from the tank budget.

I celebrated along with all the villagers at the festive occasion of the formal breaking of the first sod for tank construction on April 30, 1985. As is the custom for all important beginnings, an astrologer had been consulted for an exact auspicious moment for the sod breaking in order to ensure success and prosperity for the undertaking. The honorable deed was done by the local member of Parliament, dressed in impeccable white, who thrust a mamoty into the ground at 10:08 A.M., at a place decorated by colorful pennants and lined with proud villagers in their finest clothes.

Work on the concrete dam, the earthen bund and the main channel to the paddy field area continued through the dry season. All prospective beneficiaries contributed labor: Women prepared meals, crushed stones, and fetched sand; men mixed concrete and built the dam; everyone, including children, helped with the digging and transporting of earth for the bund and channel. Shortly after my departure from Sri Lanka (late October 1985) the main catchment area was complete and the tank filled with water when the rainy season began. Villagers wrote to me that the tank was beautiful, attracting aquatic birds and other wildlife in the jungle setting. An engraved marker stone was later placed, giving the date and the name of Suduwatura Ara Tank. I felt a distinct pride in being part of the project, and I was truly hopeful that it would improve the standard of living of the villagers.

Disappointing Outcome. To my disappointment, in spite of the many precautions taken during the field study period in order to make the land proposition satisfactory for all the inhabitants, a year later the tank was still not close to serving its purpose of irrigating an acre of paddyland for each household. The irrigation canals to the paddy fields were not yet built and the paddyland had still not been redistributed. The letters and reports I received from my assistant, and occasional letters that came from various farmers, attested to the fact that many hard feelings and jealousies still existed; and solutions to these problems were far from being in sight.

Worse yet, the water in the tank had even been the source of much contention. There were incidents of some villagers going to the police to report that community water had been "stolen" when other enterprising farmers opened the sluice gates to irrigate their fields before the distribution was settled. It was a classic "dog-in-the-manger" situation: "If I and the other people cannot use this community water, then nobody should be able to use it." Although the three acres of highland per house-hold had been settled, the government officials were not going to proceed with the official distribution of paddyland until the villagers could show some unity, doing their part in maintaining the tank and cutting the channels. In the meantime the water in the tank stagnated and evaporated in the sun. And so did village develop-ment, with the lines of factionalism more solidly drawn, but with new boundaries and new factions.

Sadly this situation prevailed through the years. With some consternation I re-alized that I had unwittingly interfered in the social dynamics of the village. What had seemed like a well-prepared and well designed mini-development scheme—perhaps because I had wanted to see it that way—had turned into a reflection of the envy and factionalism lurking under the surface in a subsistence village. My would-be philanthropic endeavors had involved water and land distribution—the two things at the very soul of agricultural life. I had naively *over*estimated the villagers' willingness to cooperate as a group and accept equal shares of land; and I had naively *under*estimated the precariousness and sensitive nature of water/land issues and the long-term consequences they could have. Factionalism proved to be so strong that it pushed aside the usual tendencies I had observed for coping with un-certainty. Namely, villagers were willing to do without tank-irrigated paddyland rather than give in to an oppositional group.

The paddyland in the command area of the tank was still not distributed when I returned a decade later. Making the case more glaring, the tank had been en-larged, the bund had been strengthened, and the main canal to the paddy acreage had been constructed at great expense using government funds under the Village Re-Awakening program in 1991–92. Thus a large artificial lake was present in this village of settlers who view paddy farming as the highest form of cultivation. And yet not one drop of that water had been used in the past ten years to irrigate the fifty-one acres of land in the command area of the tank. The situation was exacer-bated by the fact that the village had grown considerably in size—from 43 house-holds to 108—and many of the newcomers were quick to say that they also had a right to paddyland.

The New Factions

By the time of the second fieldwork in 1994, the four original factions described above had largely disappeared due to intermarriage. Indeed, they were even unified in the sense that they were all living in Suduwatura Ara at the time of the paddyland distribution talks in 1985 and had all received three-acre deeds to highland. The vil-lage had increased in population at the southern end, as more settlers migrated from various parts of the country. The boundaries circumscribing Suduwatura Ara, now an official village, had been extended to the north, south, and west.

To my dismay the tank and paddyland had become the focal point for various new factions:

10.2 Ten years after building the tank, it still serves only as a swimming and fishing hole. Due to factionalism, not one drop of water has been used for its purpose of irrigating paddy fields.

1. *The forty-three households.* This with their adult children (making a total of fifty), who were in the 1985 survey and had agreed to accept one acre of tank-irrigated paddyland, comprise one group. They cut across the original four factions.
2. *The offspring of the above households.* These started their own families and now made claims to paddyland. They were included in the seventy-eight families that participated in the Village Re-Awakening campaign that enlarged the tank.
3. *The nine families who cultivate one acre or more of paddyland in the command area of the tank, but without using tank water.* They are the pioneering families who feel they "developed" or "civilized" the wilderness. Although they all agreed in 1985 to accept just one acre of paddyland, none of them at this point was in any hurry to have the fifty-one acres of paddyland officially distributed. If redistribution should occur, they would possibly get a poorer or more distant parcel of land than they now cultivate; and those who cultivate more than one acre now would lose acreage after distribution. Although they did not openly argue this point, they felt

that what they now cultivate in the tank's command area, irrigated by a stream and not the tank's water, has been rightfully theirs since the earliest days of frontier settlement. These are all Welimada migrants.

4.   *The new settlers who arrived during the past nine years, settling particularly on the southern side of the village near Galtammandiya.* At the time of my second fieldwork they complained about lack of communication with the other groups and the fact that they are rarely informed about village activities. In this group were some politically active newcomers who campaigned hard for the new political party that came to power in 1994, the People's Alliance (PA). They were eyed with suspicion by the original settlers, who had always been supporters of the United National Party (UNP); but because of underlying fears that they could be punished—directly or indirectly—by opposing the new government, the former UNP members now claimed to be PA followers.

Another bone of contention was the fact that the politically active newcomers, one of whom is a small shopkeeper, were working to get bus service to the village—but only to the southern side, with the last stop being in front of his shop and some 4 to 5 km away from the houses in the central and northern areas. "He wants everyone to go to the shop and drink tea as they wait for the bus," it was said to me by some who resented him.

Also in this new group were fifteen families that joined Suduwatura Ara when the boundaries of another village, Kahambana, were shifted to facilitate administration at local level in 1992. These families referred to themselves as living in the hamlet of Kuda-Oya, geographically closer to Galtammandiya; they rarely participated in Suduwatura Ara societies or functions. When a member of one of the oldest groups helped me with a sketch map of Suduwatura Ara and its new boundaries, he left off the fifteen Kuda-Oya families. Other informants pointed this out, some noting that the Kuda-Oya people did not really belong to Suduwatura Ara, even though their houses were officially within the boundaries.

The factions had shifted and now transected one another. The large tank, which served no function other than swimming hole, place to bathe or wash clothes, and a source of fresh fish, was a constant reminder—for me and for the inhabitants—of the disunity and rivalries in the village. During my second stay in 1994–95, the greater part of the fifty families of yesteryear tugged at me, asking me to try to do something to get the Agrarian Services Department to finally give them a deed to the one acre of paddyland they were promised in 1985. At the same time some of the newer families argued that all households should get one-quarter acre of paddy. The nine families already cultivating one or more acres for many years in the tank's command area simply sat back smugly and observed the squabbles, feeling rather secure in the fact that village unity as well as government action—and thus redistribution of paddyland—was nowhere in sight.

SHIFTING VALUES

While I could see a shift in village values as reflected in the changing behavior of the children between the two different visits (see p. 105), the behavior of the adults was also shifting—from cooperation to individualism. This change in values could be seen in various aspects of village life, such as the declining number of people who showed up to help their friends and neighbors with house building or house reparations, and the reduction in willingness to share one's material goods—be it a bicycle, a winnowing machine, or a fishing net. It was also reflected in the low attendance at meetings called on matters concerning the whole village.

The values shift was particularly illustrated by the behavior of one pioneering family together with their married son's family, both of whom enjoyed a relatively prosperous standard of living and had fine houses; the son's family had one of two motorbikes in the village as well. This large family with their several grown, unmarried sons were on the forefront of community development ten years ago, taking the lead in many *shramadana* projects and donating much in the way of labor, food, and material goods to village endeavors. Ten years later three of the sons had left Suduwatura Ara for salaried jobs. The elder married son was the target of gossip about the possible stealing of community funds. He and his family were absent from community gatherings of any kind; and they no longer shared their material goods and labor. When the time for planting and harvesting came, the nuclear family members themselves in the two generations were the only ones helping each other. It was whispered that they cared only about accumulating wealth for themselves.

While I realized that this change in values was a phenomenon seen around the world in agrarian societies, it made me nostalgic for the "good old days," knowing all the time that I might be remembering the community cooperation of those days more ideally than the real situation had been.

VILLAGE JUSTICE

While Suduwatura Ara has a few wise elders whose judgement is respected, it is rare that anyone will go to them for advice in the settlement of disputes. Because of the existing factionalism and lack of leadership, it is more common for villagers to immediately involve the local police of Moneragala or Okkampitiya when they have a complaint or quarrel.

During both my first and second fieldwork periods it was common to hear of incidents being reported to the police, or even to see the police come to the village to investigate. Examples of such cases include the reporting of someone suspected of setting fire to another's house (case dropped due to lack of evidence); assault and battery by a drunken person in an interfamily quarrel (case taken to the low court); the investigation of *ganja* (hashish) cultivation that one villager informed on another (no evidence found). The police were even sent for when a village matron slapped a young man who failed to give her son the money she had entrusted to the former (the police sided with the woman).

An interesting practice engaged in during my first fieldwork but that had apparently diminished by the time of my second stay was that of posting "jungle newspapers" *(kaele pattara)*. These were anonymous handwritten slander messages that were tacked on trees along the main village road, defaming a particular family. In one sense they served as a leveling mechanism, as they were usually directed at the better-off families that were trying to get ahead financially. A result of the messages was, for example, that the family got less community help at the time of planting or harvesting. The "newspapers" also served as a kind of village justice when a police complaint met with little action.

The written items mainly had to do with sexual morality. For example, a young unmarried man was reported to have been seen leaving the house of a married woman at night; another example wrote that an older man had formerly been involved in the rape of a young girl. A "newspaper" that mortified the elder son in one of the more prosperous families said that he had been seen peeking at me through the bushes when I went to the pond at night to bathe.

Gossip and social ostracism—as was directed at the farmers with more individualistic values—are additional ways of controlling behavior and putting down those who try to benefit themselves at the expense of others.

On several occasions during my first stay the villagers demonstrated that they would not hesitate to carry out justice their own way. An example is the case of a man who severely injured another with a knife over the question of a wife's infidelity, which had several ramifications: The knife-wielder was caught and jailed; shortly thereafter his house was burned down and his family was forced to flee. Most villagers expressed no regrets at the expulsion of this man's family, and a summary police investigation found no party guilty of arson.

An interesting case of supposed suicide (but suspected murder) occurred during my first week's residence in Suduwatura Ara in 1984. I was visited by one of the village elders who brought the shocking news about an eighteen-year-old girl who was found hanging from a tree on her compound, less than a half-mile from my house. I was requested to go in my jeep to pick up the *grama seveka,* the coroner, the police, and the district medical officer, so the girl could be cut down and an autopsy performed. There was no official vehicle available from the police, and the hospital's jeep-ambulance could be released only to use for living patients. None of the officials could come, the representative said, unless I picked them up and took them home. Wanting to help and sensing a fascinating case, I agreed, and the village elder accompanied me to town.

Most of the day was spent tracking down the officials in different parts of the district. When we finally arrived at the lugubrious site back in Suduwatura Ara at 5:00 in the evening, some hundred villagers were gathered on the compound of the girl's family. The body was still hanging and decomposing after a long day in the sun. I watched from a distance as the girl was cut down and a postmortem examination done on the spot.

The young victim was the householder's wife's sister's unmarried daughter. She was six months pregnant by her uncle, the householder. A short inquiry followed at the compound site. The district medical officer declared the case to be suicide. The mother, grieved and scandalized by the whole situation, said there would be no funeral, and the girl's body was wrapped in a mat on which she had lain for the summary autopsy and put in a bare grave near the house.

There had been many whisperings about murder among the people gathered at the compound. When I was taking the officials home, I asked them if there would be further investigations. "No," said the medical officer. "This was suicide, because the girl first drank insecticide and then hanged herself." It looked obvious that the officials did not like to be bothered with a case involving the death of a subsistence farmer girl.

The victim's family departed early the next morning and was never seen in the village again. An interview with one inhabitant reflected a popular view at that time:

> That was a case of murder. The girl was pregnant by her uncle, who forced her to take a large number of malaria tablets and drink arrack (liquor) to get an abortion. When the abortion didn't occur, he hit her and killed her, then strung her up. His little boy even said he saw the deed. But the officials were bribed to say it was suicide. The man's father sold some of his land to come up with the bribe money.
>
> We would have driven those murderers from this village and they knew it— so they got out of here fast. But no family would have stayed in that house anyway, for Bodilima will continue to haunt that area, the demon who lives where a mother with unborn child is buried.

The informant made it clear that this family was no relation of any of the Welimada group in Suduwatura Ara, the group to which he himself belonged. He also made it clear that the villagers would take justice into their own hands if they thought it was necessary.

Some months later I talked with a neighbor who said he had been cutting grass for thatch near the compound where the girl was buried, when he had been struck hard on the back of the neck and had almost fallen unconscious. He ran quickly from the area, leaving the cut grass behind, for he was convinced he had been attacked by Bodilima. Another villager confirmed that she had heard Bodilima in that vicinity, wailing in her traditional way like a mother giving birth to a child.

I had enjoyed reading Leonard Woolf's personal accounts of his work as a Ceylon civil servant from 1904 to 1911, some of which time he spent in an area similar to that around Suduwatura Ara. I could relate to his feelings when he wrote,

> I fell in love with the country, the people, and the way of life which were entirely different from everything in London and Cambridge to which I had been born and bred. To understand the people and the way they lived in the villages of West Giruwa Pattu and the jungles of Magampattu became a passion with me. In the 2 $^3/_4$ years in Hambantota, it is almost true to say, I worked all day from the moment I got up in the morning until the moment I went to bed at night, for I rarely thought of anything else except the District and the people, to increase their prosperity, diminish the poverty and disease, start irrigation works, open schools. There was no sentimentality about this; I did not idealize or romanticize the people or the country; I just liked them aesthetically and humanly and socially. (Woolf 1961:180)

Perhaps Woolf, as well as I, had naively thought we had not idealized or romanticized the people or the country. My second trip had brought me to reality. Call it a maturing process with fieldwork, or just life experience. There were so many village people whom I admired, respected, and even held up as models, but I could now see more clearly their human foibles and the rivalries that had stymied the tank project. I could easily forgive them, however, knowing the importance of land and water and the dangers and uncertainties that plague their way of life. And of course Suduwatura Ara still remains one of my favorite places.

11 / The Nation, the Village, and the Future

I asked the smallest children at the village school to make a picture of "our village." All of the pictures represented the village through three borrowed symbols: tank, paddy-field, and stupa. These are the three national symbols of rural order, and it mattered little that one of these had only recently been rebuilt, the second provided work for only a fraction of these children's parents, and the third did not yet exist. The children had been provided with a visual mnemonic for "our village" which, more than anything, made "our village" an integral part of the nation as an imagined community of villages.
—from A Sinhala Village in a Time of Trouble by Jonathan Spencer, 1990

The above words written by Jonathan Spencer about a village in a different part of the island might well have been referring to Suduwatura Ara. In fact, the three symbols he mentioned—the tank, the paddy field, and the stupa (bell-shaped shrine in a Buddhist temple complex)—were often in drawings made by the schoolchildren in my English class. The same situation also applied as in Spencer's village: The tank was new; only a portion of the families had paddy fields, and the village had no temple with stupa. The children all identified with these national symbols, however, which are associated with a traditional lifestyle in prosperous agrarian villages. They are symbols that illustrate the stories and lessons in school books, and successive governments have used them to foster a sense of unity among thousands of Sinhalese villages.

The symbols served their purpose well. It was evident to me from my very first visit that these were proud people who had clear-cut views of their ancient heritage. I remember an early interview with one of the elders and village pioneers, who stated to my assistant, "The white lady has traveled to many places around the world; but as for me, I know in my heart that Sri Lanka is the best place." I thought about the universality of ethnic pride and how I had heard an elderly gentleman in the Netherlands say the same thing about his country; and if I was honest I could recognize the same feelings in myself about the United States. These were functional feelings for linking people together in groups with whom they could identify. But the feelings could also lead to hatred and ethnic violence, such as Sri Lanka was experiencing between the Sinhalese and the Tamils.

Thinking about this violence always saddened me. It was the first thing that people in the United States or elsewhere associated with Sri Lanka: "You were in Sri Lanka? Wasn't it dangerous with the civil war going on?" From my side it was the first thing I pushed to the back of my mind, and perhaps the reason I have not touched on the subject until this last chapter. Maybe I was a bit naive, but I did not feel endangered while doing fieldwork—no more than I would in crime-ridden, big U.S. cities. A village like Suduwatura Ara, not located in a Tamil-dominated area (mainly in the north and along the northeastern to central eastern coast), will generally experience only indirect effects of the ethnic violence.

Could I say anything about why the fighting continued, they would ask. "Not really," I had to answer. The complex causes were rooted in hundreds of years of cultural differences between two groups. However, it was not a religious war between the Tamil Hindu minority and the Sinhalese Buddhist majority. As in so many such cases of ethnic strife around the world—for which there are many differing opinions as to the cause and no single right answer—the problem seemed to lie in the economic sphere. The northern Sri Lankan Tamils felt discrimination in the areas of education and job opportunities, with the Sinhalese majority controlling the government, the military, and most large businesses. An industrious people who proved themselves under the British, receiving good education and occupying relatively high positions in the colonial government, the Tamils had grown to feel disadvantaged and persecuted after independence from Great Britain. The extremists among them forged a separatist campaign for an independent Tamil nation, an idea that seemed ludicrous and dangerous on such a small island in the eyes of the Sinhalese. And thus the fighting went on.

During my first stay in Sri Lanka (October 1983–October 1985), not long after the tremendous summer violence of 1983 that brought a festering situation to a head and caused the world to take note, the villagers seemed hopeful that the Sinhalese/Tamil problems could be solved, that enmities could be smoothed over, and that the groups could live in harmony. A decade later, however, after years of attacks and reprisals, the people made no attempt to hide from me their deep-seated feelings of prejudice. I had followed the tragedies on both sides from afar, lamenting the irony that here was a strife-torn nation, predominantly Buddhist, where the schoolchildren recited a pledge every day to kill no living thing.

ETHNIC PRIDE

The Sinhalese, who make up 74 percent of Sri Lanka's population, are a proud people. They are believed to be of Indo-Aryan origin, having first come from North India about 500 B.C. when the legendary founding father of the Sinhalese, Vijaya, arrived. They gradually replaced the first inhabitants, people of the Yakka and Naga tribes, of whom perhaps only a few hundred remain today, known as the Veddhas.

According to the great literary epic, the *Mahavamsa,* compiled by Buddhist monks in the fifth or sixth century A.D., Vijaya is said to have arrived shortly after the death of the Buddha (c. fifth century B.C.), having been driven out of his kingdom in northern India. Just before the passing away of the Buddha, he supposedly told the Hindu god Vishnu to protect Vijaya and some seven hundred of his followers, who would go to Sri Lanka and establish Buddhism there. Vijaya was the son of King Sinhabahu, who was fathered by an ancestral lion *(sinha).* So the Sinhalese people have a totemic origin, being by legend descendants of the lion, which is still their national symbol and the central figure on their flag.

The above story underscores the close relationship between the Sinhalese origin and the Buddhist religion—an important source of the people's identity. This relationship is further cemented by the account of the powerful Indian Emperor Asoka, a devout Buddhist, who sent a mission to Sri Lanka in the third century B.C. led by his son Prince Mahinda. The latter converted the Sinhalese King Tissa to Buddhism; and through examples of benevolence the common people were also converted. The close ties between Buddhism and the nation have continued from that time up to the present.

The Sinhalese divide themselves into two groups, the Low Country Sinhalese (approximately seven million) and the Up-Country or Kandyan Sinhalese (approximately five million). The latter are an extremely proud people, strongly believing themselves to be the most pure, because the Low Country Sinhalese mingled from the early sixteenth century onward with the Portuguese and Dutch colonials. Additional pride comes from the fact that the hill country was the last area of Sri Lanka holding out against European invaders and colonists, finally surrendering to the British in 1815.

Most of the inhabitants of Suduwatura Ara are originally from villages near Welimada in the up-country. Thus, even though they are poor subsistence farmers, and they migrated as squatters to this new frontier, they still have a strong sense of ethnic pride. They frequently refer to their Welimada origins, and sometimes they will seek a marriage partner in their up-country village for one of their children.

The self-esteem of the villagers is augmented by the fact that all but three of them belong to the *govigama* or cultivator caste—the highest caste in Sri Lanka after the royalty caste, which no longer exists. This ancient caste system, based on occupations in the king's retinue (e.g., fishermen, soldiers, cinnamon peelers, toddy tappers, tailors, laundry washers, potters, barbers, keepers of the sacred bo tree, drummers, bearers of the king's palanquin, dancers, mat weavers, etc.), still plays a significant role in modern Sinhalese society. In spite of successive governments trying to eliminate caste distinctions, they still remain endogamous groups and may play a role in one's occupational opportunities. The cultivator caste is by far the most populous one in this traditionally agrarian country. In the case of Suduwatura Ara, the homogeneity of caste helps equalize status among the villagers and generally elevates their feelings of pride.

LIVING IN A COUNTRY TORN BY STRIFE

Ethnic Strife

The ethnic violence between the Tamil minority (18 percent) and the Sinhalese majority (74 percent) has been simmering since 1958. The violence in the form of riots, burning, and looting exploded in ernest in the summer of 1983 after a Sinhalese army patrol was ambushed and killed by Tamil extremists. My departure for the first fieldwork period had to be postponed for several weeks, and I even feared a possible cancellation of the project.

The ethnic strife has continued intermittently with reciprocal retaliations up to the present (time of this writing), as the Tamils have fought for their separatist cause. It was frustrated from 1987–90, when the Sinhalese government struck an agreement with India by which an Indian peace-keeping force occupied northern and eastern Sri Lanka, a situation opposed by the most radical of the Tamil groups, the Liberation Tigers of Tamil Eelam (LTTE, known as the "Tamil Tigers"). It was also opposed by the Muslims and the Sinhalese leftist opposition parties, including a resurgent group of young Marxist revolutionaries, the JVP (*Janatha Vimukthi Peramuna,* People's Liberation Front). The Sinhalese groups feared Indian influence and were afraid there would be a sellout of non-Tamils in the northeastern and eastern parts of the country.

By 1990 when the Indians pulled out, the Tamil Tigers had become an effective guerrilla force. Torture, intimidation, and massacres were common on both sides. By the end of my second fieldwork period at least 25,000 people had died in the twelve years of Tamil separatist insurrections and nearly a million people had been displaced. Needless to say, the Sri Lankan economy had been crippled by the civil war.

Although the area in and around Suduwatura Ara is marked by ethnic homogeneity, the fear of ethnic violence and terrorism has also been felt in the village. Hostile feelings toward Tamils were readily apparent when I was there in 1994–95. The people were even suspicious of the Indian-estate Tamils who worked on a nearby rubber plantation and who had kept out of the conflict between the indigenous Sri Lankan Tamils and the Sinhalese. The denigration of Tamils by the villagers was evident in the socialization of their children. For example, as I was looking through a photo album with five-year-old Singithi, she came to a photo of herself that she hated because her skin looked dark. She said to me, "That's not Singithi, that's a little Tamil" ("Demelee").

Still fresh in the minds of the villagers were events that took place in 1991. By the spring of that year the Tiger terrorist guerrillas had infiltrated the jungles down the east coast and were perpetrating surprise attacks on random Sinhalese villages. In April on the Sinhalese and Tamil New Year's Day they attacked the village of Ethimale, about 30 km away. First killing the dogs whose barking might have warned the villagers, they broke into the houses and hacked the inhabitants to death with large machetes. Only one young girl survived. Shortly thereafter the terrorists attacked the small jungle village of Niyadella, only about 15 km away, killing twenty-three people.

The villagers in Suduwatura Ara were deathly frightened. The government distributed twenty guns to village men who would serve as "home guards." The latter stayed in houses around the village center, and many people came to these houses to sleep at night. Others left their houses in the evenings, sleeping in jungle caves or camping under trees. The period of fear lasted about three months. Many were afraid that Tigers would be hiding in the line-houses on a nearby rubber plantation. Although the Indian-estate Tamils who live there are themselves not terrorists and have no direct connection to the separatist cause, it was feared that they might cooperate.

Because of the bitterness and hatred on the part of the villagers toward Sri Lankan Tamils, and prejudice against any Tamils, I was a bit surprised to see how much respect they have for the Tamil ritual priest at the *devale* (Hindu deity shrine) in a neighboring village, and how many people from Suduwatura Ara go there for his healing services. At the same time, some villagers confided that they would rather not sit next to a Tamil on the bus. They described the table manners of a Tamil as uncouth, saying that Tamils squeeze their food and get it up to their elbows when eating.

Political Strife

In addition to the ethnic troubles, there was a Sinhalese political situation that had a permanent impact on several Suduwatura Ara families. In 1987–89 the Marxist radicals of the JVP party, unsatisfied with the government's conservative line, struck out against the ruling UNP (United National Party) government, terrorizing the central and southern part of the country and engaging in political murders of those especially active in the UNP. The government, under President Premadasa in 1988, retaliated by killing thousands of (mostly young) people suspected of being JVP members. Estimates run up to 17,000 killed in political terrorism in three years.

In Suduwatura Ara a small shopkeeper, Piyasena, was a politically active member of the UNP. It is thought that he probably informed on some JVP members in the area, young radicals who infiltrated the jungle and sometimes turned up at village houses asking for food. One night a group of uniformed men arrived in a jeep and told Piyasena to come with them to discuss some matters. His wife and four children never saw him again. Villagers think he was murdered by JVP henchmen for informing on their members. The same thing happened to the sons-in-law of two other Suduwatura Ara families, young married men with children living in neighboring villages.

Because Piyasena's case was one of the thousands of "disappearances," and there is no death certificate for him, the widow and her family have no claim to insurance and no compensation of any kind. The bright young son of the family, fifteen years old when I was there, had to stop his education and do the hard field labor normally done by men, as his older brother suffers from epilepsy. What happened to Piyasena and other such occurrences stimulate the villagers to avoid political activism of any kind. Except for hanging posters of the ruling party leaders, I found that few would voice much interest in national politics.

PROSPECTS FOR THE FUTURE

In spite of the factionalism in Suduwatura Ara, which has frustrated the distribution of paddyland and the use of the tank, most inhabitants are optimistic about the future of their village. They look back and see great strides since the earliest pioneering days, and they are confident that it will continue to develop, even if the progression is slow. Some are more skeptical, however, noting that Suduwatura Ara has traditionally been a UNP (United National Party) village, the party that was defeated by the new PA (People's Alliance) in the elections of November 1994 during the second fieldwork period. The electoral defeat of the UNP occurred after their presidential candidate was assassinated in a suicide bombing (attributed to the Tamil Tigers) at a UNP political rally in November that killed fifty-seven UNP politicians and left their party virtually leaderless (the wife of the assassinated candidate was placed on the UNP voting ticket). The week before that occurrence the Tigers bombed a ship in the Trincomalee harbor while peace talks were going on.

Some villagers felt that the new moderate-leftist People's Alliance headed by President Chandrika Bandaranaike Kumaratunga (the daughter of Sirimavo Bandaranaike, the world's first woman prime minister and widow of assassinated Prime Minister Solomon Bandaranaike) had too little political experience. They were hesitant to make a judgment call on the new president so early in her term of office, but they were doubtful if Suduwatura Ara would be on a priority list for any government programs to develop rural villages, given its UNP background. The PA political leaders spent their first months in office enumerating the abuses, corrupt practices, and excesses of the former UNP government, the same thing that the UNP government had done when it came to power in 1977, defeating the government of the new president's mother, Sirimavo Bandaranaike. The people of Suduwatura Ara also had grave doubts about the ability of President Kumaratunga to negotiate a peace settlement with the Tamil separatists.

The villagers had grown numb to the matter of peace talks by the time of my second stay. They had seen too many aborted truces to have any optimism for peace prospects. The more vociferous men were adamant in stating that any supposed peace agreements are merely a stalling mechanism and a distraction so that the LTTE can regroup and plan new terrorist activities as in the past. The more pessimistic villagers felt that no peace could be arrived at between the two ethnic groups short of first having an all-out war against the Tigers. Others believed that the stronger, developed countries should put pressure on the Tamil separatists. No one felt that concessions should be made: "If you give in and give them too much federal autonomy, they'll want more and more, and eventually we'll be the Sinhalese minority."

Even in the final weeks of this case-study fieldwork, as international news was printing reports of realistic prospects for successful peace negotiations, villagers were fearfully telling that their local bus had been stopped and checked for guns; Tamil terrorists were again suspected of infiltrating the jungles down the eastern coast. There had indeed been a cessation of hostilities in the first six months of Mrs. Kumaratunga's presidency in preparation for formal peace discussions. She had granted a number of concessions, including relaxing the embargo on the North for items such as arms, explosives, gasoline, diesel fuel, electrical equipment, helmets, and binoculars. But the embargo was reinstated on the same day as my farewell party after new violence occurred. The nation was again on "maximum alert," the peace talks were postponed, and I found myself succumbing to the pessimistic view held by the villagers.

Indeed, a year after my return in 1996, as I was finishing the manuscript, peace was still a distant dream. I received a letter from my assistant, Mr. Senanayaka, who had just visited Suduwatura Ara, saying that the people were living in fear, the gate to the school premises had been barricaded, and young men were again serving as armed "home guards."

THE SINHALESE AND TAMIL NEW YEAR

For the majority of Sri Lankans the most important holiday of the year is the Sinhalese and Tamil New Year *(Sinhala-Demala Aluth Avurudda)*. It is celebrated by both these cultural groups throughout the nation—though with somewhat different rituals—so in a symbolic way it can be said to unite the people. It represents the way the subsistence farmers of Suduwatura Ara look toward the future, not with a long-range perspective, but year by year, and with a host of ritualistic prescriptions designed to help them avoid the potential dangers that may be ahead. It is a crowning example of the theme of this book, namely that diverse beliefs in the supernatural and the accompanying ritual practices are enmeshed in all aspects of village life, helping the people cope with their insecure position in the future. That is one of the reasons that I postponed treating this festival until the end of the book. Another reason is that it coincided with my last fieldwork days in Suduwatura Ara.

The Sinhalese and Tamil New Year was originally an agricultural festival rather than a religious celebration, and it has maintained its predominantly secular associations. It marks the entry of the Sun, the giver of life, into the first sign of the zodiac, Aries, from the twelfth sign, Pisces, after its transit through the twelve signs and months of the year. Thus it celebrates the completion of the solar circuit and takes place in mid-April. Because it is astrologically determined, the New Year does not begin at midnight on a day of the Gregorian calendar, but the exact time is slightly different each year as determined by a team of state-employed professional astrologers. They also determine the auspicious moments for all the ritual elements involved in the New Year celebrations.

Occurring in April just after the main paddy harvesting season, the most prosperous time of year for farmers, the New Year is celebrated with great elaboration in the Sri Lankan villages. Suduwatura Ara is no exception. I was flattered when villagers stopped by to confirm that I would be present in Suduwatura Ara for the New Year, for they wanted to share the festivities with me. Many started weeks ahead getting their house cleaned, repaired, and whitewashed, and putting aside money to buy the traditional new clothes. A week or so beforehand I observed adults as well as children playing gambling games such as *pancha,* which have come to be associated with the "fat" time when the harvest is in, one of the few times of the year when villagers have surplus money on hand.

In 1995 the end of the old year was calculated to be on April 14th at 4:07 A.M. That was the moment which would conclude the old year and mark the beginning of the interim period between the old and the new, the *punya-kalaya* or neutral period, which can be of diverse lengths of time from year to year. Because it falls neither in the old nor the new year, it is considered a rather dangerous time. Traditionally the people fast, drinking only a bit of water; and they do not engage in any work, for that could lead to harm. It is said to be a time for meritorious deeds, such as going to the Buddhist temple to offer flowers or incense sticks or to meditate. In Suduwatura Ara few people go to one of the temples, which are a forty- to fifty-minute walk away. Playing games or just sitting around and talking are the common activities.

As cooking is considered to be work, the women in Suduwatura Ara were busy the day before and deep into the night preparing the many traditional sweets that are eaten on New Year's Day, especially oil cakes that are shaped like a woman's hair in a bun, called *konde kaevun*. I went to a couple of neighbors' houses to observe, all the while thinking of how I could get out of sampling the heavy sweets that would inevitably be presented with pride in every house, each woman having her slightly different and personal way of making *kaevun*. Other popular traditional sweets are *kokis* (wagon wheel-shaped cookies), *aggala* (grainy balls of meal and sugar), *dodol* (a dense, oily sweet), and *thala goolee* (rolls of sesame seeds, oil, and sugar, wrapped in tissue paper)—all being oily delicacies that my palate and stomach came to know too well.

Not wanting to waste these special foods that were brought to me in newspaper-wrapped gift packages by so many families, and not wanting to offend any of the givers, I had to think of creative ways of redistributing the sweets. Great quantities were eaten by the children who stopped by my house, and some I took to large families with many mouths to feed. Unable to cook such sweets myself to give away on New Year visits, I had to compensate with little gifts for the mother and children. Items like tape measures, fingernail clippers, or small photo albums were appreciated by the women; and children were always delighted by the novelty of any manufactured toy—however small or cheaply made—for toys are a rarity in the households.

In all the compounds the last-minute cleaning was done, a new hearth was made (often simply three stones), and each person took his or her last bath of the old year before the start of the neutral period. In 1995 the astrologers had announced the New Year as beginning at 12:26 P.M. on April 14th. Just before that auspicious moment for lighting the hearth, all across Sri Lanka, mothers were standing with a match in hand, looking at the clock; for the lighting of the kitchen hearth is the first act of the new year, bringing abundant—or at least sufficient—food to the kitchen if done at the correct moment.

I was in the house of Soma, my dear friend with five daughters and two sons, who had specifically invited me to observe the New Year celebrations in her home. She had worked hard the night before making a new built-in clay hearth out of cow dung and earth. She now stood ready for the designated moment, facing south (the opposite direction of the devil), the auspicious direction determined for the event. She was wearing new clothes in the lucky color, this year declared by astrologers to be white mixed with another color. At precisely 12:26 she struck the match and lit the fire under a new earthenware pot containing milk. Firecrackers could be heard around the village. The milk came to a boil and the froth flowed over to the south, a positive sign (flowing over equally on all sides would also have been good). Most villagers have no milk, as only a few families have cows, so they will light the fire for making milk-rice *(kiribath)* using coconut milk, which does not involve overflowing froth.

With the lighting of the hearth the New Year has begun in Sinhalese tradition, but certain activities must still await their auspicious moments as specified by the astrologers. In this particular year the next *neketa* was designated at 1:51 P.M., the time for starting work, exchanging money, and eating—all to be done as close to that auspicious time as possible. With less than an hour and a half between the two *neketas* in this year, there was not really enough time to cook an elaborate rice-and-curry meal. Soma and her daughters did cook the traditional milk-rice treats, some rice for a meal, and two curries. They then got the table ready and organized some items for the official starting of work in the new year.

At precisely 1:51 P.M., Soma and her eldest daughter were ready with a mamoty to dig a hole and plant young banana trees in the yard—their choice for the symbolic commencement of work as farmers. The three children who were in school took school books and started reading them out loud. To join in the ceremonies, I took my jotting notebook and video camera to record the events. Thus we had all started some of our work at the auspicious moment to ensure a favorable outcome during that year—and my mind could not help but turn to hopes of the manuscript for the village ethnography coming to successful fruition.

Shortly after the above ritual acts, the family members went back inside to do the exchange of money (*gana-denu,* literally "give-and-take"). Soma's husband Somapala was not present, for he had gone to a wealthy merchant's house in Okkampitiya to carry out the money-exchange ceremony. Many villagers will say that the money-exchange should simply be with someone close to you, or someone who is honest and has a good character. At the same time, most do believe that it is beneficial to have the first money exchanging transaction with someone who is prosperous. This is thought to ensure good fortune in money matters in the new year. In Okkampitiya there are sometimes long lines of people outside wealthy gem merchants' houses waiting to have a turn at the ritual.

In Soma's home the children lined up, facing south, each with a small amount of money wrapped in a betel leaf. The amount should be an odd number, for example three or five rupees. The children approached their mother in succession, each bowing as she offered them a betel leaf with money. They accepted it with both hands, then gave her a betel leaf containing a little more than they had received. If Somapala had been present, the husband and wife would have first made the ceremonial exchange, with him giving her a betel leaf, and her returning one with a slightly increased sum. Then the children would exchange with their father.

Soma and I exchanged betel leaves with money after I had videotaped her ceremony with the children. Some villagers commented later that her family had covered all bases to make sure they had a prosperous year: Somapala in Okkampitiya at a wealthy man's house, and Soma inviting me (they considered me to be rich). Soma denied this, saying my good character was the important factor. I stood by her loyally, explaining the truth of the matter to anyone who made a comment—namely, that I was delighted to be able to share and observe all the ceremonies in a large village household for my research, and Soma was the first person to extend a personal invitation.

The next important activity to be ritually done for the first time in the new year was eating. In this case the children again lined up facing south, approaching their mother. They first kneeled down to "worship" her; then Soma broke off a small piece of *kiribath* and banana and put it in their mouths in turn. After this formalized first eating, everyone was free to partake of the different sweets on the table and to have a rice meal when it was ready.

Firecrackers continued to pierce the air intermittently for the rest of the day. There was a lot of visiting each other's houses, offering food to guests, and sometimes giving gifts of cloth to make clothes. The most conspicuous activity was the playing of gambling games. Even the youngest children of six and seven were rolling cowrie shells in the game of *pancha* for stakes of a few rupees. For higher stakes, often irresponsibly high amounts (Rs. 500–1000) for subsistence farmers who had just received cash for their harvests, groups of men gambled illegally in card games such as *booruwa* (similar to poker) until deep in the night.

Another popular gambling game engaged in by all ages and both sexes is *keta gahanawa*. In this year it was played in Gamini's house, an enterprising young man who went to town and bought a large number of goods or "prizes" attractive to villagers, such as a tea kettle, a bucket, a mirror, a broom, a kerosene lamp, a jerry can, plastic containers, lengths of cloth, cans of fish, and boxes of cookies. By wagering a given amount, people who wanted the particular item that Gamini was holding high for their viewing could take a chance on winning it. They had to throw a large die against a wooden board and bet on the number that would come up. The atmosphere was bustling and carnival-like. People were admiring each other's new clothes, eating, and enjoying themselves. There were many other games also going

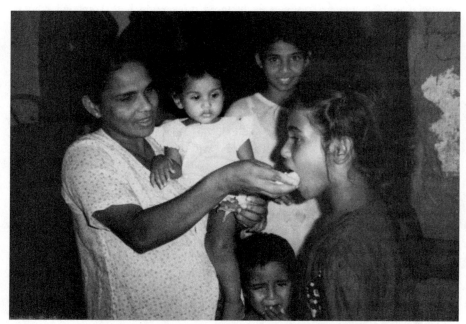

11.1 Soma gives her daughter Dinusha a piece of banana and kiribath *as the first food in the new year. This is one of the ritualized "firsts" in the Sinhalese and Tamil New Year ceremonies.*

on in Gamini's compound. He earned a nice sum for his efforts, and the lucky prize winners were happy with their new goods.

Activities with merrymaking went on throughout that day and the following day, when a big cricket match was organized. The next morning, on April 16th, the most important of the New Year rituals was to be done at 9:56 A.M., as calculated by the official astrologers: the anointing of oil *(isa-tel ganawa)*. It is associated with good health in the coming year, and it is usually performed by the family's grandfather or an older respected person. Before the anointing ceremony villagers do not take a full bath (getting the head and hair wet) in the new year.

I was especially happy when invited to join the oil-anointing ritual held at Sudu Banda's house, an esteemed elder who had been a valued respondent for me in various interviews, and who was well versed in *pirith* chanting and the prescriptions for

11.2 Respected patriarch Sudu Banda anoints a village girl with oil at the state-announced official propitious moment for this ritual. Many have lined up to be anointed.

many traditional ceremonies. I remembered well the serious but gentle way this white-haired old gentleman had carried out the first haircut ritual I had observed sometime earlier.

When I arrived at his house at 9:45, a large group of villagers of all ages had gathered in his compound. A chair had been put outside to serve as a table on which the ritual items were placed: a cup containing a mixture of coconut oil, water, and herbs; and a small branch of an *imbul* tree. On the ground was a large pestle and a little branch of a banyan tree. The two kinds of branches, one to be at the feet of each anointee and one to be held over the head, are specified each year by the astrologers, for the different planets involved are associated with certain kinds of trees.

As the propitious moment grew near, the people to be anointed lined up facing south, parents carrying their toddlers and infants, all listening to a transistor radio that would accurately announce the exact moment. At 9:56 A.M. the first person in line (usually another respected person) was anointed by Sudu Banda. The latter, with the *imbul* branch in his right hand and the cup with oil in his left, dipped his fingers in the oil and rubbed them on the head of the anointee, all the while chanting *pirith* blessings. The anointee then stepped over the pestle and the banyan branch, and the next person moved forward to be anointed in the same way.

I was last in line because I wanted to videotape the procession, but I was grateful to be included among those anointed by Sudu Banda. This wise keeper of traditions, who anointed us to ensure our health, was badly injured in a bus accident shortly after my departure. He later died from his injuries, leaving the village mourning the demise of one of its most loved and respected citizens.

There is one last *neketa* in the new year, namely leaving the house to go to work when one has a job outside the house. This was set for Monday morning, April 17th, at 6:44 A.M., but it applied to few villagers. Those who had a job and were home for the holidays, such as a man in the army, did adhere to the ritual. They left the house at the auspicious time; and then they could turn around and go back home if still on holiday leave, for the games, reciprocal visiting, and festive eating would go on for several days.

In the symbolism of the Sinhalese and Tamil New Year, the sun had concluded its passage through benevolent signs, neutral signs, and malevolent signs. It had emerged, untarnished, giving strength and vitality to the people and starting them on a journey through the months and planetary signs once again. The New Year was a time for renewal and reunion. It was a time for the people to take stock of achievements and failures in the old year, on a personal level as well as a national level, and to rededicate themselves to the tasks ahead with fresh hope and resolve—for development, prosperity, and peace.

Every parting leaves an empty feeling, a slight touch of cosmic loneliness. It is hard not to begin at once forgetting that fieldwork consists largely of intense boredom, loneliness and

mental and physical disintegration. A golden haze descends . . . the ritual becomes more stir-
ring, the past is restructured as leading inexorably to some great purpose of the present.
     —from The Innocent Anthropologist: Notes from a Mud Hut *by Nigel Barley, 1983*

Several friends had given me a copy of Barley's *The Innocent Anthropologist* when
it came out in paperback a year after my return from the first fieldwork period
(1986). Perhaps they had meant it to be an antidote to my romanticizing of village
life in Suduwatura Ara. I had read Barley's book with great amusement, but I had
trouble relating to many of the messages written in his satirical style. Sure, there are
bouts of boredom and hardships to endure, but fieldwork is also fascinating—with
new cultural revelations that can occur at any time, and a chance, as in my case, to
experience our universal humanness through deep friendships with people from a
totally different culture. Still, there were lines from Barley's work that struck a
chord, and I was starting again to feel the emptiness he was talking about as my second fieldwork time drew to a close.

The Sinhalese and Tamil New Year celebrations were among my last experiences in Suduwatura Ara before writing this book. A few days later, my assistant,
Mr. Senanayaka, had organized a small van from Colombo to come pick me up with
my goods, and I was relieved that the road was passable. My dearest friend, Sudu-
Menike, had staved off the visitors and children as I tried to put together a photo
album to leave in the village, and as I tried to cram my clothes, books, notes, and
souvenirs into two suitcases.

At the farewell party staged by the villagers, during a chain of speeches, I had
time to reflect on the two fieldwork periods and the modest changes that had taken
place in the past ten years. I thought about the ways the people had tried to cope
with the many uncertainties of an agricultural subsistence way of life. Some had
stopped by my house the day before, apologizing profusely that they would not be
able to attend the farewell party, because it was market day in Okkampitiya and
they could not miss the income from selling their produce. It drove home the tenu-
ousness of their steps toward a higher standard of living.

After the lengthy speeches, presentations, and songs sung by special friends
like Leela, I asked the villagers to assemble under the bo tree for a group photograph. Forcing a cheerful smile, I looked around for Sudu-Menike. True to her quiet
and generous character, she was in my house organizing the last rice meal and
preparing some packages of my favorite snacks and fruits for the trip.

Having checked off all last-minute items from the list, I emerged from the
house, a mixture of emotions darting through heart and mind. Sriyani had remembered that I once said I was interested in getting a metal tube in which a protective
amulet is worn around the neck. She had bought me one as a farewell gift; and
Punchi Rala had inscribed a thin copper sheet with protective mantras to put in it.
When I stepped outside, he put the *suraya* amulet around my neck, chanting *pirith*
blessings along with several other elders.

The day was another scorcher, the sun's rays almost palpable as the van pulled
away. The waving villagers became shimmering splotches of color as I left them
behind, my neck craning until the last one disappeared from view. I was on my way

back to Colombo, then back to America. I fought back the cosmic loneliness—not without a twinge of guilt—as I looked forward to my comfortable, air-conditioned home in Florida, an easy chair with a good reading lamp, television, a refrigerator with cool drinks—the list would easily be long enough to span the nine-hour ride.

But I would go back to Suduwatura Ara again as I had promised. Something else that Barley had written, near the end of his first book's sequel, *A Plague of Caterpillars,* vaguely came to mind. As the van bounced over the washed-out road, I made a note in my jotting book to look it up when I got back: "The fact that so many return to rather uncomfortable and sometimes dangerous parts of the world is eloquent testimony to . . ." I could not help but fill in my own answer here: testimony to the fact that fieldwork has a profound and lasting impact on the anthropologist. "A trip terminated brings a sense of sadness at the passing of time, the rupturing of relationships. . . . Combined with this is a very basic sense of relief at returning, relatively unscathed, to a world that is secure and predictable. . . . It leads too to fresh ways of seeing ourselves." Yes, I would surely return.

Orthographic Notes and Glossary

The Sinhala language (sometimes called Sinhalese, although the preferred term in Sri Lanka is Sinhala) has many sounds that are difficult for the non-native speaker to pronounce or even to distinguish as being different from other sounds. The Sinhala alphabet has fifty-six letters: sixteen vowels and forty consonants (though a few are not used in contemporary writing).

Rather than use a complex set of orthographic symbols, I have used transcriptions that are commonly given by educated bilingual Sinhalese people. The subtleties of pronunciation are lost in this way, however. Those interested in a more accurate pronunciation can start by referring to the book *Colloquial Sinhalese,* Part 1, with audiotapes (see entry in References Cited).

A few tips to aid in pronunciation of the Sinhala words transcribed in this book are given below.

- The *a* sound is often the *a* in "far" but is also frequently the *a* sound in "ago." The word *bana,* for example, contains both sounds.
- The vowel combination *ae* stands for the approximate sound of *a* in "cat."
- A single *e* at the end of a word is given a long *a* sound; for example, *kale* is pronounced "ka-lay."
- The Sinhala language has two *d* sounds and two *t* sounds, which are difficult for the untrained non-native ear to distinguish. They are distinguished in the spelling in this book by *d* or *dh, t* or *th.* The *th* sound is not the strongly aspirated sound of *th* in "thank," but somewhere between a *t* sound and the soft *th* in "thin." For example, *kiribath* sounds closer to "kiri-bot" and not at all close to the English word "bath."
- When a word is spelled with double consonants, this indicates that there is a very slight pause between the consonants.

achchi: great grandmother or grandmother
affinal kin: kin members related through marriage
AGA: Assistant Government Agent
aggala: grainy balls of meal and sugar; a traditional sweet
aiya: older brother, or older male parallel cousin
akka: older sister, or older female parallel cousin
akuru kiyaweema: ritual of reading the first alphabet letter to a child, at an astrologically auspicious moment, to ensure educational progress
amba: mango
ambaruwa: honorific term for a bull, used on the threshing floor
amma: mother
animism: the belief that animals, plants, and inanimate objects can have a soul or spirit
ata-pirikara: special alms package of eight prescribed items to give to Buddhist monks
attamma: great grandmother or grandmother
ayurvedic: traditional medicine stressing naturopathic healing and herbal remedies
bade panuwo: intestinal worms
baela tana: blade of grass used in the "first milk" rite of passage
baena: son-in-law, or husband of niece on either side
bahirawa: a category of potentially evil spirits
bambara: a kind of wasp that produces wild honey
bana: Buddhist sermon
bappa: father's younger brother, a classificatory father

Bath kaewa da?:   a greeting when meeting someone near mealtime; literally, "Have you had your rice meal?"

beheth: medicine

betel leaves: leaves that are chewed together with a bit of areca nut (betel nut) and chalky lime as a mildly addictive stimulant

bhikku: Buddhist monk or priest

Big Man: a type of leader in Melanesia who gains status by giving away wealth, especially through sponsoring pig feasts

bim-kohomba: a jungle plant boiled into tea for bringing down fever

bo tree: in Sri Lanka, believed to be trees that are all descendants from a branch of the tree under which the Buddha achieved enlightenment; thus they have a sacred character; *ficus religiosa*

bodhi pujawa: an offering ceremony to the sacred bo tree; used to offset possible negative influence of the planets when a person's horoscope shows he or she is in an inauspicious period

bodhisattva: a being on the way to becoming a Buddha

Bodilima: a female demon that haunts the area where a mother with unborn child has been buried

bohoma istuthiy: thank you very much

booruwa: a gambling card game similar to poker

Buddha govi: cultivated rice belonging to the Buddha

bulath vita: a betel chew; a betel leaf in which a bit of areca nut, tobacco, and chalky lime are rolled for chewing

cadjan: woven palm fronds used for enclosures or partitions

caste: a social class in which membership is determined by birth and does not change throughout life

chena: Sri Lankan English word for a highland field, usually prepared for cultivation by slash-and-burn

classificatory kinship terms: terms that refer to more than one category of kin members, e.g., "mother" may refer to mother's sisters as well as to one's biological mother

consanguine kin: kin members related through biological or blood ties

cross-cousin: the children of a person's mother's brother or father's sister

curries: spicy vegetable, fish, or meat dishes eaten with rice

dana: an offering of alms or food, for example to Buddhist monks, or to local deities in a ceremony

deva dana: a sweet, sticky rice with sugar and cardamoms, prepared as an offering to local deities for a good harvest

dath panuwo kanawa: tooth decay; literally, "teeth eaten by worms"

dehi-kepima: lime-cutting ceremony, used for ritual healing

devale: temple of Hindu deities

diyaredda: a bathing cloth

dobi: laundry washer caste

dodol: a dense and oily traditional sweet

dowry: goods that the bride's family gives to the new couple or to the groom at the time of marriage

duwa: daughter, or niece on either side

endaru: a twig used for cleaning one's teeth; when broken off it exudes a milky, bitter liquid

endogamous: marrying within one's own social group

"Epa, epa":   "No, no, I don't want any."

eswaha-watura: evil-eye water, used in curing the effects of the evil eye

ethnocentrism: the tendency to judge another culture by one's own norms and values; the belief that one's own culture is superior

ethnography: the description of an individual society and its culture

Gam Udawa: governmental Village Re-Awakening program of 1991–92

gana-denu: the ritual exchange of money during the Sinhalese and Tamil New Year; literally "give and take"

Ganesha: the elephant-headed Hindu god; helps remove obstacles and is a patron of learning

ganja: hashish leaves

goda govitena: nonshifting highland homestead cultivation

gona: bull or ox

gotu-kola: edible wild leaves (also cultivated) used as a vegetable and as medicine for worms

govigama: the cultivator caste, the highest caste after the (no longer existent) royalty caste

grama niladhari: the village officer, the formal head of a *grama seva* division

grama seva division: the smallest administrative unit in Sri Lanka

grama seveka: former title of the village headman, or the administrative head of a cluster of small villages

hath-malu: a special curry made of seven kinds of vegetables, given to a new mother on the seventh day after she has given birth

hen govitena: shifting, slash-and-burn highland cultivation

hiramanaya: a low stool with a saw-toothed coconut scraper blade attached

hisa kes kepeema: ritual for a child's first haircut

huna: gecko or small lizard, said to have predictive powers

ilattattuwa: dish on a pedestal for spreading out betel leaves to present to guests

illuk: tall grass used for thatching roofs

imbul: a kind of tree

incest: having sexual relations with or marrying a close relative, as determined in a particular culture

indul katagaema: first rice (solid food) ritual for four- to five-month-old babies

isa-tel ganawa: the anointing of oil; an important ritual at the time of the Sinhalese and Tamil New Year in order to ensure good health in the coming year

istuthiy pattara: a printed and framed statement of appreciation; "thank you letter"

jackfruit tree: large, tropical tree that produces immense fruit; in Sri Lanka it is categorized as a "milk tree" and associated with women and children

JVP: *Janatha Vimukthi Peramuna;* People's Liberation Front, the party of young Marxist revolutionaries

kadawaraya: a kind of demon prevalent in jungle village locations

kale: water pot

Kalukumaraya: Black Prince; one of the trinity of principal devils, who may cause irregular menstrual periods or miscarriages

kamata: circular threshing floor

kan-wideema: ear-piercing ritual for little girls

kaele pattara: anonymous, handwritten, slanderous note tacked on trees along a road; literally, "jungle newspaper"

kaevun: oil cakes; a traditional sweet

kapurala: Hindu ritual priest

karanda: twig used for cleaning one's teeth

kasippu: homemade liquor

Kataragama: the Hindu god said to reign in the southeastern region of Sri Lanka, especially in the area around the town of Kataragama; the Hindu god Skanda, god of war

kattadiya: ritual healer

kenda: rice porridge

keta gahanawa: a popular dice game for prizes, typically played around the Sinhalese and Tamil New Year

king coconut: orange-colored coconuts, the water of which is used as a refreshing drink and as an intravenous infusion for hospital patients

kiriamma: great grandmother or grandmother

kiriammalage dana: a special almsgiving ceremony held when a child is suffering for an extended period in order to end the malady; "offering to nursing mothers" *kiribath:*   milk-rice, a common treat cooked for festive occasions

Koheda giye?:   a greeting; literally, "Where did you go?"

Koheda yanne?:   a greeting; literally, "Where are you going?"

kohomba: margosa; the leaves, when hung over a sick person's door, are said to protect them from evil spirits; also made into a bitter oil for weaning infants

kokis: cookies in the shape of wagon wheels; a traditional sweet

konde kaevun: oil cakes shaped like a woman's hair in a bun; a traditional sweet

kotu-paninawa: a game similar to hopscotch

kudu: lanterns

kulla: small winnowing basket

kumbhandas: a category of evil spirits

kunukatuwa: hump-nose viper, a mildly poisonous snake

leli: daughter-in-law, or wife of nephew on either side

leveling mechanism: a practice that serves to even out wealth or differences in status in a social unit

levirate: the custom in which a widow marries a brother of her deceased husband

lingam: symbolic male phallus, generally associated with the Hindu god Shiva

loku aiya: big elder brother

loku amma: mother's older sister, a classificatory mother

loku appa: father's older brother, a classificatory father

LTTE: Liberation Tigers of Tamil Eelam; "Tamil Tigers," a radical Tamil group fighting for a separate Tamil state in Sri Lanka and reputed to use terrorist tactics

maama: uncle other than father's brother

mae: long beans, similar to green beans

maha: main cultivation season (October–March) using rain from the northeast monsoon

Mahasohona: Great Graveyard Devil; ferocious member of the trinity of principal devils, who lives in cemeteries and can cause mental illness

Mahavamsa: literary epic that chronicles the Sinhalese kings, written by Buddhist monks in the fifth or sixth century A.D.

mal-bulath putuwa: chair prepared to hold ritual items used in a healing ceremony

malli: younger brother, or younger parallel cousin

malpela: small shrine stand woven from young coconut palm fronds on which to place offerings to deities

mamoty: Sri Lankan English word for a large hoe, the main agricultural tool in Sri Lanka (Sinhala: *udella*)

mandape: decorated enclosure in which the participants in a *pirith* chanting ceremony sit; a dais

mantra: a mystical formula to be chanted or inscribed as an invocation to supernatural forces

mapila: cat snake, one of the mildly poisonous species of snakes in Sri Lanka

massina: brother-in-law, or male cross-cousin

minibiri: granddaughter, or great granddaughter

mudiyanselage: a high official under the last Kandyan kings and during the British colonial period

munubura: grandson, or great grandson

murunga: tree that bears long, stick-shaped vegetables, called "drumsticks" by English-speaking Sinhalese

naanawa: to bathe, which includes getting the head and hair wet

naena: sister-in-law, or female cross-cousin

Naewe da?:   Did you bathe?

Nagas: one of the indigenous tribes of Sri Lanka

nangi: younger sister, or younger female parallel cousin

nembiliya: ridged bowl for finding small stones in uncooked rice

nenda: aunt other than mother's sisters

neketa: astrologically determined auspicious moment for carrying out a ritual *nona:* lady; madam

NUFFIC: Netherlands Universities Foundation for International Cooperation

nul bandinawa: tying of threads with knots around the neck, wrist, or arm after invoking blessings from deities to drive away evil spirits; ritual of the charmed thread

PA: People's Alliance; the new government political party that came to power in 1994

paddy: unhusked rice; rice plants

padikkama: spittoon for chewed betel leaves

pancha: a gambling game with cowrie shells, typically played around the Sinhalese and Tamil New Year

pan-sil: the first five Buddhist precepts, in which one pledges not to lie, steal, kill any animal, drink alcohol, or engage in sexual misconduct

pansukula: ritual carried out during a funeral; close relatives of the deceased hold on to and pour a pitcher of water into a cup, which overflows into a basin, symbolizing the collection of merit for the *prethas* (spirits)

papadam: fried unleavened bread crisps

parallel cousin: the children of a person's mother's sister or father's brother

participant observation: method of gathering ethnographic data by living among those being observed and described; the researcher may participate in the observed group's lifestyle to varying degrees

patrilocal residence: residence pattern in which a married couple lives near the husband's father's family

Pattikaraya: the demon that lurks around cows in the night, who carries a golden stick and milk pot; he is dangerous for people who encounter him

Pattini: Hindu goddess of health and chastity

pela: small shelter or hut used when guarding agricultural fields against animals at night

pel-kawi: traditional songs sung in the *pela* at night while guarding crops

perehera: a religious procession

pirith: chanting of Buddhist discourses to invoke blessings of the "triple gem" (Buddha, his teachings, and the Buddhist monks) as well as the gods and deities in a particular area

pirith-mandape: dais or enclosure where the *pirith* chanters sit

podi aiya: little older brother

podi nangi: little younger sister

polanga: Russell's viper, a highly poisonous snake

pori: fried paddy seeds

Poson: festival on the full moon in June, celebrating the advent of Buddhism to Sri Lanka

potlatch: Northwest Coast Indian ceremony in which property is given away or destroyed to raise the giver's social status

pottuwa: dark brown dot on the forehead of a child, used as protection against the evil eye

poya: full-moon day; sacred for Buddhists, and a holiday in Sri Lanka every month

pretha: spirits of deceased persons, especially those who were sinful or who left some unresolved problem

punchi amma: mother's younger sister, a classificatory mother

punya-kalaya: the neutral period between the old and the new year, as calculated for the Sinhalese and Tamil New Year

purana: traditional or ancient

putha: son, or nephew on either side; also a term of affection for a child, male or female

ran-kiri katagaema: "first milk" rite of passage for newborns

Ranwela: local deity called the "ferryman," to whom travelers must make a small monetary offering at a shrine to ensure their safe passage through his territory

Reeriyaka: Blood-Sucker; one of the trinity of principal devils, who lives on human blood and influences the human blood system

rites of passage: culturally defined, formalized practices that mark the transition from one stage of life to another

sadu, sadu, saaaadu!: blessings!

Saraswathie: Hindu goddess of learning

sari: the traditional dress of Indian and Sri Lankan women, consisting of six yards of thin, draped cloth

sarong: a tube-shaped piece of cloth wrapped around to resemble a long skirt, worn by men

Sarpayek awa!:   A snake has come!

satsande: a medicinal root

seettu: a system used by the Women's Society to pool and redistribute rice by lottery in order to help women who might otherwise have to borrow money to pay for expensive obligations

sembuwa: a small water pot

shramadana: unpaid community labor for completing a project or task

SIDA: Swedish International Development Authority

sil: eight Buddhist precepts, observed by pious followers; dressed in white and seated on mats, participants meditate, read religious scriptures, and listen to sermons

silmaeni: female Buddhist monk not attached to a particular temple

sinha: lion

Sinhala-Demala Aluth Avurudda: Sinhalese and Tamil New Year, celebrated in mid-April

slash-and-burn: a form of cultivation in which farmers slash down natural vegetation and burn the remains in order to enrich the soil; cultivators may shift to a new area after a few years when the soil is depleted; swidden cultivation

SLFP: Sri Lanka Freedom Party; a liberal government political party

socialization: the transmission of a society's culture from one generation to the next; enculturation

sororate: the custom whereby a widower is encouraged to marry one of his deceased wife's sisters

sprats: tiny dried fish

stupa: bell-shaped shrine in a Buddhist temple complex; a Buddhist reliquary

sudu: white

suniyam: powerful evil force

suraya: a small metal tube worn on a string around the neck, containing a thin copper scroll on which a ritual healer has written and drawn protective mantras or symbols

syncretism: the combination of different beliefs and practices, especially those related to religion or belief in the supernatural

taatta: father

taboo: a prohibition, especially one backed by fear of supernatural sanctions

talagoya: monitor lizard

tank: an artificial lake or water reservoir (Sinhala: *waewa*)

thala goolee: rolls of sesame seeds, oil, and sugar, wrapped in tissue paper; a traditional sweet

totem, totemic: a stipulated ancestor (esp. animal) of a human group; e.g., the Sinhalese people are said to be descended from an ancestral lion

tunpali: the trinity of principal devils: Mahasohona, Reeriyaka, and Kalukumaraya

UNICEF: United Nations Children's Fund

UNP: United National Party; conservative government political party

unu-watura: boiled water or hot water

up-country: the mountainous region in central Sri Lanka

vandinawa: to bow down and "worship" as a sign of respect

vedamahatmaya: traditional doctor or ayurvedic physician

Vedas: collections of the earliest Brahmanic religious verses, dating from the second millennium B.C.

Veddhas: the original, indigenous peoples of Sri Lanka

venivel-geta: a thick jungle vine used as medicine or as a source of water

Vesak: important Buddhist festival on the full moon day in May, celebrating the Buddha's birth, passing, and enlightenment

Vishnu: important Hindu god, protector and preserver of the world, and restorer of moral order

wee govitena: wet rice or paddy cultivation
wela path kade: a preliminary astrological chart, requested from an astrologer at the time
   of a child's birth
waewa: water reservoir or artificial lake; "tank" in Sri Lankan English
Yakkas: one of the indigenous tribes of Sri Lanka
yaya: an area of paddy fields
yuga: the chanting of Buddhist stanzas by pairs of chanters, two-by-two

References Cited

Baker, Victoria J. *Going to School in Black-Thicket Jungle: Education in a Disadvantaged Sri Lankan District.* NUFFIC Colombo Research Report No. 6. Leiden: Institute of Cultural and Social Studies, University of Leiden, 1986.

Baker, Victoria J. *The Blackboard in the Jungle: Formal Education in Disadvantaged Rural Areas—A Sri Lankan Case.* Delft: Eburon Publisher, 1988.

Barley, Nigel. *The Innocent Anthropologist: Notes from a Mud Hut.* London: British Museum Publications, Ltd, 1983.

Barley, Nigel. *A Plague of Caterpillars: A Return to the African Bush.* New York: Viking Penguin, Inc., 1986.

Beeby, C. E. *The Quality of Education in Developing Countries.* Cambridge: Harvard University Press, 1966.

Bowen, Elenore Smith (Laura Bohannan). *Return to Laughter: An Anthropological Novel.* New York: Harper & Brothers, 1954.

Dhammananda, N. *History of Uva. (Uva Itihasaya.)* Colombo: M. D. Gunasena and Sons (in Sinhala), 1966.

Fairbanks, Gordon H., James W. Gair, and M. W. S. DeSilva. *Colloquial Sinhalese, Part 1.* Ithaca, New York: Cornell University South Asia Program, 1968. Reprint, with audiocassettes, Audio-Forum, Guilford, Conn., 1981.

Malinowski, Bronislaw. "Magic, Science and Religion." (First published in 1925.) In *Magic, Science and Religion and Other Essays,* 17–92. Garden City, N.Y.: Doubleday Anchor Books, 1954.

Ondaatje, Michael. *Running in the Family.* London: Victor Gollancz Ltd., 1983.

Percival, Robert. *An Account of the Island of Ceylon.* London: C. and R. Baldwin, 1803.

Spencer, Jonathan. *A Sinhala Village in a Time of Trouble: Politics and Change in Rural Sri Lanka.* Delhi: Oxford University Press, 1990.

Van Gennep, Arnold. *The Rites of Passage.* Chicago: University of Chicago Press, 1960.

Wolffers, Ivan. *Changing Traditions in Health Care: Sri Lanka.* Ph.D. diss., University of Leiden, 1987.

Woolf, Leonard. *The Village in the Jungle.* London: Edward Arnold Limited, 1913.

Woolf, Leonard. *Growing: An Autobiography of the Years 1904–1911.* New York: Harcourt, Brace & World, Inc., 1961.

Woost, Michael D. *Constructing a Nation of Villages: Development and Community on the Sinhalese Frontier.* Ph.D. diss., University of Texas at Austin, 1990.

Wickramasinghe, Martin. *Madol Doova.* Translated by Ashley Halpe (1976). Dehiwala, Sri Lanka: Tisara Prakasakayo Ltd., 1947.

Wickramasinghe, Martin. "Village Craftsmen" from *Our Village (Ape Gama).* Translated by Lakshmi de Silva. In *Stories from Sri Lanka,* edited by Yasmine Gooneratne 39–43. Hong Kong: Heinemann Asia, 1940.

Yalman, Nur. *Under the Bo Tree: Studies in Caste, Kinship, and Marriage in the Interior of Ceylon.* Berkeley: University of California Press, 1967.

INDEX